Craft Traditions
of the World

Bryan and Polly Sentance

Craft Traditions
of the World

Locally Made, Globally Inspiring

with 480 illustrations, 475 in color

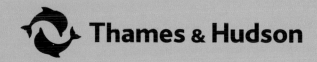
Thames & Hudson

For Tansy, Lisa, Dylan, Rachel, Luke and Kieran

"I marvelled at the subtle genius of men in distant lands." Albrecht Dürer

page 1: Painted ceramic bird, Puebla, Mexico.
pages 2–3: Paper cutout, Lowicz, Poland.
page 4: Carved sandalwood statuette
of the Hindu god Ganesh, India.
page 5, left: American quilt in the Amish 'New Hope'
pattern by Pippa Moss.
page 5, right: Gourd with incised and scorched
designs, Cochas, Peru.
page 6, left: Hungarian earthenware plate with slip-
trailed pattern.
page 6, right: Coiled grass basket, KwaZulu-Natal,
South Africa.
page 7, above, left: Turkomen *okbash*, a felt bag for
the ends of yurt poles, Central Asia.
page 7, below: Spoons with celadon glaze, China.
page 7, right: Aboriginal hunting boomerang, Australia.

First published in hardcover in 2009 in the United States of America
by Thames & Hudson Inc., 500 Fifth Avenue, New York,
New York 10110

thamesandhudsonusa.com

Library of Congress Catalog Card Number 2009900126

ISBN 978-0-500-51466-5

Printed and bound in China by C&C Offset Printing Co., Ltd.

Contents

Prologue: The Sultan Who Became a Weaver

There was once a Sultan in a far off land. He was wise and beneficent, just and merciful, a father to his people. But one day he turned to his Vizier with a troubled look upon his handsome face.

'What am I to do, my friend?' he asked. 'I am rich and powerful with servants to supply my every need, I have a beautiful wife and children who are the joy of my heart yet I am restless and unfulfilled.'

'Well, my lord,' answered the Vizier. 'You must learn a craft. Every man should learn a craft! I will call all the master craftsmen to the palace to demonstrate their skills and you can choose from amongst them.'

So the Vizier summoned the master craftsmen, the master potter, the master carpenter, the master copper smith and the most skilful artificers of every trade, and they demonstrated their skills before the Sultan. The Sultan watched and finally he called the master weaver to him and engaged him as his teacher.

Every day the master weaver came to the palace and showed the Sultan how to set up the warps on his loom, how to open the shed, how to send the shuttle flying across from side to side and how to beat the weft down tight. Every day before he sat in court or held audience the Sultan practised on his loom. Every day his skill increased and he found a sense of peace and contentment come upon him.

The Sultan became skilful on the loom and particularly adept at weaving a pattern of flowers. He made rugs for his wife and his children, for his Vizier and for his favourite courtiers, all with the pattern of flowers.

Now, one night the Sultan called the Vizier and, as was their practice, they went out in disguise to see how things were amongst their subjects. Returning home before dawn they were set upon by a band of robbers who mistook them for a pair of merchants. The brigands tied them securely and locked them in a house in a back alley intending to sell two such healthy specimens to a slave trader for a good price.

'Wait!' said the Sultan. 'I might be worth more to you if you don't sell me. I am a skilled weaver and my weavings would fetch you a great deal of money.'

The robbers were intrigued and set up a loom in the courtyard and watched as the Sultan's shuttle flew back and forth and the pattern of flowers began to appear.

'Now that is what I call weaving!' exclaimed the chief of the robbers who was used to handling expensive merchandise even if it was usually stolen. 'When he has finished we could sell this at the royal palace.' And indeed when the Sultan had finished the chief of the robbers himself took the rug to the palace and showed it to the first courtier he met.

'Just wait here,' ordered the courtier who recognized the pattern of flowers. 'The Sultana herself should see this. I am sure she would pay a lot for such fine workmanship,' and he hurried off to show the Sultana. The Sultana, who had been beside herself with anxiety over the mysterious disappearance of her husband, instructed the courtier to give the robber a large bag of gold for the rug but to have him followed when he left. The delighted robber chief swaggered home with the gold but as he entered his house the armed men the Sultana had sent rushed in, rescued the Sultan and the Vizier and arrested the band of robbers.

After he had returned to the embraces of his relieved family, the Sultan sat upon his throne and had the robbers summoned into his presence.

'Take these men away,' he said, 'And lock them in a cell with a loom. When they have learned how to weave a carpet you may let them go. After all, it is my firm belief that every man should learn a craft!'

opposite: Shirvan flatweave kilim, Caucasus, Iran.

Introduction

Craftspeople, either professionals or those who practise craft as an integral part of their daily life, are among the most inventive and adaptable people in the world. Although they have not generally achieved the status given to the artist, a good artist must be a craftsman and a good craftsman is often an artist. Artists and craftspeople around the world may have different materials available to them and may belong to different cultures, but their approach to problems is often very similar.

above: Ceramic vessel for pouring water, made by the Quichua people, Ecuadorian Amazon.

below: Nampeyo, the matriarch of a pottery dynasty on the Hopi Reservation in Arizona, North America.

Art and craft

True craftspeople develop their skills after much practice. Historians postulate that it was only when food was abundant (for instance, when agricultural practices became sufficiently efficient or when a coastal group had a plentiful supply of fish) that a society did not need all its members to be involved directly with food production and so specialists were able to develop their skills. Thus the manufacture of pottery, which is labour intensive and requires a sedentary lifestyle, is generally considered to be one of the indicators of the birth of a civilization.

In many cultures the distinction between 'art' and 'craft' is not clearly defined. Both are dependent on the application of manual skill and the knowledge of materials. Just as a basketmaker would gather and prepare willow or palm fronds before interlacing them into a basket or a weaver might spin and dye yarn before weaving cloth, so the painter would grind pigments and prepare a suitable surface before creating a picture.

In Renaissance Europe the status of the artist was higher than that of the other guild craftsmen as they were considered to be intellectuals.

Recognition for craftspeople

Craftspeople have often been viewed as artists when their creations have become as aesthetic as they are functional. This may occur in an affluent society where functionality is not an important consideration or it may be a perception that comes from historical or geographic distance. For example, craftspeople whose work was originally made for traditional, practical purposes, but has now become collectable for aesthetic reasons may

become famous. For instance, in North America the Washo basketmaker Datsolalee (c. 1835–1925) or the innovative Hopi potter Nampeyo (1860–1942) and in Nigeria the Yoruba master-carver Areogun (c. 1880–1954) or the potter Ladi Kwali. The Japanese, however, have always had a greater respect for craftsmen, celebrating the work of men such as the ceramist and lacquer maker Honami Koetsu (1558–1637) or more recently the basketmaker Hiroshima Kazuo (b. 1915).

Since most of our everyday objects have been industrially produced, a new respect has been granted to craftspeople whose work is now looked at from a more aesthetic viewpoint. In Cornwall in England, for instance, the early 20th century saw a revival of copper working at Newlyn and also the development of the craftsman potter movement spearheaded by Bernard Leach and his Japanese friend Shoji Hamada at St Ives. We have come to appreciate that however efficiently goods can be manufactured by machine, a handmade object has not only individuality, but also a personality stamped on it or woven in by the mind and hand of the maker.

left: Horizontal loom set up for weaving silk, Tokyo, Japan.
above: Bamboo basket by Hiroshima Kazuo, Hinokage, Japan.
opposite, below, right: Ritual ablution vessel, Central Iran, c. 1000 BC.

far left: Chinese carpenters at work, after a 17th-century woodcut.
near left: Michael Callaghan, maker of toys from recycled materials, Cape Town, South Africa.
opposite, left: Weft ikat silk textile from Siem Reap, Cambodia.

Supernatural craftsmen

The crafts of many cultures have become entwined with myth and folklore. In Peru, Greece and parts of Africa, where pottery is one the foremost skills, myths frequently tell how the Divine Creator, like the August Personage of Jade in China, made the first people from clay. However, in northern Europe, where the foremost material was the wood of the forests, the great god Odin and his brothers carved the first man and woman from wood as did the gods in the Admiralty and Banks Islands in the Pacific. The Ata of Mindanao and the Igorot of Luzon in the Philippines, who are skilled basketweavers, believed the first couple were woven from grass. The universe too was made by supernatural artificers. The Norse Frigga spun the clouds, the Finnish Ilmarinen forged the sky and, according to the West African Fon, Mawu-Lisa made the earth itself from clay in the shape of a giant calabash.

The act of creation is such a magical process that the invention of many crafts is credited to gods and heroes. According to the ancient Greeks the goddess Athene was the greatest of weavers, while in the American Southwest the Navajo rub spider webs on the arms of their daughters in the hope they will become accomplished weavers, remembering how Spider Woman taught their ancestors the craft. It is the smith, however, working magical transformations in the forge and crucible, who is best represented among the gods. In Greece it was Hephaestus, in Scandinavia Volund, in Ireland and Wales Goibniu and Govannan and in Nigeria Ogun. The forging of metals is one of the most far-reaching of technological developments providing the tools of agriculture, industry and perhaps most significantly military power and so the smith plays a pivotal role in history. But the blacksmith was not always the tool of the mighty, sometimes he has stood for the rights of the common man. In the Persian epic *The Shahnama*, it is Kava, the mythical smith, who leads the people in rebellion against the demon Zohak, while it was the historic blacksmith Michael Josef, also known as An Gof, who led the Cornish in revolt against King Henry VII in 1497.

Many inspired enough to invent or teach craft skills have frequently achieved mythical status. Among the greatest of all legendary craftsmen and inventors was the Greek Daedalus whose adventures seem to have taken place during the time of the Minoan culture. Having learnt smithcraft from the versatile goddess Athene, he supposedly developed the lost-wax metal casting process, invented the saw, compass, axe and auger, cut the first dovetail joints, made the first animated dolls and designed the first sails for ships as well as a pair of wings that famously cost the life of his son Icarus.

Craftspeople have believed in placating the gods and holy patrons of their craft to ensure success either with a prayer or an offering. Chinese potters, for example, make a small 'god' from clay to watch over the firings of their kilns. They also traditionally invoke craftsmen deified for their services: Sun Piu, god of cobblers, who is credited with

right: Two Moroccan Berber coiled baskets stitched with the wool of their sheep rather than the more conventional plant fibres.

inventing shoes in the 4th century BC, T'sai Lun who invented paper in the 1st century AD and Lu Ban, the god of carpenters. Christians, too, have assigned numerous saints to serve as patrons of crafts from basketry (St Anthony) and blacksmithing (St Dunstan or St Eligius) to shoemaking (St Crispin) and pottery (St Radegunde or St Sebastian).

Materials, Techniques and Pattern

When studying crafts around the world there are striking similarities between the work in places divided by many miles. For example, the chip-carved patterns on the woodwork of Wales, Zanzibar and Pakistan and many of the patterns on wool-stitched coil baskets of the Moroccan Berbers and the Iranian Qashgai. This may be because of an exchange of ideas through trade or a shared belief system that dictates a certain repertoire of motifs, but in many cases the likeness is dictated by the limitations of the medium and the technique employed: a carver must respect the grain of the wood whether he lives in Europe or Asia and there is a finite

number of ways in which a group of coloured squares of fabric can be arranged. Climatic and topographic environment plays an important role as craftspeople will have similar materials at their disposal, resulting in the production of similar craftwork.

left: Roughing out the basic shape of a carving from a wooden block with an axe, Mas, Bali.

Changing Markets, Changing Attitudes

For thousands of years people have created the tools and requisites of daily life and many, especially in less industrialized regions, continue to do so today. However, the natural world has been affected by development, climate change and social migration, changing the balance of available materials and now a woman in Borneo, Thailand or Mexico may construct a basket in the way her mother taught her, only making it from strips of plastic instead of bamboo. As the times change so needs and challenges change and the availability of new materials and technologies may lead to the development of crafts such as the telephone-wire basketry begun by night watchmen in South Africa or the establishment of workshops specializing in non-traditional crafts such as the pottery workshops set up in Australian Aborigine communities in the 20th century. Frequently these new crafts have found a market abroad, providing income for communities that might otherwise break down as the young struggle to find employment in the cities.

The spread of global culture has had an impact and the need for cash in the modern world has led to a change in the craftspeople's market. The Inuit have no word for 'art' and once their skills were used to construct functional objects, decorated with auspicious and magical designs, but nowadays the environment and lifestyle of people in the Arctic regions has significantly changed because of poor hunting due to the decrease in winter ice so 20 per cent of the Inuit are now involved in the manufacture of 'art' for sale to outsiders. In Bali, on the other hand, woodcarving was formerly carried out almost exclusively for religious purposes, but now thousands of carvers make their living from carving objects to be exported or sold to tourists. Some may be crudely turned out, but many are still exquisitely carved.

The tourist market is important as it is often the only outlet for the exponents of ancient skills that might otherwise expire and may also encourage a craftsman, freed from convention and functional requirements, to develop new skills and ideas. Even if an artefact is only a copy one should keep in mind that this often requires the same skills as making the original and that it may still be judged on the quality of its workmanship.

Craft and Conservation

Working with the hands using natural materials promotes an empathy with the natural world. It is essential to be aware of the individual strengths and weaknesses of materials to be able to use them well and not cause them to tear, snap or disintegrate. So the craftsman learns respect and becomes aware of the need to conserve and protect resources. When the materials come from a local source it is easy to monitor their sustainability, but when a global market arises, as it did for tropical hardwoods, catastrophe hovers.

Craftspeople faced with the depletion of local resources have often looked around and adapted their skills to whatever is to hand. For many, the cheapest and most plentiful source is the detritus of the modern world and many have avoided hunger and poverty by creating useful or entertaining items from bottles, tin cans, newspaper and plastic. This resourceful attitude has affected the developed world where the issues of conservation, pollution and recycling are being taken more and more seriously.

About this Book

To include every craft technique from every region would require many volumes and so writing a book like this, where space is limited, demands the making of choices. We have endeavoured to include a range of techniques and disciplines from as many countries, regions and cultures as possible. We have tried to pick examples that are representative of lifestyles and cultural attitudes. The choice is unashamedly personal and leans towards the traditional arts and crafts of ordinary people that are so often both practical and imbued with the honest joy of life. By juxtaposing examples from different places now and then we have tried to provide an opportunity to compare and contrast different solutions to the same tasks.

Old crafts may employ new materials and traditional materials may be used for new crafts. As old markets have closed, new ones have opened. There are still millions of people around the globe who weave their own cloth, carry their goods in a handmade basket, eat off locally made crockery or sit on chairs made by traditional craftsmen. Some old skills have been forgotten but many are still in use. It is our task to keep them alive either by learning the skills ourselves or by supporting the craftsmen by buying their produce both at home and aboard. The first step along this road is to open our eyes and see how craftsmanship can enrich our lives and hopefully this book will contribute to this knowledge or engender enthusiasm for the handmade. Don't forget the Sultan who became a weaver.

above: Bulldozer made from recycled Coca-Cola cans, Vietnam.

1

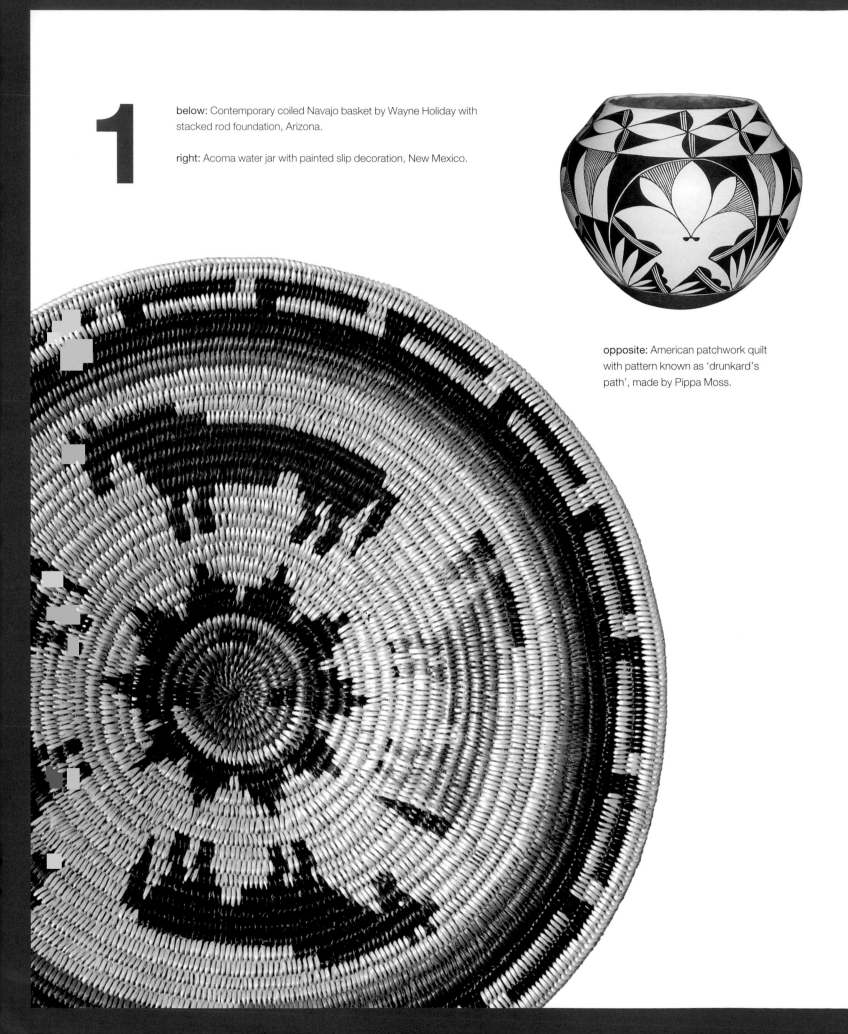

below: Contemporary coiled Navajo basket by Wayne Holiday with stacked rod foundation, Arizona.

right: Acoma water jar with painted slip decoration, New Mexico.

opposite: American patchwork quilt with pattern known as 'drunkard's path', made by Pippa Moss.

North America

Introduction

During the last Ice Age a land bridge was exposed across what is now the Bering Strait, allowing hunters in pursuit of mammoths and mastodon to cross from Siberia to Alaska and to migrate across North America.

In each region some people settled and established a lifestyle and culture based upon local resources. For instance, on the Pacific Northwest coast the settlers found plentiful supplies of shellfish and salmon while the forest provided abundant stocks of timber. They built houses from cedar planks, carved canoes and ceremonial objects from wood and made clothing and baskets from shredded bark and tree roots. On the wide Prairies they remained nomadic, basing their culture around the animals they hunted, eating their flesh, wearing their hides and also using them to make their homes. In the South and East communities became established, cultivating squashes, beans and corn as well as cotton for weaving cloth.

The Coming of the White Man

European settlers arriving from the 16th century onwards brought with them their own traditions and skills from home. These often became localized to specific parts of North America as those with the same beliefs or of the same nationality tended to settle in the same areas. In Pennsylvania there was a tradition of German-influenced joinery while in the Hispanic communities of the South silverwork flourished. Women from England and Wales developed an American style of quiltmaking, drawing on the traditions of their home countries, while potters employed techniques native to the English West Country. As pioneers travelled west, crafts were often adapted or honed down to the basics and new skills had to be learnt quickly in order to survive. These factors endowed the objects they made with a vigour and spontaneity that is now considered characteristically American.

Cross Cultural Exchange

Although the influx of European immigrants ultimately almost led to the extermination of the Native Americans

above, left: Shoshone tipis with buffalo hide coverings, 1870s, Wyoming.
above, right: Bark-paper cutout of an Otomi pineapple spirit, Puebla State, Mexico.

right: Flying 'V' log cabin dating from the 1830s, Pioneer Living History Village, Arizona.
below: 1880s Arizona trading post, photographed by Frank Wittick.

and their confinement to small pockets of land, there has always been a level of trade. This had been established by travelling traders and was followed up by the establishment of trading posts providing a market, and subsequent income, for craftspeople, exchanging cash, materials or consumables for craft items as well as acting as a forum for the exchange of ideas. Many trading posts still operate today and are a wonderful opportunity to see and buy outstanding craftsmanship. New materials and ideas opened up new craft developments. Metal tools facilitated crisper carving, glass beads made possible embroidery that was more elaborate than could be achieved with porcupine quills and trade cloth saw the development of new styles of needlework such as the ribbon appliqué popular among the Osage. New skills could also be learned, for instance, silverwork taught by the Spanish in the Southwest. Commissioned craftwork also introduced a new design repertoire and sometimes dictated a change of product. The Navajo, for instance, stopped weaving blankets in around 1890 and instead began weaving rugs which were more appealing to the colonial market.

Today, the distinctions have become blurred and while many Native Americans work in traditionally European trades, many whites have chosen to learn the skills of the indigenous peoples.

above, left: Iroquois 'false face' mask, Canada.
left: Nuu-chah-nulth (Nootka) wrap-twined basket, Salt Spring Island off Vancouver Island, Canada.
above: Basketmaker from Second Mesa on the Hopi Reservation in Arizona.

Wicker plaque from Third Mesa on the Hopi
Reservation in Arizona. Once ceremonial or
functional, many baskets are now made by
the Hopi to be sold to outsiders.

Marine Ivory

According to Inuit myth, Sedna married against her father's wishes and in different versions of the myth her husband was a dog or a seabird, but either way it was not a happy marriage and her father came to rescue her. As they escaped across the sea a terrible storm arose and, in a panic, the father threw his troublesome daughter from the boat to save himself, but she clung to the side and he was forced to chop off her fingers to break her hold. As Sedna sank she became transformed into a powerful spirit and her severed fingers turned into seals and whales. The harvest of sea mammals is thanks to Sedna's sacrifice but, like the Arctic Sea, she is moody and changeable and must be placated. When the harvest is bad it is the shaman's task to visit her beneath the sea and comb the tangles from her hair, a task she cannot perform for herself with no fingers.

The Harvest of the Sea

Although times have changed and most Inuit now live in settlements, Sedna's generosity was for a thousand years vital to the survival of the Inuit and traditionalists still consider hunting an important part of their culture. Nothing was wasted. Flesh

was eaten (the liver of seals provided vitamins obtained in other cultures from plants), skins were used for clothing, waterproof garments were made from gut, sinew was used for thread and cordage, bones were used for tools, oil made from blubber was used for lighting. The highly prized ivory obtained from the tusks of the walrus and the teeth of whales is an excellent material for making harpoon heads, hooks, pots, combs, needles and many other tools and utensils. It was also used for making amulets and objects of mysterious esoteric significance used by shamans.

Inuit Art

The peoples of the Arctic have no traditional concept of 'art'. Carving was historically either functional (as in the making of harpoon points), decorative (applied to functional objects) or for talismanic or magical purposes. This last group attracted the attention of collectors in the 1950s which stimulated many Inuit to devote greater amounts of time to carving. The market was mainly for realistic work but over the years many Inuit have become full-time professionals and their work has become imbued with an increasingly personal vision and a cultural or spiritual significance.

left: Contemporary walrus carved from marine ivory by Yup'ik eskimo Aaron Oseuk from St Lawrence Island in the Bering Sea.
above: Inuit engraved pot made from a section of hollow walrus tusk, probably early 20th century, labelled 'Simpson Collection'.

Techniques

Ivory is a very hard material but is traditionally carved with knives, rasps and drills. Many modern Inuit now prefer to work with electric, flexible shaft rotary grinders that save considerable time and effort and also allow for greater precision and delicacy.

Another popular technique involves scratching designs into the surface. Whalers from North America and Europe also excelled in this artform, which became known as 'scrimshaw', and produced delightful, often naïve scenes usually depicting ships and whales.

Today

The international trade in ivory, both marine and elephant, has been curtailed by the threatened status of marine mammals and ivory carving has diminished. Substitutes have been found in caribou antler and fossilized Siberian mammoth tusks while many artists have taken to stone carving which provides the added advantage of working on a larger scale. The decision to purchase ivory today should not be made without first considering both ethical and legal issues.

top: A replica of a scrimshaw walrus tusk. Due to the restrictions on trade in marine ivory there are now many replicas like this on the market.
left: Inuit craftsman using a bow drill to make holes in a cribbage board made from a walrus tusk, 1902, Bering Strait.
above: Sami knife, c. 1900, northern Sweden. The handle and sheath are made of reindeer antler.

Totem Poles

The totem pole is perhaps the most iconic artefact of the Pacific Northwest coast. Once the villages nestled into the bays and inlets of British Colombia and Alaska were filled with totem poles, conspicuous indicators of an affluent society with a sufficiently plentiful food source to allow the development of time-consuming artforms.

Lifestyle and Culture

The success of the coastal tribes of the Northwest, the Haida, the Nuu-chah-nulth, the Kwakwaka'wakw (formerly known as the Kwakiuł) and many others, was due to the super abundance of salmon brought by the ocean currents. The salmon could be smoked or preserved for consumption over the winter months; the tribes' diet included other fish and shellfish, marine mammals, deer and elk as well as more than forty species of fruit, nuts and roots. This allowed free time in which to develop an elaborate system of ceremonies, dances and storytelling as well as advanced craftsmanship in basketry and cedarwood carving which provided everything from spoons, masks and rattles to plank houses, large canoes and totem poles.

Poles

There are four types of totem pole: massive poles erected outside a house and through which entry was sometimes gained; the interior house pole; the freestanding pole erected to commemorate events such as the accession of a chief or the giving of a potlatch; and finally the mortuary pole which may house the cremated remains of a chief. Depicted on the poles are a number of motifs such as bears, killer whales and eagles, stacked one above the other depicting the totemic animals of a clan or stories attached to them. Particularly common were images of the trickster Raven who was responsible, among other feats, for bringing light to the world.

The coming of white traders had brought an influx of metal which the locals adapted into traditional tools such as the adze, the chisel and the 'D' adze that had previously been made from stone or the incisors of beavers.

The erection of a pole was accompanied by feasting during which the carvers danced around their work with their tools in their hands. The pole subsequently decayed or fell as the damp coastal climate dictated.

Decline and Revival

Although initial contact with Europeans had been friendly, it eventually proved disastrous for the culture of the region. Between the 1850s and the 1880s 90 to 95 per cent of the indigenous peoples were eradicated by viral infections to which they had no immunity such as smallpox carried by Europeans. The government banned many local practices such as the potlatch ceremony, a conspicuous giving away of possessions, and banned the speaking of native languages. The result was the loss of a great deal of tradition and culture. Totem poles decayed and were no longer replaced.

above: Kwakwaka'wakw dance mask, Coastal British Columbia, Canada.
opposite, above, left: Totem pole carved in 1999 and dedicated by Kwakwaka'wakw carvers Sean Whonnock and Jonathan Henderson to their Salish ancestors; erected in Thunderbird Park on Vancouver Island.
opposite, below, left: Replica of a Haida mortuary pole carved in 1955 by Mungo Martin, Henry Hunt and David Martin in Thunderbird Park on Vancouver Island.

A small number of enterprising craftsmen had managed to preserve their skills by making small items from wood and argillite to sell to outsiders. Foremost among these was the Haida Charles Edenshaw (1839–1920) who, like the Kwakwaka'wakw Mungo Martin (1879–1962), provided the inspiration for carvers such as Bill Reid (1920–98) and later Robert Davidson, Edenshaw's great-grandson. In the second half of the 20th century, thanks to these men, craftsmen were active in the cultural rebirth of the nations of the Pacific coast, providing the artefacts for ceremonies and dances and the totem pole, that conspicuous statement of tribal identity.

below, right: Totem pole with clan motifs outside a Kwakwaka'wakw house, 1899.

Horns, Quills and Claws

Once the Plains of North America were home to vast herds of buffalo so numerous that they might take several days to pass a single spot. However, during the 19th century the herds were virtually eradicated by professional white hunters, supplying the lucrative hide market. During the 1870s a million buffalo were killed each year. This caused starvation among the indigenous peoples of the Plains and also shock and disgust at the wanton slaughter. A trail of rotting corpses was left as only the hides were taken. The approach of the Indians had been sustainable, more respectful of the buffalo, killing only what was needed and letting nothing go to waste.

Waste Not, Want Not

From Alaska to the Gulf of Mexico, the philosophy of the indigenous peoples all over North America was to use every possible part of the animals they hunted. The meat was eaten or smoked or preserved for later consumption. Fat was eaten or employed as a base for paint mixed with earth pigments or used as a hair and skin treatment. Skins were used as rawhide or tanned for leather, and brains for tanning. The stomach was used by the Assiniboin of Saskatchewan for cooking: it was placed in a hole in the ground and filled with water heated by dropping hot stones into it. The sinews were used for thread; bones for needles, hide scrapers, spear points and beads and certain body parts were crafted into prestige objects or used as decoration.

above: Brulé Sioux High Horse (Tasunke Wankatuya) in 1900 wearing a shirt embroidered with porcupine quills, Dakota.

below: Dakota Sioux baby-carrier hood with porcupine-quill embroidery made in the 1860s.

Horns and Antlers

In California, the Hupa and Yurok ground down elk antlers to make spoons, while the Tlingit in the Northwest carved the handles of their spoons from the black horns of mountain goats. The bowl of a spoon or a cup can also be made from horn using techniques that are still employed in Scotland. The horns of sheep and goats are made up of layers that can be softened by heating and then bent or moulded easily into shape. In Europe and Asia the same techniques have been applied to tortoiseshell (actually the carapace of marine turtles), although trade has been restricted owing to the decline in turtle numbers.

Hooves, Claws and Teeth

The hooves of deer were once widely used as rattles or dangling ornaments on clothing substituted sometimes in the Northwest with the beaks of puffins. The claws of large beasts such as bears might be strung into a man's necklace, while a woman's dress was often decorated with rows of elk teeth.

Quills

Before the arrival of glass beads, porcupine quills were frequently used for creating patterns on clothing. Flattened between the teeth and dyed, the quills could be sewn down onto a shirt, dress or bag. At each stitch the quill would be folded back over itself, forming a band of tight zigzags which could be built up, using different colours, into a geometric design.

Feathers

The feathered war bonnet is perhaps the most iconic item of Native American attire. The design, however, varied enormously from one tribe to another in both its shape and the type of feathers used. Less well known are the feathered belts and baskets of the Pomo in California or the dance skirts of the Mission tribes which incorporated turkey or swan feathers reminiscent of the feathered cloaks worn by the Aztecs.

top: Made from moulded mountain goat horn, this Tlingit spoon was collected in the 1860s, Alaska.

above: Sioux chest ornament made from rawhide and bone 'pipe' beads and embellished with quill-wrapped fringes.

Shaker Boxes

In the mid-18th century English Quakers were shocked by the ecstatic whirling and convulsions that overcame some of their members during meetings. These 'Shakers' broke away to form their own sect and, after a number of run-ins with the law for disturbing church services, emigrated to North America under the leadership of Mother Ann Lee. In 1776 they acquired land in New York State for their first community and subsequently spread across New England and, during the 19th century, further afield, establishing a community in Narcoossee, Florida in 1896. One of the central tenets of the Shakers was celibacy and so, after initially inspiring thousands with religious fervour, the communities declined. At their peak during the 19th century there were 19 Shaker communities across North America and their numbers reached about 6,000; today there are less than 12 surviving adherents.

Philosophy of Work

'Hands to work and hearts to God' was another Shaker maxim. Labour and craftsmanship were a form of devotion and it was therefore important to produce goods of the best quality possible. Objects made, whether chairs, washstands, or shovels, were designed for a specific purpose and were as plain as the home was uncluttered, allowing their use to dictate the final form. 'Every force evolves a form,' they said. Produce

below: Round 'nice' box made at the Shaker Community at Hancock, Massachusetts.

was supposed to be sufficient to support the needs of the community with just a little excess to insure against hard times.

Although hand-working skills were prized, the Shakers were not against innovation or machinery, indeed the first circular saw in North America was invented by a Shaker and Shakers first packeted seeds.

The 'Nice' Box

One ubiquitous Shaker object was the 'nice' box, the basic structure of which was used, with variations of size and shape, when making objects as diverse as pails, spittoons, grain measures and herb storage. Made from wood grown on the communities' own land, they were a mainstay of the economy and are still popular today. The construction techniques are simple but effective as can be seen by the existence of similar bentwood receptacles as far away as Nepal and Japan.

above, left: European log basket made from riven wood; the technique was taken to the Americas by settlers, but was already in use by Native Americans.
left: Oval cherry wood 'nice' box with the swallowtails and copper rivets typical of Shaker boxes.

Techniques

Round or oval, the top and bottom of the box are traditionally cut from pine and form the 'bones' of the structure. The sides of the box and lid are made from 'riven' or split hardwood, usually maple, walnut or cherry. These are softened in a steamer or by immersing in hot water. Once soft, the sides are bent around the softwood formers of base and lid and tacked into place with copper pins chosen because they do not discolour the wood when aged and oxidized. One of the most distinctive features of Shaker boxes is the use of 'swallowtails' cut with a knife into the end of the piece forming the sides which is not only attractive, but also allows the box to flex with changes in humidity and temperature.

above: Punnet made in Poland by interlacing strips of split pine.

below: The Shaker Community at Hancock, Massachusetts. The Round Stone Barn in the centre was built in 1826.

Patchwork Quilts

Growing up in North America in the 19th century, a girl would spend a great deal of her leisure time preparing quilts to place in her 'hope chest' in anticipation of her wedding day. Twelve was the target with an extra one to cover her bridal bed. Throughout her adolescence she would piece together squares of fabric that she would assemble and quilt when she became engaged. Sometimes this might be carried out with the assistance of her mother and sisters, but often it was an occasion when women from isolated settlements would come together for a 'Quilting Bee', a social event when the sewing was a welcome opportunity to socialize.

Basically a quilt is made from a number of layers of fabric (often recycled scraps) sewn together into a thick, padded item used most often as a bed covering but also for warm or protective clothing. The technique is found all over Asia and Africa, but was introduced to North America by European settlers, especially from Germany, England and Wales.

Patchwork

Plain 'wholecloth' quilts are not uncommon, but better known are those assembled from small pieces of fabric into a mosaic-like pattern. A girl would generally begin her sewing apprenticeship by collecting square blocks she had made from four or nine patches. When she had sufficient blocks they could be sewn together to create a large-scale geometric pattern. More advanced techniques included patterns assembled from triangles or lozenges. One classic design constructed from blocks assembled from narrow rectangular strips is the 'log cabin' quilt which could be put together to create a whole range of optical effects.

The English patchwork technique involves the use of templates for cutting the individual patches which are often

right: Patchwork quilt made by Pippa Moss in the Amish 'sunshine and shadows' pattern.

left: A quilt with an appliqué pattern known as 'penne picante' made by Pippa Moss, a quilter with Mennonite ancestry.
opposite: An Amish-style 'lone star' patchwork quilt made by Pippa Moss.

hexagonal. A smaller paper template is placed on it and the edges are folded over and tacked down before the separate pieces are sewn together. The American method requires no paper and the patches are sewn, right sides together, using running stitch.

Appliqué

Less geometric curvilinear designs may be worked by cutting shapes from material and sewing them onto the surface of the quilt. A fine example of this is the 'Princess Feather' motif which was originally derived from a pattern popular in the north of England. Pictorial quilts could also be made in this way by cutting out whole images such as flowers or birds and sewing them on. This was a very popular way of using fabric that had worn out, but retained intact, attractive areas.

Quilting

The defining characteristic of a quilt is that it is assembled from a number of layers of fabric. The structural integrity is ensured by

'quilting' stitches worked right across and right through the quilt. Although subtle and sometimes virtually invisible, incredible care may be taken over this stitching, working complex designs in tiny running stitch. Stunning examples of this are to be seen in the work of Amish women. The Amish, a strict sect of Mennonites originally from Switzerland, renounced the use of vain ornamentation in their lives and became known as the 'Plain People'. Nevertheless, their quilts can be distinguished by the use of bold geometric designs made from large pieces of fabric in surprisingly bright colours. On close inspection, however, it can be seen that the surface is covered in geometric designs worked with exquisite, tiny stitches.

Rustic Furniture

With simple tools and a sense of urgency, the first buildings were cabins built from the felled logs and the first furniture was made from the smaller branches.

Later Americans, in the changing world of industry and capitalism, have yearned for the pioneer spirit of their forebears and like the Romantics, the poets and philosophers, such as Ralph Waldo Emerson, Walt Whitman and Henry David Thoreau, they have dreamed of a life closer to nature. Early rustics were obliged to employ the materials available and work with the natural bends, twists and forks rather than to force a piece of timber into a shape it did not want to assume. Modern rustics find this one of the most exciting disciplines of the craft and build what the timber suggests. There is also the appealing fact that the materials are cheap and often even free. The craftsman can afford to make mistakes while learning and start again.

The arts of carpentry and joinery could be defined as taking a tree, reducing it to regular, geometric pieces and assembling them into something completely different. However, with rustic woodwork, which uses and even emphasizes the natural shapes of the materials, the end object remains something that is identifiable as having once been a tree and gives the impression of retaining the memory of its former state. With a rustic chair there is always a sense that you are sitting in a tree.

Rustic Philosophy

Rusticity was not always an aesthetic choice. Pioneers and settlers making a new life for themselves in the New World (just like their ancestors settling in Western Europe a thousand years earlier) began by clearing land for crops and building a home.

Types of Rustic Furniture

The type of furniture built is dictated mainly by the availability of materials. Arguably the best materials are those harvested by pruning or coppicing on a trip to the woods. Wood is best cut in the winter when the sap is not flowing and needs to be allowed to season and dry out. Peeling away bark is easiest if

wood is cut while the sap is running as a tree comes into leaf. Those who live by rivers or the sea may use smoothed and bleached driftwood while those in towns may choose to recycle pallets and packaging or reclaim timber from demolition sites or skips. The

advantage of this type of timber is that it is already seasoned and can be used immediately.

Another type of rustic work uses freshly cut 'green' wood such as willow that can be easily bent around a frame before it dries out. Style varies, ranging from the chunky ranch house style popular in the Southwest to the elegant charm of Daniel Mack's peeled maple.

Techniques

While green wood is best bent and interwoven or nailed to avoid splitting during drying, seasoned wood can be assembled with traditional carpentry techniques. The most common joint is the mortise and tenon. In its most basic form this can be made using just a knife and a hand auger, but today many rustics use an assortment of hand and power tools including chainsaws, electric drills and mortise cutters.

Finishing is a matter of taste. Bark may be left on or stripped, the wood may be left natural or polished. The best effect is suggested by the wood itself.

left: Chair made by school children from Devon, England, using driftwood collected on local beaches.

opposite, left: Rustic chair using the natural shapes of branches to decorative effect, made by Daniel Mack from Warwick, New York.

opposite, right: High-backed chair by Daniel Mack, New York, using wood with the bark intact.

above, right: Peeled wood armchair by Daniel Mack, New York.

American Folk Art

Folk artists were historically mainly amateurs or local craftsmen making and decorating goods for their own use or for the community who reached a creative peak in North America during the 19th century. The current popularity of the genre has led to the appearance of many professionals working in the field today.

Americana

The repertoire of the American folk artist drew upon a sense of national pride, calling upon icons of history and the natural world. Great American presidents such as George Washington and Abraham Lincoln were popular subjects as was the allegorical figure of Uncle Sam in his top hat and striped trousers. Less specific were carvings of soldiers or Native Americans, the 'noble savages' who had been displaced by colonists and settlers. Certain animals, too, expressed the attitudes of the people, notably the indomitable bear so admired by Theodore Roosevelt and the bald eagle, a symbol of freedom, which in 1782 was chosen as the official emblem of the United States. Incorporated into many pieces is the Stars and Stripes, the American flag, or its bold red, white and blue colours.

Wood

Timber was the most plentiful material, easily obtained from the extensive woods for the construction of buildings, houses, furniture and utensils, many of which were enhanced with brightly painted carving. Decoys for attracting ducks, for example, were carefully shaped but stylistically painted. To observe the strength and direction of the wind there were 'whirligigs', human in shape with arms that whirled like a windmill. Signs and shop fronts were often distinctive and no cigar store was complete without a life-sized carving of an Indian outside its door. Larger than life were the carved animals on fairground rides and the imposing figureheads of sailing ships.

top: American Eagle carved and painted by J. P. Uranker, a craftsman from Martha's Vineyard, Massachusetts.
left: Life-sized carved wooden Native American, a figure once commonly seen outside American stores selling cigars.
above: Wooden bear, Rico, Colorado.

Metal

A village blacksmith had to turn his hand to making many things and farmsteads were often equipped with a forge of their own. Weather vanes, a common feature of the landscape, were frequently moulded from copper into the striking forms of cockerels or Native Americans with bows and arrows, while even a humble object such as an iron boot scraper might take an unexpected form like that of a dog or chicken.

Textiles

The quintessential North American textile is the patchwork quilt, but many women were also adept at embroidery or weaving. Today, the rugs of the Navajo sometimes show narrative scenes calling upon the folk art genre rather than traditional style.

Contemporary Navajo rug depicting a reservation trading post. Rugs with more traditional designs can be seen hanging at the back of the store.

Painting

Folk art painting was generally very direct in its approach. The subjects of sedentary painters included scenes of the local area or visions of more biblical or heavenly landscapes. Others, such as the famous Grandma Moses (1860–1961), chose scenes from daily life. Among the few professionals were 'limners' who earned their living travelling from settlement to settlement and painting portraits of the inhabitants.

Plains Bead Appliqué

The Great Plains of North America form a vast, grass-covered prairie stretching from Saskatchewan in Canada to New Mexico two thousand miles to the south in North America. The plains were ideal grazing for deer antelope and buffalo, providing a rich hunting ground for many semi-nomadic tribes who depended on such animals for food, clothing, shelter and most of the necessities of life. Here, among many others, roamed the Blackfoot in Alberta and Montana, the Sioux and Cheyenne in Dakota and the Comanche into Texas. Although this way of life has now been swept aside, many tribes still continue to preserve their traditions and will dress in the finery of those lost times as an expression of tribal identity and pride.

History

The abundance of game allowed leisure time during which the various tribes developed distinctive styles of decoration for their clothing. Before the coming of the white man the most common decoration on the hides worn by the Plains tribes was fashioned from elk teeth or porcupine quills. The latter could be dyed, flattened and sewn down in geometric patterns. Although they were used extensively by the peoples of the Northeast, beads made from marine shells, known as wampum, traded second or third hand were expensive and therefore used sparingly.

Styles changed with the introduction of glass beads by white traders in the late 18th century. By 1805 the Crow in North Dakota were using a combination of porcupine quill and bead embroidery and by the mid-19th century quillwork had virtually disappeared. The Crow were particularly enamoured with the blue beads and were prepared to trade a horse for 100 beads. These comparatively large 'pony' beads were supplanted in the 1840s by smaller seed beads that allowed more delicate work.

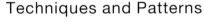

above: Pair of gauntlets embroidered with cut-glass beads from the Plateau region.

Techniques and Patterns

Rather than sew beads individually, the Plains tribes preferred to thread several at a time and sew them down at once in a series of short parallel rows, a technique called 'lazy stitch'. A greater number of beads can be sewn down in one go if the thread is laid in position and secured at intervals of two or three beads with an 'overlaid' or 'spot' stitch. The Crow would often sew several rows of beads using lazy stitch and then secure them all at once with a thread sewn at right angles across the back, rising to the front to tack the rows down one at a time. This is often known as 'Crow stitch'.

While the tribes of the Northeast Woodlands sewed individual beads down into sinuous and intricate floral designs, the technique used by the people of the Plains, sewing several beads simultaneously, dictated the use of straight lines which formed geometric patterns worked in solid blocks. Often these represented clouds, the sun, lightning, tipis, hills or buffalo.

Patterns were initially strongly influenced by the patterns used with quillwork, but became increasingly floral during the 19th century.

The Use of Plains Beadwork

Beadwork was often used to decorate the borders, cuffs or seams of clothing and sometimes the entire surface of festive clothing. Some of the most beautiful beaded items are moccasins, the soft leather footwear of the Plains. For someone important or a treasured child these were occasionally intensively beaded even on the soles. Other beaded items included bags for pipes or mirrors and the covers for cradle boards.

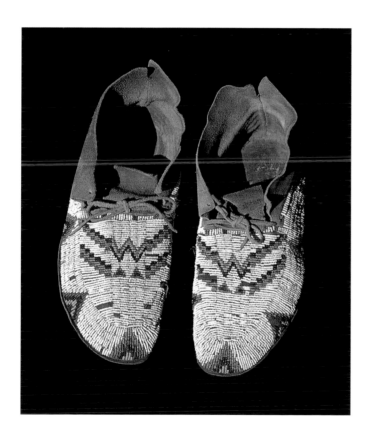

above: Sioux or Cheyenne moccasins with extensive beadwork made in the late 19th century. Some fancy moccasins even had beadwork on the soles.
right: Blackfoot mirror bag made in the 1880s. Blackfoot territory stretched from Alberta in Canada to Montana in North America.

Rawhide and Buckskin

The Cherokee believed that the love of the Great Spirit for mankind could be seen in the fact that it took the brain of one antelope to tan the hide of one antelope. In parts of North America the First Peoples were able to weave clothing from the hair and wool of animals, the bark of cedar and basswood or from the fibres of certain plants such as nettles and milkweed. Some, however, like the tribes of the prairies, depended solely on the hides of the animals that they also hunted for food for clothing and other requisites. Many animals were hunted but the best hides were obtained from buffalo, deer and elk.

Rawhide

On the prairies the hunting of animals was the task of men, but the arduous preparation of the hides was the work of women. Once an animal had been skinned, the hide was pegged out on the ground and the flesh and tissue was scraped off. It was dried in the sun before scraping again to thin and smooth it and then the hair was scraped off. At this stage the skin, now known as rawhide, is tough, flexible and waterproof. When wet it can be moulded into shape to dry stiff and hard.

Rawhide was ideal for making both shields and drumskins as it could be stretched into shape before shrinking tight. It was also good for making saddles, boxes and for parfleches, large envelopes, that could be folded up for transporting dried food and valuables. The skin could also be cut into strips and used as thongs. In the cold north it provided the lacing for snowshoes.

Leather

After cleaning, a hide could be tanned by rubbing it with a paste made from brains and then soaking for several days. After wringing out and stretching, the hide could be softened by pulling back and forth around a thong or by stretching and scraping again. In this cured state the hide or leather remained soft and supple and could be further preserved by smoking which also gave it a darker colour. The softest, and whitest, leather was obtained from the skin of deer and is known as buckskin.

Leather was used by the Plains Indians for making all manner of bags and pouches and was ideal for making clothing such as shirts, dresses, leggings and moccasins. A man's shirt

above, left: Pair of Sioux beaded buckskin moccasins, 1890s.
above, right: Contemporary shirt in the style of those made in the 1880s; brain-tanned buckskin painted with earth pigments and decorated with seed beads and horsehair tassels.

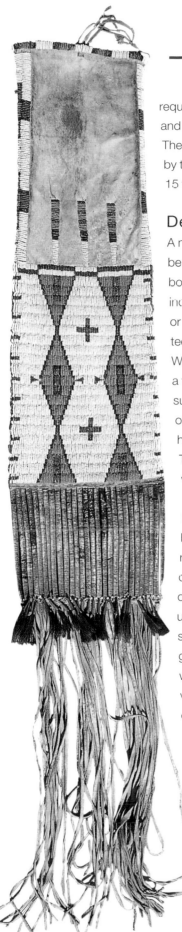

required two deer or antelope skins and a woman's dress two elk skins. The covers for the conical tipi favoured by these nomads required on average 15 to 20 buffalo hides.

Decoration

A number of techniques might be employed to decorate hides, both rawhide and tanned leather, including the cutting of fringes or the attachment of beads, elk teeth or porcupine quills. The Western Apache were adept at a form of appliqué in which they superimposed one layer of hide over another in which patterns had been cut out with a knife. The simplest form of decoration was painting.

Before painting, leather must be sealed with a size made from beaver tail glue, cactus sap or rendered horn. Over this patterns could be painted using pigments obtained from minerals or later using commercial paints. While some designs were abstract and geometric, others were imbued with the symbolism of dreams and visions. Some, like those painted on the shirts of the Ghost Dancers of 1890, were believed to protect the wearer from injury, even making them bulletproof. On occasion large 'exploit' robes of buffalo hide were painted with scenes of heroism and visions. With the decline of buffalo numbers this became a genre of painting on paper and cloth.

left: Teton Sioux buckskin pipe bag with beadwork and porcupine-quill wrapping, late 19th century.
below: Sioux pouch made from painted rawhide, Pine Ridge Reservation, North Dakota.

Pueblo Pottery

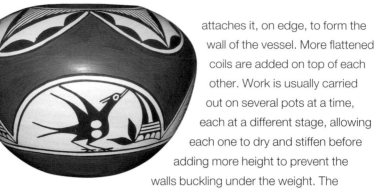

The basic forms and construction methods used today have much in common with pottery dating from 1,500 years ago found in the Southwest. Pottery skills are still passed down from mother to daughter or niece in the Pueblos of New Mexico and Arizona and even today it remains a predominantly female occupation. Until recently, when ceramics have become a source of cash, men were seldom potters with the exception of men who chose to live as women such as the Zuni-trained Arroh-ah-och, working at Laguna, who was one of the most famous Pueblo potters of the 19th century.

With the exception of reduction-fired blackwares, Pueblo pottery is decorated with polychrome patterns painted with slip before firing.

Preparation

Many Pueblo families continue digging their own clay, often some distance from home, a task now made easier with wheelbarrows or pick-up trucks. The clay is dried and impurities are removed before it is mixed with water and kneaded. Temper made by grinding fragments of broken pots is added to the mix. This gives the pot greater strength, prevents warping and allows the escape of air during firing, thus reducing the potential damage caused by thermal shock.

Construction

First the potter forms a base in a concave *puki* formed from an old pot or a bowl. She then rolls out a coil of clay, flattens it and attaches it, on edge, to form the wall of the vessel. More flattened coils are added on top of each other. Work is usually carried out on several pots at a time, each at a different stage, allowing each one to dry and stiffen before adding more height to prevent the walls buckling under the weight. The finished form is then scraped and sanded until smooth.

Decoration

Several coats of slip (liquid clay) are applied to the pot with a brush or a piece of cloth or leather and allowed to dry before patterns from the family's repertoire are applied with a fine brush traditionally made from a chewed yucca stem. Finally, the surface is burnished by rubbing with a smooth pebble.

The traditional base colour varies: Zuni, Acoma and Laguna potters, for example, prefer a white base while Hopi potters choose yellow. Most Pueblo pottery features stylized and geometric motifs which often represent clouds or animals. Acoma jars are sometimes decorated with large parrots,

above, left: Slip-painted canteen, Laguna Pueblo, New Mexico.
above, right: Water jar made by Eleanor Pino Griego, Zia Pueblo, New Mexico.
right: 'Migration pattern' pot by Bonnie Nampeyo, a design handed down through the family since the first Nampeyo (*c.* 1859–1942), Hopi Reservation, Arizona.

while Zuni jars frequently feature a deer with a heartline (an arrow from its mouth to its heart). Many designs are now common to several villages.

Modern Hopi pottery owes a great debt to Nampeyo (c. 1859–1942) who developed the curvilinear Sitkyatki style inspired by sherds of ancient pottery found near her home.

Firing

Items to be fired are stacked in a sheltered spot on a grid over glowing embers before being covered with potsherds or pieces of metal to protect them from flames. The heap is then covered with cow or sheep dung that is ignited by the embers. The fire burns at a high steady temperature reaching up to 940°C (1724°F) for just an hour or so. Once the pile has cooled and the pots are extracted, the colours of the decoration are revealed as being far brighter than when applied.

above: Slip-painted wedding vase, Jemez Pueblo, New Mexico.
right: Jar in the Zuni style by M. Antonio, New Mexico. The deer with a heartline is an iconic Zuni motif.

Navajo Jewelry

left: Gilbert Hamilton, a Navajo silversmith from Coyote Pass, New Mexico, stamping motifs onto a silver bracelet.
below, right: Silver Navajo bracelet inset with turquoise.
below, centre: Navajo bracelet of hand-pulled silver wire set with turquoise.

The Navajo, who call themselves 'Dineh' which means 'the people', occupy the largest reservation in North America, situated mainly in northeast Arizona with adjoining territory in New Mexico and Utah. Today they are one of the most successful tribes balancing traditional beliefs and customs with aspects of the modern, economic and industrial world.

The Long Walk

Things have changed considerably since the 1860s when the tribe were subjugated by forces led by Colonel Kit Carson. Their orchards were destroyed, their flocks slaughtered and 8,000 Navajos were forced to make the 'Long Walk' to Bosque Redondo (Fort Sumner) in eastern New Mexico. Hundreds died

on the walk and during their five-year-long exile. On returning home, however, many Navajo realized the opportunity of using their craft skills to earn money from their white overlords. Blanket making was adapted into rug weaving and the newly learned silversmithing thrived. The main outlets were the trading posts run by men such as Lorenzo Hubble at Ganado.

Silverwork

Atsidi Chon ('Old Smith') is reputed to have been the first Navajo silversmith, learning his trade in the 1850s from itinerant Mexican silversmiths known as *plateros*. For a long time silver was obtained in the form of silver dollars or pesos which were hammered out and decorated by stamping, filing and piercing. One popular and simply made item was

below, left: Silver squash-blossom necklace with *naja* pendant, *c*. 1950.
below, centre: On this silver necklace with *naja* pendant the silver balls are made from two hammered hemispheres soldered together, 1954.
below, right: This silver squash-blossom necklace with *naja* pendant is set with turquoise, *c*. 1945.

the *concha*, a silver disc that could be attached to belts or hatbands.

Later a technique referred to as 'sand casting' was learned although the mould is not actually of sand but is hollowed out, in two sections, from a piece of soft volcanic stone. This method is used to make bracelets, *ketoh* (bow guards) and *najas*.

use of turquoise in silverwork has become almost omnipresent and it is the combination of silver and turquoise that for many people epitomizes the craftwork of this enterprising nation.

left: Broad silver bracelet set with turquoise. The design is inspired by the guard worn on the wrist when using a bow, Navajo.
below: Nineteenth-century Navajo silversmith displaying a belt decorated with silver *conchas*.

Naja

The *naja* is a form of crescent used as the pendant for necklaces copied from Spanish jewelry of the 19th century. The Spanish, in turn, had borrowed the motif from the Moors who regarded the moon-shaped crescent as a talisman against the evil eye. Often the arms of the crescent terminate in little hands reminiscent of the Islamic Hand of Fatima, also a powerful protective amulet.

Squash Blossoms

Many *naja* necklaces are adorned with strings of hollow silver squash-blossom pendants. These too are motifs acquired from Spanish jewelry, specifically imitating the little silver pomegranates that adorned the capes and trousers of gentlemen from the city of Granada of which the pomegranate is an emblem, a symbol of fecundity.

Turquoise

Turquoise is a beautiful blue or green stone deeply embedded in Navajo myth and legend and jewelry is often decorated lavishly with it. Once the stone was abundant in the region although now it is often imported from abroad. Turquoise had been drilled and strung into jewelry since ancient times but the technique of setting stone was not learned until 1880 and since then the

Coiled Baskets in the Southwest

North America is rich in traditions of basketry among both First Americans and the descendants of European settlers. According to the uses to which the baskets are put and the locally available materials a considerable range of techniques and styles has developed encompassing coiling, plaiting, twining and stake and strand. Many fine baskets are still produced in the Southwest mainly using the coiling technique although due to the effort and time required to make a good basket the number of women making them has fallen dramatically over the last hundred years as young folk seek jobs with regular wages and many of the remaining basketmakers are now quite old. However, baskets continue to be an important part of the spiritual life of some groups such as the Hopi which promises the survival of skills for some time to come.

Practical and Ceremonial Baskets

Since prehistoric times, as evidenced by archaeological remains such as those in the cliff dwellings of the Ancient Puebloans (once referred to as the Anasazi), baskets have played an important part in the daily life of the people of the Southwest. They have been employed to gather and carry food, to winnow seed and to store grain. Some have been used in leisure activities as gambling trays or as drums and the techniques have also been used in the construction of both hats and shoes.

Other baskets are traditionally used in marking rites of passage and the celebration of births, marriages and deaths. Baskets full of corn pollen are an important part of an Apache girl's Sunrise, when she becomes a woman, and a distinctive basketry bowl is made for a Navajo wedding. The Hopi, in particular, place great importance on baskets and give plaques, often decorated with images of Katchina spirits, to children to help develop their link with the spirit world.

Techniques

The basic technique of making a coiled basket is very similar to making a coiled pot. Plant fibres are curved around and around in a spiral to form the body of the basket and are stitched into place. The foundation material may be made up of a bundle of fibre such as grasses or it may be composed of pliable rods.

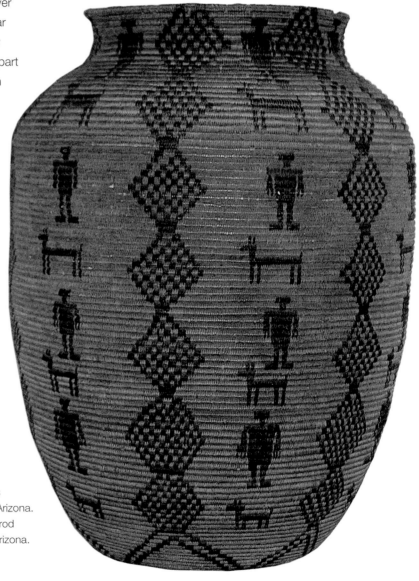

above: Coiled Hopi basket with a coil foundation of galleta grass stitched with yucca, Second Mesa, Hopi Reservation, northern Arizona.
right: Western Apache *olla*, a large storage basket, with a three-rod foundation stitched with willow and black devil's claw, eastern Arizona.

The stitches that fix the coils in place are sewn using a flexible fibre such as yucca or stems of shrubs such as willow or sumac that have been split into splints.

The composition of the coils and the materials used vary according to location and tribe and may be used for the purposes of identification. The Papago (the most prolific basketmakers in the Southwest), for instance, use bundles of beargrass stitched with willow or yucca, the Pima use bundles of cattails stitched with willow and devil's claw and the Hopi use galleta grass bundles sewn with yucca. The Paiute use a foundation of three bunched rods sewn with sumac, while the Jicarilla Apaches employ three or five and the Western Apache three rods sewn with willow and devil's claw. The Navajo, on the other hand, traditionally use two rods and a fibre bundle stitched with sumac. There are many variations.

Basketry Today

The materials used to construct a basket were once gathered from the immediate environment, but as plants have become scarcer a woman may have to travel for hours to find what she needs. So the traditional distinctions due to the choice of materials has sometimes become blurred as substitutes are made. Designs have also changed as the maker alters her repertoire to suit her market and some contemporary basketmakers now produce designs that are a fusion of motifs from the traditions of other tribes.

above, left: Papago (Tohono O'odham) 'man in the maze' basket with a foundation of beargrass stitched with yucca and devil's claw, southern Arizona.

above, right: Yavapai basket, made by Effie Starr, with a three-rod foundation stitched with willow and devil's claw, Prescott Reservation, western Arizona.

Mexican Painted Ceramics

Mexico is a country bursting at the seams with vibrant craftwork. Many women have become proficient potters, making all the crockery required for the storage, preparation and serving of food. The city of Puebla and the town of Dolores Hidalgo in Guanajuato are famous for their brightly coloured lead-glazed pottery, a technique learned from the Spanish in the 16th century, but the vast majority of Mexican pottery is unglazed earthenware, either plain or simply decorated in earth colours with slips and oxides. The exceptions are the brightly painted pieces produced for festivals, skeletons, saints and nativity scenes, which, in the 1960s, became much sought after by collectors of folk art such as Nelson Rockefeller. The ensuing recognition and demand gave many a chance to rise out of poverty and develop their work in new ways. Today in Oaxaca, arguably Mexico's most artistically inspired state, 400,000 out of a population of three million are involved in the creation of folk art.

be made and fired separately for attachment afterwards using pieces of wire or springs. Firing takes place outdoors in a kiln which is a brick or adobe wall to protect a fire from uneven draughts that would spoil the pottery. The raw wares are stacked inside the wall and the fire is fed through an opening in its base. Work intended to be painted is fired once for up to eight hours.

above, left: Three-footed dish decorated with acrylic paint, Guerrero, central Mexico.
below, right: Brightly painted Day of the Dead candlestick, Izucar de Matamoros.

Construction

In Oaxaca the digging, preparation and firing of clay is traditionally carried out by men while women focus on the actual construction. This skill is still passed down from mother to daughter as it has been from time immemorial but, now that serious money may be involved, men also play a part in the making and decorating processes.

Pottery is made indoors or in the shade either at a table or working on the ground. Like pots, large shapes are built up from coils of clay while figures and details are pinched into shape with the fingers. Clay is scraped with a piece of gourd, smoothed with a piece of old felt and details added using a needle or the spine of a cactus. The shapes of flowers or other repeated elements may be moulded and then attached while other pieces may

left: Painted clay figure in the style typical of Ocotlán, Oaxaca.

left: Skeleton candlesticks for the Day of the Dead, Izucar de Matamoros.

Once cool, work is painted using acrylic paints in the bright colours so beloved by Mexicans.

Subjects

Many of the models made these days represent scenes of daily life or episodes from local legends such as La Sirena, the lazy girl who turned into a mermaid, La Matlacihua, the demon who disguises itself as a beautiful woman to lure men to their doom, or La Llorona, the weeping woman who is cursed to wander forever after killing her own children. Other popular subjects include figurines of the Virgin Mary and popular saints. Increasingly common are models of women at the market selling fruit, flowers or even parrots.

Large structures smothered with flowers and figures represent the Tree of Life, *arbol de la vida*, often with Adam and Eve at the base and family members in the branches. Other distinctive models are associated with the Day of Dead, a festival celebrated on 2 November when folk remember their lost loved ones. The festivities are filled with eating and drinking and many representations of skeletons.

right: Mexican ceramic *arbor del amor* (Tree of Love). These exuberant sculptures sometimes include dozens of figures.

Hojalata: Tincraft

Often referred to as the artistic capital of Mexico, Oaxaca is teeming with arts and crafts, known in Spanish as *artesanias*. Inventive masterpieces, both festive and functional, can be found made of anything from clay to papier mâché and from bones to gourds. Among the brightest are gaily painted tin figures, including suns, moons, mermaids, parrots and animals, that make great decorations for Christmas trees. These are a modern application for the contemporary market of a craft that reflects the history of Mexico itself.

Tin in Mexico

Although it has now mostly perished, tin was being worked in Mexico before the arrival of the Conquistadores, used for making ornaments and other small objects. The introduction of Catholicism by the Spanish had far-reaching consequences in many aspects of daily life including the development of tin craft for making apparatus and paraphernalia for use in the churches. These ranged from frames for religious pictures and niches (*nichos*) for statues of saints to wall sconces and chandeliers all of which could be cut to shape with simple tools and decorated with stamping and tooling. On a smaller scale small ex-voto offerings or *milagros* were also made of sheet metal, sometimes even of gold. These still function as tangible prayers, pressed with the shapes of body parts, kneeling figures or animals, and are attached to the clothing of the Saints to invoke their aid with sickness and worries.

Tin craft reached across the border into New Mexico during the mid-19th century at a time when canned food, glass, wallpaper and cheap religious lithographic prints were among the many goods being shipped down the Santa Fé Trail from the East. Tin cans could be recycled and some, like the five gallon lard cans, could provide large sheets of tin. The Hispanic community took advantage of these new ideas and materials and produced elaborate frames and *nichos* that were decorated not only with tooling, but also with painting on the reverse of the glass or panels of wallpaper.

While the craft expired in New Mexico during the 1940s, it has thrived in Mexico, finding new techniques and a new market in the form of visitors from abroad.

left: Mexican painted tin rocking elephant, Oaxaca City, Oaxaca.
above: Contemporary painted tin mirrors and decorations, Oaxaca City, Oaxaca.

left: Painted tin *milagro* commemorating the victim of a shooting, Mexico, 1972.
below: Found in Mexican churches, stamped brass *milagros* or ex voto tangible prayers like these are attached to statues of saints.
bottom: A tin and glass *retablo* frame containing the image of the Virgin of Guadalupe, patron saint of Mexico.

The Material

Sheet tin is in fact a sandwich made of steel coated on both sides by dipping in molten tin. The tin content may be as little as two per cent. The steel provides rigidity, while the tin provides a shiny surface that prevents rust as long as it does not get scratched. Sheet copper or zinc may also be used but tin is cheap and readily available, particularly when in the form of recycled cans. Food cans often have the added appeal of being lacquered gold on the inside, creating extra decorative possibilities.

Techniques

The tools required for tin craft are few and simple, making a large workshop superfluous. Shapes are cut from a metal sheet using shears or tin snips. Curvature of the surface may be achieved by hammering or by scoring lines with a chisel and bending. The surface is frequently enhanced with scored lines to emphasize the form depicted or decorated with patterns that may be either indented, by punching from the front, or embossed, by punching from the back. Separate modules may be joined together, for example when making a mirror frame, using solder melted with a hot iron or simply by tying together with wire. In former times the decoration was purely texture, but the availability of a vibrant palette of commercial paints has been exploited here in an expression of the Mexican love of exuberant colour.

2

left: Head wrapping, from Guatemala, made in tapestry weave with supplementary wefts.

above: Women with their babies in traditional costume, Cusco, Peru.

opposite: Appliqué mola from the San Blas Islands off Panama.

Central and
South America

Introduction

Conventional wisdom has it that the early Americans who had crossed from Asia to Alaska during the last Ice Age gradually migrated south and east through Central America, heading south all the way to Patagonia. Finds showing possible human settlements in Pedra Furada in Brazil and Monte Verde in Chile 33,000 years ago have suggested that settlers may have arrived before this, travelling by boat along the coast or even across the ocean. Evidence has shown that the peoples of ancient times were skilled, inventive and adventurous.

Geography

Central and South America can be divided into a number of climatic and topographic zones and the indigenous cultures should be categorized by these rather than by political boundaries. To the west lies a long strip of coastal plain which rises abruptly into the valleys and high plateaux of the Andes. To the east of the mountains lie the vast humid forests of the Amazon Basin and to the south the grasslands of the Pampas and the cold dry wastes of Patagonia. The physical demands of life are basically the same for those living at altitude in the Andes whether they live in Ecuador, Peru or Chile and are considerably different from those who live on the coastal planes in the same countries.

Pre-Columbian Cultures

Due to the challenging terrain, early civilizations in the region were mostly isolated until united by colonizing

nations such as the Aztec and the Maya in Central America and the Inca in South America. The secret of their success lay in their exploitation of the skills of the peoples they subjugated who in turn drew upon the techniques developed by their forebears just as the craftspeople of the present draw upon them. Among these were the pottery of the Moche in northern Peru and the sublime weaving of the Paracas peninsula. At the heart of the story of the downfall of the Incas is the working of the gold, known to the Incas as 'the tears of the sun'.

left: Copy of a pre-Columbian drinking vessel used by the Carchu people (1200–1500) of Peru.

below: Yekuana basket from the rainforest of Venezuela decorated with armadillo motifs.

opposite, above, left: Silver crucifix made in Cuenca, Ecuador.

opposite, below, left: Carved seat in the shape of a jaguar made by animist Achuara Indians in the Amazon rainforest. The forest animals are believed to possess great spiritual power.

opposite, below, right: Ceramic church used as a roof decoration, made in Ayacucho, Peru.

left: Male weaver using a backstrap loom in Urubamba, Peru. In the Andes weaving is traditionally women's work, but men have taken up the craft for commercial gain.

below: Prayer flag consisting of a woollen 'god's eye' made by the Jivaros in the forests of the Oriente, Ecuador.

below: Metal fastening for a *manta* or shawl used by the Mapuche people of Chile.

Catholicism and the Old Ways

Driven by the search for gold, the Spanish conquered South America in 1530 under the leadership of Francisco Pizarro who travelled south from Panama which had already been annexed by Columbus. In only five years the conquistadors had gained control and began to impose European values onto the indigenous population. Foremost among these was Catholicism. The indigenous peoples had previously placed their faith in belief systems in which patron deities were constantly invoked and at the heart of which was the idea of sacrifice and blood. With its army of saints and focus on the sacrifice of Christ, Christianity was a religion that the people could identify with and to this day many pagan beliefs survive disguised by the skin of Catholicism. The images depicted in crafts have changed, as have many of the techniques used, but they are created with the same ancient, colourful fervour. The conquistadors did not seriously challenge the established way of life in the rainforest and here old beliefs and skills have survived largely untouched into the present. Now, however, the threat lies not in religion but in the destruction of the habitat in a rapacious quest not for gold, but for agricultural land, timber and oil.

above: Appliqué panel depicting a farming scene with a smoking volcano in the distance, Cotopaxi region, Ecuador.

Alfombras: Guatemalan Flower Carpets

For a thousand years before the arrival of the Spanish in the late 15th century, Central America had been under the sway of a succession of colourful cultures of which the best known were the Maya and the Aztecs. Religious and ceremonial life was embellished with precious stones, gold, feathers and flowers. In 1523 the gold hungry conquistador Hernando Cortez sent Pedro de Alvarado into what is now Guatemala, leading to its consequent subjugation and subsequent enforced conversion to Catholicism. To succeed in their mission the new rulers employed a combination of brutality and colourful pageantry to rival that of the culture they had supplanted.

Semana Santa in Antigua

Throughout Latin America feasts such as Corpus Cristi are accompanied by the parading of the images of the saints around the town or village. The most important feast is Easter and the week leading up to it, known as Semana Santa (Holy Week), is a spectacular occasion attracting both worshippers and tourists in their thousands to Antigua city in Guatemala. The effigies may weigh as much as three and a half tons and require teams of 80 to 100 penitents to carry them around the cobbled streets. Locals began cushioning the hard stones by strewing them with pine needles before realizing the decorative possibilities. Today, neighbourhoods compete to create the most amazing carpet or *alfombra* before it is trodden underfoot and destroyed.

Making Alfombras

Pine needles are still used to make the colourful carpets, but are now combined with flower petals, and large quantities of brightly dyed sawdust, all of which may become dangerously slippery when walked on. Sometimes the footsteps of the penitents are further hampered by the inclusion of fruit and vegetables in the designs.

below: Alfombra on the streets of Antigua City in Guatemala during Semana Santa (Holy Week). Time-consuming work shortly to be destroyed underfoot during the Easter processions.

The sawdust is spread across the pavement and kept in place by regularly spraying with water. Motifs may be worked by hand, but it is common to use stencils and templates which are often kept from one year to the next.

Well Dressing

In Derbyshire and a few other counties in England another ephemeral artform is the Dressing of Holy Wells. A pro-Christian festival, it is intended to ensure a plentiful supply of water. Wooden boards are soaked and coated with mud or clay before being decorated with images constructed mainly from early summer flowers. Once the subjects of the designs were predominantly biblical, but more contemporary themes are now also popular.

Sand Paintings

Large sand designs thought to have spiritual or healing properties are exactingly drawn by Tibetan Buddhists and by the Navajo of southwestern North America. The accurate execution of the design is an act of devotional focus and invocation but the beautiful results, which may have taken hours or even days to draw, are deliberately destroyed at the end of the ceremony. Tibetan designs take the form of a geometric *mandala*, whereas the Navajo employ more figurative images such as supernatural *yei* figures specific to particular healing rites.

above, left and above, right: Creating alfombra patterns by sprinkling coloured sawdust through a stencil.
below: A well dressing with flowers pressed into clay at Tissington in Derbyshire, England in 2004.

Molas: Appliqué of the San Blas Islands

above, left: Mola with stylized design inspired by natural forms.
above, right: Panel with four variations of a fish design. Wildlife plays a major role in the design repertoire of the Kuna.
opposite, above: Mola with a pair of doves, possibly inspired by imported packaging.

Off the Atlantic coast of Panama lie the San Blas Islands, an archipelago inhabited by the Kuna people who are believed to be descendants of the original Carib Indians after whom the Caribbean is named. Despite increasing tourism they have managed to maintain their traditions and way of life. The society is matrilineal with a man moving in with his wife's family after marriage and property passing down the female line. Although the men wear drab modern dress, Kuna women wear a colourful and distinctive costume consisting of a patterned, blue sarong, a red and yellow headscarf, arm and leg beads, a gold nose ring and earrings and a blouse decorated front and back with appliqué panels called molas. These blouses are considered such a mark of Kuna culture and identity that an attempt to ban them by the Panama government led to a rebellion which ultimately resulted in the legal recognition of the islands as an Autonomous Territory in 1938.

The Mola

The mola is a panel sewn onto a woman's blouse to fit between the bust and waist. Usually a pair is made, one for the front and one for the back, using variations of the same design or even the same design with a different colour sequence, the most popular colours being red, black and orange. Traditional motifs may be geometric designs derived from body painting, abstracted patterns based on local wildlife or scenes from Kuna mythology. Today, molas are sometimes worked for sale to tourists and then designs may be chosen from imported cultural sources

such as television, posters, food labels and magazines. Traditional molas often come onto the market second hand as their makers tire of their old clothes and make new panels for their blouses. These are usually of better quality than those made directly for sale.

So much time is taken up with embroidery that it has been said that the mola is in effect a form of diary, recording the joys and vicissitudes of a Kuna woman's life.

Mola Construction

In spite of attempts to introduce the sewing machine during the 1970s, Kuna women prefer to sew by hand. The technique used is reverse appliqué which in its simplest form involves laying one piece of fabric over another, cutting a slit or hole in the top layer and tucking the edges under to reveal the layer beneath. The edges are notched before tucking to avoid bunching and are then sewn down. Molas are special because as many as seven layers may be superimposed to produce vivid multi-coloured designs. Occasionally pieces of cloth may be added into a space using conventional appliqué to create an accent. Finally, surface detail is sometimes added with embroidery.

Similar Techniques

Reverse appliqué is popular in India for use on quilts and hangings and is frequently used to decorate the costumes of the hill tribes of Southeast Asia and China. However, the use of multiple layers, like on the costumes of the White H'mong in Laos, is much more unusual. The Seminole Indians in Florida once used a similar distinctive technique in North America for the embellishment of the borders of clothes and blankets, but by 1910 the introduction of the sewing machine and trade cloth resulted in the traditional technique being supplanted by the quicker and better known Seminole patchwork.

below: A purely abstract design which shows how the colours of the design are revealed in the underlying layers of fabric.

Modelled Foodstuff

Whether Tutankhamun in his tomb in Egypt, Raedwald in his ship burial at Sutton Hoo in England or the nobles buried in the permafrost of Pazyryk in Siberia, the respected and the loved have often been sent on their journey into the next world equipped with everything they might need. A Saxon lord might have his sword or an Amazon tribesman his blowpipe, while a Chinese emperor or Sumerian king might be accompanied by a whole army made of terracotta or even real flesh and blood. All were supplied with food, often in the form of bread.

Masapan

Bread dough has been modelled in Europe and Egypt for thousands of years and was probably introduced to South America by the Spanish. In Ecuador the making of dough models, called *figuras de masapan*, has become a serious business. Dolls were originally made with crosses painted on their chests to celebrate All Souls' Day, but their popularity has become such that they are now often made as Christmas decorations, genre scenes or even earrings. Subjects vary from the Three Wise Men and their camels to complex tableaux of market traders in traditional costume with stalls full of fruit and vegetables.

The dough is a mixture of flour and water with salt added to preserve it. Usually the ratio is two parts flour to one part salt but variations are used for greater stiffness or elasticity. Once shaped, the dough is lightly baked in an oven, although it can be air dried, and then painted with food colouring or commercial paints and finally varnished.

In Ecuador the figures were once made in moulds at a local bakery but are now modelled into imaginative forms by enterprising women who have recognized the appeal of cheap, colourful souvenirs for tourists.

El Día de los Muertos

All Souls' Day is celebrated in Christian countries on 2 November and is known in Latin America as El Día de los Muertos, the Day of the Dead. In Ecuador *figuras de masapan* are placed in cemeteries for the departed to eat. In Mexico a colourful festival has grown up in which families dine out by the graves of their loved ones, often eating *panes de muertos*, the bread of the dead, which is shaped like small people and decorated with sugar. For several days houses are filled with representations of skeletons made of paper, clay or plaster and skulls made of sugar decorated with tin foil, icing and sequins. Although edible offerings may remain after the festival, it is believed the dead dine contentedly on the essence and the smell.

In many lands carved or moulded offerings of foodstuffs are given to the spirit world. Among the most spectacular were the larger than life sized sculptures of deities paraded at Tibetan festivals and made entirely from butter.

Potato Paste

In Peru the branding of cattle during August was once accompanied by a ritual in which offerings of food and coca leaves were placed before a portable shrine. When the doors of these *retablos* were open two floors were revealed, the top containing the patron saints of animals and the bottom showing

top left: Salt dough decoration in the form of a stylized turtle, Cuenca, Ecuador.
above, left: Salt dough figure in local costume, Cuenca, Ecuador.
top right: *Retablo* made in Lima, Peru, depicting a textile shop.
above, right: Sugar skull made for the Day of the Dead in Mexico.

a rustler being reprimanded. The figures were made from plaster mixed with potato paste. Since the 1940s *retablos*, especially those from Ayacucho, have become a popular folk art and are collected by tourists. There may now be several floors and dozens of brightly painted figures. The scenes may depict the Nativity, the Last Supper or craftsmen and shopkeepers.

A *retablo* with three registers. Although subjects were originally religious, those to be sold to visitors today often depict scenes of daily life.

Filigree

The Ancient Greeks and the Etruscans used the filigree technique of decorating metalware and jewelry. It consists of intricate designs drawn with wire, plain, twisted or plaited, and predominantly using gold or silver. Openwork filigree is often reminiscent of the delicate skeletal structure that remains after the flesh has decayed from autumn leaves.

Wire

The first wires were made from metal in one of two ways. The first method was to hammer the metal into a sheet and cut it into very thin strips which were then rolled between two flat surfaces, usually of stone or bronze, until it had become round. The second method was to take a strip and twist it into a spiral that resembled cord. By Roman times a third technique had been developed in which the metal strip was pulled forcibly through a draw plate. This was drilled with a number of holes of diminishing diameter through which the metal was pulled in succession, becoming thinner and longer each time. The resulting wire may be used as it is or it may be twisted or plaited into cords for extra decorative impact.

below: Pair of fine filigree earrings decorated with birds; made in Chordeleg, Ecuador.

left: Earrings from Chordeleg, a small town near Cuenca in Ecuador, famous for its filigree work.

Filigree Techniques

Wire decoration has been popular in many parts of Europe and Asia since ancient times and was introduced to North Africa and Spain by the Moors. Spanish craftsmen, skilled at working with silver, subsequently introduced wire work to South America where false filigree was already in use. Most filigree work here is of silver with some work in Chile being made from alpaca wire, an alloy containing only a small amount of silver.

The easiest, and therefore commonest, form of filigree is to bend lines of wire into a design and solder them onto a metal base. The spaces in the work may serve as settings for stones or be filled with enamel. Gallery wire is a term used to describe borders of pattern made by twisting wire around rows of nails in a board before soldering onto the base.

A jour filigree requires an even higher degree of manual dexterity as the wires must be shaped and assembled into an openwork design without the use of a base to provide

a foundation. This technique has become popular in South America for the creation of intricate jewelry often inspired by the natural world. Fine examples can be found at Catacaos in Peru, Mompós in Colombia, where much work is in gold, and Chordeleg in Ecuador where pieces range from peacock-shaped earrings to large-scale virtuoso sculptures of horsemen.

False Filigree

Although the techniques are entirely different, false filigree is similar in appearance to filigree and in fact may be made by taking a cast from a true filigree matrix.

The conquistadors were responsible for the melting down of enormous quantities of pre-Columbian gold work, but a sufficient quantity has survived to show the techniques they preferred. Among these was the cire perdue or lost-wax method of casting which was used in Colombia for making votive figures. Strands of wax were often attached to the matrix before casting which appeared in the finished piece much like wire.

The technique of granulation imitates twisted wire work, another pre-Columbian technique, in which patterns are formed from tiny droplets of metal soldered onto the base.

Appliqué Pictures

The towns and markets of South America are filled with handicrafts. Many of these handicrafts, such as weavings and pottery, are traditional while others have sprung up to please the tourist. Among these are the lively scenes, worked in appliqué by local women, called *telas recordas* in Spanish. Most are about the size of a pillowcase, but a few are larger than bed sheets.

Genre Scenes

In a changing world where baskets and pots are rapidly being replaced by plastic buckets and embroidered blouses are being superseded by T-shirts, traditional culture would appear to be a fragile thing. However many aspects of everyday life in Latin America have changed little over the centuries and the agricultural techniques employed are still often much the same as those used by the Incas and Aztecs. The rich mix of old animist beliefs and Catholicism has produced a range of festivals filled with exuberant colour and enhanced emotional fervour. Scenes like these, of daily toil and festive joy, are now painted, sculpted or sewn as a source of income. The same skills formerly used to make clothes and utensils are now turned to profit. Although some collectors scoff at articles made for the

tourist trade, it is often only the exploitation of this market that keeps those skills alive.

Techniques

Appliqué scenes are turned out quickly and in great numbers, often being made by groups of women working side by side. In spite of the repetitive subjects and the limited number of motifs, each piece is unique as the choice of colour and the way texture is created, for instance when depicting the leaves on a tree, is decided spontaneously by the maker and may be done differently each time.

Although appliqué was originally derived from the need to mend and recycle old fabric, a great deal of the materials, such as the blue cloth for the Andean skies which appear in most of these pieces, are now bought specifically for sewing. Templates may be used for some of the more awkward motifs such as llamas and used either way round for variety, but mostly the different elements are

cut by eye. The stitches used to sew down the individual pieces are basic and even crude, demonstrating the speed at which the scenes are assembled but the results are probably more full of fun and energy than work assembled with fastidious planning and meticulous needlework. On some pictures additional materials may be used for details including tiny wooden spades and tools tacked to the hands of labourers.

Other Media

Genre scenes are also worked in many other media; paintings on boxes and furniture or on paper made from sheets of bark are particularly common. Paint is extremely versatile and so the style varies considerably from one artist to another according to the choice of subject, to their drawing ability and the choice of bold or subtle colours.

Clay, papier mâché, bread dough and wood are among the many materials used. In Brazil brightly painted ceramic figures of bandits, soldiers and footballers are popular. In Colombia, Ecuador, Peru and Bolivia clay buses are ubiquitous. These depict the local open-sided vehicle, the *chiva*, and are packed with passengers, their roofs overladen with sacks of grain or vegetables and baskets of fruit. In Peru model shops may be filled with potato paste tradesmen and in Ecuador tableaux are made from bread dough.

above: Appliqué picture with wooden tools depicting Andean farming scene, Ecuador.
opposite, above: Appliqué picture of a village from Colombia.
opposite, below: Appliqué street scene from Bolivia.

Knitted Hats

When the conquistadors arrived in the early 16th century the Aymara and Quechua peoples of the Andes, subjects of the Incas, dressed simply, the men wearing a tunic and cape and the women a wrap-around skirt and mantle. Under the Spanish a different code of propriety was enforced and a costume like that worn by Spanish peasants was imposed, the men wearing a shirt, trousers and blanket or poncho and the women a blouse, skirt and mantle. By the 19th century this had become, with some variations, the traditional costume of the Andes topped off, in the case of women, by a felt or panama hat or, in the case of men, a knitted hat called a *chullo* which was usually equipped with earflaps.

Knitting

There is no evidence of knitting in pre-Columbian Latin America and it seems likely that it was introduced when the Spanish began to bring their womenfolk from Spain. Weaving was of a very high standard, however, and this understanding of textile structures enabled the folk of Peru and Bolivia in particular to become extremely adept at working complex designs and even writing into their knitting. A considerable number of women now depend on knitting for their livelihood, selling their hats, sweaters (a non-traditional item) and costume dolls in the markets and by the road sides of the Andes. Unfortunately the popularity of 'ethnic' wares has led to the introduction of knitting machines in the cities, producing cheap wares that undermine prices and so making labour-intensive quality work economically less viable and threatening the survival of craftsmanship.

right: Knitted woollen hat or *chullo* from Bolivia with bands of patterns similar to those used in woven belts.

Camelid Fibres

Sheep's wool is widely used for knitting in South America but is rivalled by the wool of the llama, alpaca and vicuña. These animals are the result of selected breeding in ancient times of the wild native guanaco, a ruminant closely related to the camel. The vicuña is now very rare whereas the llama is omnipresent and valued as a pack animal as well as for its wool. The alpaca, however, is kept purely for its beautiful, soft coat.

Camelid fibre and sheep's wool can be white, brown, grey and black and are often spun and knitted in these pleasant natural hues although dyed wool, increasingly bought ready dyed, is very popular.

The Chullo

The knitted hat, the *chullo*, is worn exclusively by men and boys. They are usually knitted by women but on Taquile Island on Lake Titicaca men learn from an early age to knit their own hats, the *chullo Santa Maria*, which unlike other *chullos* have no earflaps. Boys' *chullos* have a white tip, while those of married men have a red tip.

The better the quality of the wool and the more finely it is spun, the more delicately the patterned bands of a *chullo* can be knitted. Frequently these may be geometric with sequences of lozenges or chevrons, but often they are based on natural forms such as birds or vegetation. Knitting for sale to tourists, predictably, is likely to feature bands of stylized llamas or people holding hands. The most intricate work involves lettering such as the name of the knitter, place of origin or date of manufacture.

Styles of hats vary regionally. Alpaca fibre is preferred in southern Peru and Bolivia while sheep's wool is more typical further north. Although patterns worked for sale may have no local significance, many traditional patterns are used exclusively by a community, tribe or family.

above, left: Knitted child's hat bought in Pisac, Peru.
above, centre: Knitted Peruvian hat with the maker's name worked into the pattern.
above, right: Finely knitted hat with delicately worked animal designs from Bolivia.

The Backstrap Loom

left: Weaving on a backstrap loom attached to a handy post, Cusco, Peru.
right: Guatemalan woman's blouse or *huipil* with supplementary weft patterning woven on a backstrap loom.

Since ancient times, the backstrap or body-tensioned loom has been in use in Central and South America and Southeast Asia as can be verified by its depiction on pre-Columbian pottery and in the codices of post-conquest times. Traditionally it is a device used by women to meet the needs of the family, but today many items are woven on it as a source of income. On a loom of this type it is only possible to weave cloth up to a metre wide and larger textiles must be sewn together from several strips, but this very narrowness can also be an advantage as it is ideal for weaving complex designs using sophisticated techniques that can be cumbersome on wider apparatus.

Below: Peruvian woman's belt or *chumpi* worked with traditional motifs and the word 'felicidad' which means happiness.

The Loom

The basic structure of any loom requires a bar at each end to which the warp elements are attached, evenly spaced along their length. The warps must be kept under tension so that they are kept in sequence during weaving, a problem most often solved by fixing the end bars into a frame. With the backstrap loom, however, one end bar is attached to a fixed object such as a tree or a house post and the other is attached to a cloth or leather strap which passes around the waist of the weaver who creates tension by leaning back. Because it is light and not rigid when not in use the loom can easily be rolled up, carried around and set up in another location. It is a common sight now in Peru, Ecuador or Bolivia to see women weaving at the roadside or in the market place beside a stall where they have set out their wares.

Weaving Techniques

To weave a length of plain cloth the weaver must be able to open two sheds (through which the weft can be threaded), one by raising the even warps and another by raising the odd ones. On the backstrap loom a flat shed stick is threaded in and out across the width of the weaving. By turning this on edge alternate warps are raised to open a shed while laying the stick flat will close it. The second shed may be created with the use of a heddle or leashes which consist of a stick laid across the work to which loops passing around the other set of alternating warps are attached. When this stick is raised the warps are lifted to create the shed.

For the creation of sophisticated patterns, both geometric and figurative, many weaving techniques may be employed. Some, like tapestry weave, may be worked using the basic two sheds but only passing the weft part way across the work. Other techniques may depend on the opening of a number of different sheds with extra heddles or shed sticks. The weaver may also use a pattern stick which she threads in and out of the warps as required without first opening a shed.

Backstrap Textiles

Today the majority of textiles woven on the backstrap loom in Central and South America are made from cotton or wool, but plant fibres such as maguey (agave) were once very common. Although commercial yarn and chemical dyes are now readily available, many weavers continue to spin and dye their own yarn. Commonly used dyes include indigo blue, cochineal red and marigold yellow with secondary colours created by mixing or over dyeing.

Many items of traditional clothing may be woven on the backstrap loom including the sleeveless *huipil* of Mexico and Guatemala and the *manta* (a cross between a shawl and a carrying cloth) of Andean Peru. Some of the most complex designs are worked on the belts and sashes worn throughout the region: embellished with intricate patterns, writing or bold heraldic creatures.

right: Elaborate belt made on a backstrap loom by a Quechua weaver in Bolivia or Peru.

Vegetable Ivory

Along the banks of tributaries of the River Amazon in Ecuador, Peru and Bolivia grows a palm known to the indigenous peoples as the tagua nut palm. Its botanical name is *Phytelephas aequatorialis* which means literally the equatorial elephant plant. The name refers to its seeds or nuts which have the creamy colour and hard density of elephant tusks thus its common name 'vegetable ivory' in English.

The Tagua Palm

Growing under larger rainforest trees, the tagua nut palm is dioecious, which means it is either male or female. The female palm annually produces fruits the size of small melons with a hard, spiny case called a cabeza in which the seeds, about 5 cm (2 in.) long, are clustered in a manner similar to brazil nuts. When dry, these seeds become so hard that a hacksaw is needed to cut them. Their similarity to animal ivory has been recognized for a long time and tagua has been extensively used in the manufacture of items such as chess pieces, knife handles and dice. During the 19th century the uniforms of soldiers and sailors in North America were fastened mainly with buttons of tagua. The more unscrupulous artisan or trader has at times exploited the similarity, passing off vegetable ivory as animal ivory, and in our modern ecologically conscious world such a substitution can be an advantage.

In a year a tagua palm can produce about 22 kgs of fruit, about the same quantity of ivory as an elephant's tusk. It is therefore a cheaper, more sustainable source of ivory than animal ivory, providing an alternative that threatens no elephant with extinction and does, in fact, offer a financial incentive to preserving the rainforest, providing a higher return than stripping the land for agriculture or grazing.

above: Rosary of tagua nuts with a crucifix made from several nuts joined together, Cuenca, Ecuador.
below: Tagua nuts picked up near the River Napo, a tributary of the Amazon.

above: Bracelet made from slices of tagua nut, Ecuador.

Other Vegetable Ivory

A number of other palms produce a form of vegetable ivory. Among these are the Caroline ivory-nut palm, *Metroxylon amicarum*, which grows on the Caroline Islands of Micronesia and the natangura palm, *Metroxylon warburgii*, which is found on Vanuatu and the Solomon Islands and *Hyphaene ventricosa* which grows beside the Zambezi in Africa.

Working Tagua

Almost indistinguishable from elephant or marine ivory, the main disadvantage of tagua is its size. For larger objects such as umbrella handles or sculptures it is necessary to grind flat surfaces and assemble several nuts into one larger piece. Most items for sale in the markets of South America are small, carved from a single nut which is often mounted upon another. The most common subject for carving is wildlife, not only that found in the rainforest, but also species from further afield such as turtles, dolphins and even pandas, rabbits and, ironically, elephants.

Tagua nut is, like real ivory, dense and very hard, too hard to carve with a knife. A hacksaw is used for cutting and roughing out shapes before defining the form with files and rifflers intended for working metal or stone rather than wood. Machinery such as stone polishing tumblers or grinders and buffing wheels may also be employed.

Each nut is covered with a brown coating which must be removed to reveal the creamy 'ivory' beneath. Often the brown is only partially removed so providing a decorative contrast. The off-white ivory colour is one of the most attractive qualities of tagua nut and, although some craftsmen do paint or dye their carvings in bright colours, it is far more common to find work that displays its beautiful natural tones.

above, left: Carved tagua rabbit mounted on a base made of a tagua nut with its hard brown outer layer left intact. Large quantities of small sculptures are made in Ecuador for the tourist trade.
above, centre: Carved tagua dolphin.
above, right: Carved tagua turtle.

Amazonian Pottery

The Amazon Basin is vast, draining an area almost as large as Australia, but today it is seriously threatened with destruction by logging, agriculture, mineral extraction and oil drilling. Scientists have acknowledged the seriousness of the threat to the planet if this vast natural resource with its pharmacy and its ability to lock carbon in its trees were to be lost. Also at risk are the people who have lived there for thousands of years: their culture and their beautiful crafts, their flamboyant featherwork, intricate basketry and fine pottery.

Pottery and Baskets

The peoples of the forest traditionally live a hunter-gatherer lifestyle supplemented with slash and burn agriculture. Moving on when the fertility of the soil is exhausted, they need to be able to travel light and live off the jungle.

Other groups who live along the banks of the Amazon River and its many tributaries are more sedentary, living off an abundant stock of fish and growing crops in the rich alluvial silt. They are also able to trade with their neighbours, travelling the riverine highway in dugout canoes. These people have the

above: Resin glazed bowls made by the Huaorani in the Amazon rainforest of eastern Ecuador.

materials and the time to develop pottery: research by Donald Lathrap in the 1970s revealed that ceramics were first made here about 9,000 years ago.

Organic Tempering

In a region where firings take place in a bonfire surprisingly pottery made in Amazonia often has very fine walls, sometimes as delicate as porcelain. In other parts of the world the strength of clay and its ability to resist thermodynamic shock is improved by mixing a tempering agent such as sand, shell or grog (ground-fired clay). Here the tempering is organic, being obtained from a freshwater sponge in the Lower Amazon and from the bark of a certain tree in the upper Amazon. Both are burnt and the ashes ground before mixing with the clay body where their long filaments of silica bind the clay like fibreglass.

Building Techniques

Amazonian pottery is hand built from thin coils of clay. As the form rises it is allowed to firm up periodically to prevent buckling under the weight of added clay. When the form has been completed it is beaten with a paddle resisted by an anvil stone on the inside. This compacts the clay, making the walls even stronger.

above: Anthropomorphic beer pot by the Shipibo-Conibo who live in the Pucallpa area by the Ucayali river, an Amazon tributary, in northern Peru.

Decoration

When the pot has dried out to the leatherhard stage it is decorated with slip coloured with minerals present in the alluvial muds. Once complete, the patterns may be burnished with a smooth river stone to make them shiny.

The patterns painted on pottery frequently refer to patterns in the natural world such as the spots on a jaguar, the carapace of a water turtle or the zigzags of an anaconda. The fine linear patterns used by the Shipibo-Conibo who live on the Ucayali river in Amazonian Peru are believed to represent a map of the night sky.

Resin Glazing

When removed from the fire, Amazonian pottery is often covered with plant resins that are easily smeared across the surface while it is hot. This helps to waterproof the clay and also gives an attractive glossy finish. The plants used for this are widely traded along the rivers.

above: Quichua resin-coated bowl, Pastaza Province, Ecuador.
below: Resin-coated bowl made by the Asurini who live in the Amazon Basin in Pará, Brazil.

Seeds, Beans and Nuts

The climate of the Amazon rainforest is such that the indigenous peoples have no great need for clothes and so personal adornment traditionally takes the form of body painting and jewelry as well as elaborate headdresses for ceremonial occasions. The materials employed for these adornments are acquired from the flora and fauna of the forest and river.

Trophies and Amulets

Often jewelry is constructed from elements chosen purely for their intrinsic beauty, their colour, their sheen or shape or the attractive sounds they make as they rattle together. Other items may be chosen to show a hunter's prowess and bravery or to endow the wearer with the nature of the source animal or plant. Still others may be chosen because of their amuletic properties, their ability to protect the owner from danger, both physical and spiritual. Among these red objects are the most highly valued. Many of the smaller creatures of the forest, such as poison dart frogs, are brightly coloured, frequently red, to inform predators that they would make an unsavoury meal as they are filled with venom. Other non-venomous creatures sometimes imitate this and by association people have come to believe that anything red can provide positive, magical protection against the ever-present risks of forest life and so hang around their necks strings of seeds or beans such as the huayruru which is dramatically

coloured red and black. Sometimes objects, including the body, may be painted red for the same reason, a favourite dye being the seeds of the achiote tree.

above, right: Necklace decorated with scales from the arapaima, a gigantic Amazonian fish which can reach 4.5 m (14¾ ft) in length, River Napo, Ecuador.
near right: Bracelet from Oriente in Ecuador decorated with iridescent beetle-wing cases. Trade in items like this is illegal.
far right: Necklace including a sea bean, the fruit of the entada species. These large seeds often fall into rivers and are washed out to sea, sometimes ending up on European shores. This one is from the River Napo in Ecuador.
opposite, above: Bracelets of knotted string and red and black huayruru seeds which provide magical protection, Oriente, Ecuador.
opposite, below: Beaded collar of huayruru seeds with a net of tiny seeds including black ones from heliconia plants.

Plants

A wide range of attractive seeds are available ranging from the tiny, glossy black ones of the heliconia to the large vegetable ivory 'nuts' of the tagua palm. The seeds of the caymito are hollow and can be fashioned into tiny rattles by cutting off one end. Another popular seed, also found in tropical Asia, is the blue-grey Job's tear which contrasts well with the usual blacks and browns.

The Animal Kingdom

The animal kingdom provides many of the most dramatically coloured materials for ornamentation, from the iridescent green wing casings of certain beetles to the brilliant reds, blues and yellows of macaw feathers. The wearing of certain items advertises the strength or skill of the wearer. You must be a strong fisherman to catch the arapaima gigas, the largest fish in the Amazon, and string up its enormous scales. Only the brave can catch the jaguar and wear its claws and only the successful hunter can boast of his skill with necklaces of peccary tusks or monkey teeth.

Techniques

It is possible to thread natural beads onto a strand of chambira or other plant fibre, but stringing may be far more elaborate. Several strands of fibre may be used braided together like the flat sennet of European macramé or worked into a ribbon of figure-of-eight looping, a technique similar to the one used for making string bags. When a broader band is worked to create a bandolier the beads, rather than being threaded on the central strand it may be attached to one edge.

Elaborate collars are also worked into a net of diagonally connected strands strung with seeds or, increasingly today when a great deal of jewelry is sold to tourists, glass beads.

Ponchos

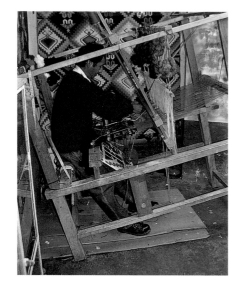

A rectangular blanket with a slit in the centre through which the head can be passed is part of the costume of men from many parts of Central and South America. Best known by the Spanish name *poncho*, it is also called a *serape* in Mexico and a *makuñ* by the Mapuche who inhabit Chile and Argentina.

The Makuñ

Among the Mapuche, the *makuñ* is a mark of cultural identity and in recent times has been worn as such in court by tribesmen accused of breaking the law in land rights disputes with the Chilean government. The colour shows the status of the wearer as blue is worn by leaders. A chief's *makuñ*, or *poncho del cacique*, is treated with great respect and may be hung on a wall, but never laid on the floor.

Huicha Huichahue

Once the wool of llamas and guanacos were used for weaving in Chile, but after the coming of the Spanish most textiles were made with the wool of sheep, spun

above, left: Tapestry weaving on a horizontal loom at Urubamba, Peru. In Chile the Mapuche use a vertical loom.
above, centre: Mapuche *makuñ* with patterns created using the ikat technique with the design dyed into the warps before weaving, Chile.

far left: Bolivian woollen poncho with a simple striped pattern.
near left: Ikat-patterned poncho woven in the Cotopaxi region of Ecuador.

upon it fine cloth with subtle patterns intended for use as blankets, rugs, bags and ponchos.

Weaving a Poncho

A poncho is basically a blanket with a hole in the middle. In many parts of the Americas this is made by cutting an opening which must then be reinforced. The Mapuche, on the other hand, create the opening as an integral part of the weaving process. They achieve this by treating the section of poncho where the neck hole is to be as two separate pieces, passing the weft from the selvedge to the opening and back on each side for the length of the slit in the same way as rug weavers leave a slit when changing colour in a pattern.

Designs and Patterns

Ponchos may be warp striped, like many from Bolivia, or striped with tapestry-woven motifs like those from northern Mexico. Many are treated decoratively with designs woven with a supplementary weft. The Mapuche repertoire consists of many motifs based on plants and objects from daily life as well as more obscure symbols with spiritual significance.

Plain woven ponchos are sometimes decorated by tying and dyeing the finished article. In some places, such as Mapuche territory in Chile and near the town of Cuenca in Ecuador, ponchos are woven with designs created using the ikat technique (sometimes known as jaspé). This is the same method as that used in Southeast Asia and is achieved by tying the warps in strategic bundles and dyeing them before they are fixed on the loom. Often these designs consist of stepped lozenges which may be combined with stripes in the warp.

More often than not the warp ends of a poncho extend beyond the woven area and are knotted to form a dangling fringe.

into yarn with a drop spindle. The loom of the Mapuche is called a *huicha huichahue* which means 'standing on the floor'. As its name suggests, it is an upright loom with the warps tensioned by the vertical side pieces of the frame. It is generally fairly crude and made from rough sticks with horizontal pieces lashed to the uprights. These cross pieces can be easily changed according to the width of cloth the weaver intends to make. This loom is used exclusively by women who were initially, according to Mapuche myths, taught the art of textile manufacture by the tutelary deities 'Old Spider' and 'Old Fire'. In spite of the loom's rustic appearance, Mapuche women are able to weave

Shigras and Mochilas

The string bag can be found all over South America, from Colombia in the north to Argentina in the south. As they are so light and portable they are carried all the time and have for many become a part of daily costume, some peoples such as the Arhuaco and Kogi men from Colombia actually wearing two bandolier style, one for coca leaves and one for other objects. The term *shigra* is generally used for small bags and *mochila* for large ones. The largest are carried by women with the weight of the load taken by a strap across the forehead. Shapes and designs vary, but all have in common the use of string in their manufacture.

left: Fishing net with looped structure made from chambira palm fibre made by Quechua peoples in the rainforests of eastern Ecuador.

below: *Mochila* of caraguata fibre with a looped structure, Gran Chaco, Paraguay.

String

Although wool is sometimes spun to be used in making bags, it is more common to use string made from one of the many suitable plant fibres depending on what is available locally. In the mountains of northern Colombia and the high Andean regions of Ecuador, for instance, the preferred fibre comes from the maguey plant (*agave Americana*) while in the Oriente (the Amazonian region of Ecuador) the fibre is taken from the chambira palm.

The maguey is perhaps the most widely used material and is prepared by soaking the succulent leaves to remove the pulp before drying in the sun and dyeing. Although traditionally natural dyes are used, nowadays makers may be supplied with fibres brightly coloured with commercial dyes.

For strength, cordage is generally produced by combining two or more lengths of fibre. The strands are tied together and held in one hand and the loose ends are kept apart while being rolled in the same direction with the other hand, often while rested upon the thigh. The two strands are then gripped and the top end released whereupon the tension created by the rolling causes the strands to twist together into a single cord. This is repeated until the desired length of twine has been achieved, adding in extra fibres as required. On a larger scale, the same principles are used in the making of ropes, particularly for sailing ships, and ports were all once equipped with a building called a ropewalk as long as the intended final length of cordage.

far left: Chambira fibre *shigra* with netted structure made by Quechua Indians, Oriente, Ecuador. The long strap stretches across the forehead when a loaded bag is being carried.

near left: Maguey fibre *shigra* with looped structure from Andean Ecuador.

Waterproof Bags

Shigras made in Andean Ecuador were once used to carry water. As plant materials expand when soaked, the tightly worked fibres swell to form a dense impermeable membrane sufficiently waterproof to carry water home from the well.

Construction Techniques

As the materials and tools required for making *mochilas* and *shigras* are so light, women may carry their work with them and stitch away with a blunt needle while watching the cooking pots or keeping an eye on their flocks and herds.

The method of manufacture varies widely according to local custom, the flexibility of available fibres and the intended use.

The once waterproof *shigras* of Ecuador are made of tightly worked looping which provides a fairly rigid structure whereas the fishing nets of the Amazon Basin may also be looped but with a much looser, more flexible structure. Variations of looping are employed: in the Gran Chaco of Paraguay and Argentina a figure-of-eight technique is used, similar to that used to make *bilums* in New Guinea. Elsewhere, in parts of the vast rainforests of the Amazon Basin, bags are constructed using knotting in the same technique as that used by European fishermen. Like loosely worked looping, this produces a bag which is strong but flexible and therefore ideal for carrying an unpredictable range of a objects.

3

background: Border of a Hungarian shift embroidered in dense chain stitch.
below: Earthenware plate with a slipware design from Beot, France.

opposite, left: German turned-wood spinning top dolls.
opposite, centre: Russian chopping board painted on one side for display when not in use.
opposite, right: Painted wooden spoon from Poland.

Europe

Introduction

below: Romanian woman in traditional embroidered costume, 1920s.
right: Chip-carved bowl shaped like a duck from Slovenia.

Europe is an industrialized continent. With mechanization, factory production by multi-national companies and the development of trade and communications networks Europeans have, on the whole, become cosmopolitan. Cheap, mass-production has undeniable advantages, but the need for some trades has disappeared and so many hand craftsmen have been driven out of business and some traditional skills are in danger of being lost or have even gone forever.

Craft in the Modern World

Many in the developed world are keen to preserve their cultural heritage. In the Shetland Islands, for instance, women still choose to knit with wool they have spun themselves by hand and knitting is taught to all school children. The Norwegian art of furniture painting, Rosemaling, is not only thriving in Norway, but also courses in the art are popular as far away as North America. In parts of Eastern Europe families still sit around the table to paint eggs for the Easter celebrations. In Europe there are many courses on, for instance, basketmaking, pottery or woodwork, which might no longer be essential to our daily existence, but give the student the satisfaction of working with their hands and a sense of identity not only with the natural world, but also with their ancestors who were dependent for survival on such skills.

Pride and Identity

Europe is incredibly diverse in terms of topography and culture and many Europeans retain a sense of national pride and also of regional distinctiveness. As well as regional foods, French bouillabaisse, Spanish paella, Hungarian goulash, or Swedish smorgasbord, we have a wealth of distinctive regional handicrafts ranging from colourfully embroidered costume to painted furniture, from slip-trailed pottery to crochet-lace. So often these crafts are restricted to a small area where local materials

above, left: Spoons made from moulded cow horn, Scotland.
above, right: An Irish *sciathóg*, a willow basket made on a frame, used to strain potatoes; made by Alison Fitzgerald.
right: Salt pot of plaited birch bark made by Salteri Jekkonen, Finland.

Introduction

have been exploited. A fine example is the way in which the inhabitants of the birch forests of Finland and Russia developed techniques for making receptacles from birch bark, one of their few assets. Scottish shepherds in a treeless landscape, on the other hand, learned to mould their porridge spoons from the horns of their sheep rather than carve them from wood. Many Europeans use or display at least a few artefacts of local or national origin, showing an identification with their culture and heritage. At times of celebration, in particular, cultural heritage is brought to the fore in dances, songs and food accompanied by the customary utensils and decorations. Consider the painted decorations in Germany or Scandinavia at Christmas time or the embroidered costumes at a provincial Polish wedding.

above, left: Everyday earthenware jug of a type found all over Spain and Portugal.
opposite: Linen shift, from the Balkans, with red-wool embroidery around the edges and openings.

right: Wooden milk jug with relief and chip-carved patterns, Sibinj, Croatia.

Painted Furniture

Much of Europe was once covered with dense forest and the inhabitants of regions such as Scandinavia and Transylvania exploited wood as a major resource. It was used to build homes and to make everything from cupboards to the *ale geese* used to serve drinks to thirsty visitors. Much of this wood was carved and often it was painted with flowers and scrollwork in the folk-art style known in Norway as *rosemaling*.

History

In Norwegian towns the wealthy eagerly followed the fashionable trends in costume and interior design of their European neighbours, decorating their homes with Baroque and Rococo carving and paintwork. The artists were often itinerant and as they travelled further from the cities they discovered a new market in the countryside. Here the introduction of glazed windows and stoves during the mid-18th century had made homes lighter and smoke free and provided the painters with a new market for their wares. Away from the influence of the towns, new ideas and motifs were tried out and amateur artists began painting for themselves. The less formal, 'peasant' style that developed was used to decorate everything from walls and doors to cupboards and boxes. Bright colours were popular and the subject was most often flowers and vines, sometimes with added lettering or genre scenes. Three main regional styles developed in Telemark, Hallingdal and Rogaland.

In Sweden the reign of Gustav III (1771–92) was a time of great patronage of the arts and a new, lighter style developed using a palette of pastel colours which has remained typical of Swedish design to this day. Painting in Finland and Denmark followed this trend, but the Norwegians have remained fond of bold, vibrant colours.

Technique

Rosemaling employed paint made from mineral pigments such as copper mixed with either turpentine, obtained from the abundant coniferous trees, or linseed oil which is acquired from flax which was grown to provide linen for clothing and bed sheets. The wooden ground was primed and then given a base coat of strong colour, often red or blue, over which flowing floral designs were painted.

The stylized simplicity of much 'peasant' painting worldwide is due to the way the brush is used. The sweeping curved brushstrokes can be linked together into a swirl or swag and grouped to represent a flower. Using a soft brush with a fine point the stroke begins with a light touch for a fine line with added pressure increasing its width until the brushstroke resembles a tadpole or an elongated teardrop. Once the basic forms have been painted in, shade and highlights are added with sweeping strokes

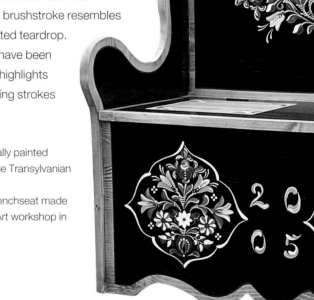

above, centre: Traditionally painted wardrobe from Sibiu in the Transylvanian region of Romania.
right: Painted wooden benchseat made and decorated in the M'Art workshop in Sibiu, Romania.

top left: Birchwood seat painted by rosemaler Ellen Bjørnsen of Nannestad, Norway.

to create a crude, but effective, impression of depth. This same technique can be observed on the 'bargeware' of English canals and the chests and cupboards of the Alps and Eastern Europe.

Today

Rosemaling has become popular again among professional and amateur artists in Norway and also in North America. Many Norwegian immigrants took painted chests to North America in the 19th century, but the revival of the art is credited to Per Lysne, a wagon painter who turned his skills to *rosemaling* during the Depression in the 1930s.

above: Swedish corner cupboard, painted in 1780, from the Rättvik area of Dalarna in Sweden.

left: Traditional furniture has been enjoying a renaissance in Romania. This painted dresser is from the M'Art workshop in Sibiu.

Frame Baskets

Before cheap industrial products were manufactured many of the needs of society, both at home and in the work place, were served by basketmakers, whether professional or amateur. Articles expected to receive rough treatment needed to be tough and resilient and baskets such as those intended for agricultural use were often constructed around a frame made with one or more hoops. The tough, uncluttered elegance of form of frame baskets displays a truth to function and fibre engineering that has led to the construction of virtually indistinguishable baskets at the opposite ends of Europe.

left: Polish basket woven from pine roots over a juniper frame; made by Stanisław Kumanrowicz.
below: A Welsh *cyntell*, a willow frame basket for collecting potatoes; made by D. J. Davies.

Potatoes

The Spartan form of frame baskets also reflects the uncompromising lifestyle of the people who traditionally made and used them. Willow frame baskets were, for example, used agriculturally in England, Wales and Ireland for several centuries, and are particularly associated with the cultivation, preparation and serving of potatoes, once the staple diet for many country people. A large, round or elliptical basket about 60 cm (24 in.) long (known in Wales as a *cyntell* and in Ireland as a *sciathóg*) was used while planting seed potatoes as well as for harvesting the crop. In some places, such as Cork and Kerry, a smaller *sciathóg* was placed over a pot for draining the cooked potatoes and then served at a table around which the family sat for their communal meal.

Riven Wood

One style of frame basket that may be encountered in such diverse places as Hungary, Portugal, Austria, the Pyrenees and the English county of Cumberland uses weavers made from strips of split or 'riven' wood. This might be maple, oak or chestnut split with a sharp blade or a maul and froe, often steamed first to open up the fibres. After a little shaping the strips are interlaced neatly with their ends wrapped over the hoop. The light coloured wood is often complemented by a hoop with dark coloured bark.

Construction

The first step is to soften a tough rod by thorough soaking and then bend it over the thigh into a hoop. Curving ribs are then lashed to the hoop lying in one direction to form the skeleton of the basket. Finally flexible rods or fibres are woven in and out from side to side, in and out of the ribs and wrapping around the hoop. To keep the tension even it is best to work from both ends towards the middle.

To form a basket with a handle two hoops are used lashed together at right angles, often with a decorative lashing of concentric diamonds called a 'God's eye'. While the upper half of one hoop forms the handle, the lower half divides the belly in two and the two sections may be formed into exaggerated bulges. Emigrants from the English county of Devon may have introduced this style of basket into North America where the bulges meant it became known as a 'buttock' basket.

Materials

Although some frame baskets can be constructed using elements made from different thicknesses of the same material, it is more common to use different material for the skeleton and weaving. For the hoop a strong but reasonably pliable material must be used. The most common choice is hazel, but many other materials are used elsewhere including juniper, briar and willow. Flexible fibres are required for the weavers and the choice includes willow, elm, wild clematis and pine or spruce root.

above, left: Spruce root Swedish basket on a frame of spruce rods; made by Jonas Hasselrot.
above: Cumberland 'swill', an English frame basket made from strips of riven oak; by Owen Jones.

Birch-bark Containers

and even shoes and was once used as a form of paper (many Medieval Russian documents were recorded on birch bark). The most impressive use is probably the graceful birch-bark canoes built by the Native Americans of the North American Woodlands.

Bark

The bark may be peeled from the tree in spring or autumn either by pulling it off in strips or by levering around the trunk. The softest part is the cambium layer at the base of the bark, but as this is the living, growing part, removal right around the trunk would cause the death of the tree. For this reason it is common practice to strip only sections of the bark or to remove it from felled timber.

The boreal forest stretches around the northern hemisphere across Alaska and Canada and from Karelia on the borders of Finland and Russia to Kamchatka in Russia.

At the heart of the philosophy of the animist peoples of northern Eurasia stood the birch tree which they saw as the Cosmic Tree that connected the material and spiritual world. By climbing a birch tree or pole, while in a drum-and-dance-induced trance, the shaman ascended through the spheres to communicate with the Supreme Spirit. In Siberia offerings for the nature spirits are wrapped in birch bark and hung from the branches of birch trees.

The Useful Birch

It is small wonder that the birch, such a useful tree, should be given spiritual significance by the inhabitants of these regions. The sap may be refined into a handy glue, while the bark makes good tinder for starting fires and contains fungicidal chemicals as well as being an effective barrier to moisture and odours, making birch ideal for food storage. The pale-coloured timber is serviceable and has an attractive grain. It is, however, the bark that makes the birch special as it can be stripped from the tree in flexible sheets. These may be made into boxes and baskets, vessels for collecting sap, pots for storing coins, roof coverings

with two layers and when they have dried out become rigid and very tough. It is not surprising that a raw material so easily obtained should inspire the ingenuity of those with limited means. A fine example is the way in which peasants could make themselves a pair of slip-on shoes, not long-lasting perhaps, but free and easily replaced. In Sweden the term *näverskomil* (birch-bark shoe mile) referred to the distance that they might last.

When first stripped, birch bark is supple and flexible and can be worked immediately. However with time it dries out, but can be softened when required by steaming or soaking.

Folded Sheets

Large sheets have often been used to cover nomadic dwellings, the most common of which, whether in Eurasia or North America, were conical or hemispherical. On a smaller scale, boxes and baskets are most often made from a single piece sometimes with the addition of a lid. The bark is first cut to shape and scored along the line of the folds before bending into shape and then secured in position with stitching, gluing or reinforcing with a wood-splint rim.

Plaited Strips

It is a simple matter to cut bark into even strips using a tool with a number of evenly spaced blades. As birch bark is so pliable it can easily be manipulated and plaited together. Generally, items made this way are constructed

above, left: A pair of *lapti*, Russian slippers made from plaited birch bark.
right: Basket of plaited birch-bark strips; from Archangel in northern Russia.

Irish Lace

Pat Earnshaw, author of *A Dictionary of Lace*, once said that lace could be defined as 'a lot of holes joined together by thread'. The construction of such an insubstantial material is extremely time consuming and hand-made lace was once a very expensive commodity worn only by the rich and the clergy. Invented in Europe, it was taken around the world by conquerors and missionaries to lands as diverse as Paraguay and the Philippines. Although the wearing of lace was an indulgence of the rich, its production has often been associated with poverty and the need for self-preservation as in Ireland during the 19th century.

Irish Lace

The production of lace began in Europe during the 15th and 16th centuries, but it was not until the mid-19th century that serious manufacture began in Ireland. The horrific suffering of the Irish people during the Great Famine caused by the failure of the potato crop saw the death of a million people and the emigration of many more. By 1900 the population had halved. In an attempt to provide much needed income to the starving poor, lace-making was encouraged in several parts of Ireland where it already took place and introduced into others. Regional styles subsequently developed, most incorporating floral motifs and frequently including the shamrock.

below: Collar of Irish Carrickmacross lace worked over a net, County Monaghan.

below: Detail of a collar of fine Youghall needlepoint lace, County Cork.

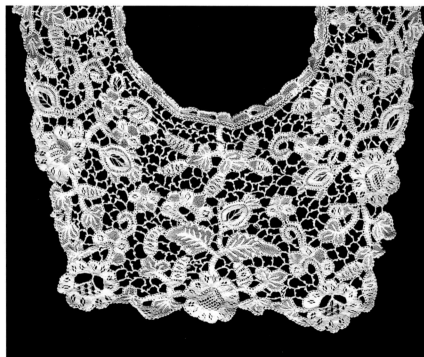

Needlepoint Lace

Made with a needle and resembling embroidery, the motifs of needlepoint lace are built up using buttonhole stitch. For structural integrity the design elements are subsequently linked with narrow strands, also worked in buttonhole stitch, which are known as 'brides' or 'bars'. These connecting strands are often decorated with tiny loops known as 'picots'. The distinctive form of needlepoint lace made in Ireland is Youghal lace named after the town in County Cork where it was first made in 1846. The pretty floral designs are enhanced with the effect of light and shade created by varying the distance between the stitches.

Net Lace

An easy way to build up a lace design is to embroider onto a ground of net. 'Limerick tambour work' is made in this way by embroidering whirls and sprays of flowers and shamrocks in chainstitch with the aid of a tambour hook. At Carrickmacross in County Monaghan a different style was developed in the 1830s. Here a layer of muslin was laid over the net and the design embroidered on top. The muslin was then cut away from the areas forming the background. Sometimes the backing net was dispensed with and the spaces left when the muslin had been cut away were then reinforced with brides.

Crochet Lace

Deigns similar to needlepoint lace can also be worked with a crochet hook, but the results are often crude. Irish crochet lace, first made in the 1840s, is however worked with a very thin steel hook and is often delicate and of very high quality.

Bobbins

Bobbin lace has been made all over Europe, but although popular in England, this method never caught on in Ireland. The work takes place on a pillow or cushion upon which many separate threads are held in place with pins. Each thread is attached to a bobbin which weighs it down. The threads are then twisted, plaited and entwined to form a structure that is woven rather than embroidered.

below: This Irish lace collar was worked with a crochet hook.

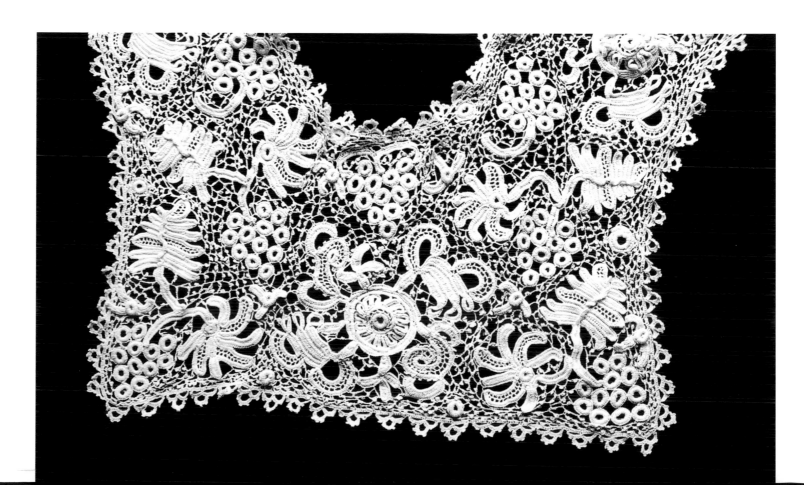

The Forge

In Oxfordshire, England, there is a Neolithic burial chamber known as 'Wayland's Smithy'. Local legend has it that should a man leave his horse there for a while, along with a silver coin, then upon his return he will find the horse shod with new iron shoes. The mysterious smith, Wayland, is none other than the Anglo-Saxon god of metalworking. This story shows the mystique that surrounds the blacksmith, the master of a craft that to the ancients seemed magical and even today there is something compellingly elemental about the smith smiting the metal on his ringing anvil by a glowing fire with the sparks flying. More prosaically, the blacksmith was viewed as the master of other craftsmen because he made everyone else's tools.

Iron and Steel

Iron-working began in earnest in Anatolia between 3,000 and 4,000 years ago when Hittite craftsmen discovered they could smelt 'pig' iron from ore at heats reached by pumping oxygen into a fire with goatskin bellows. By re-heating the iron and removing impurities they were able to produce 'wrought iron', the ideal blacksmith's raw material. They discovered iron was superior to copper and bronze as it was much harder and that when reheated it could be beaten into all manner of shapes. A blacksmith is literally one who smites (smith) black metal,

above, left: Wrought iron railings outside an office block in Glasgow, Scotland.
above, right: Blacksmith shaping a piece of hot iron by hammering it on the anvil.

referring to the colour of iron before it is heated. Today, blacksmiths often work with mild steel as it is less expensive, but it is harder to work and rusts more easily.

The Importance of Colour

The forge holding the fire in which the metal is heated is at the heart of the workplace and the anvil upon which it is beaten is placed beside it so that the smith can take the metal from the fire and 'strike while the iron is hot', as the English maxim goes. The word 'forge' is often used to describe the whole smithy or workshop. Traditionally a blacksmith needs seven years to master his trade and one of the prime skills learned is the ability to judge when the metal is at the correct heat for carrying out different processes by observing the changes in colour. Gentle bends can be made in mild steel when it becomes blood red, while sharper bends or punching holes require it to be bright red. Most work with wrought iron demands a bright yellow colour, while welding requires the metal to have become white.

The processes and techniques in the forge are essentially the same as those used in the times of the Hittites, but today welding is frequently carried out with the aid of an electric arc welder or an oxy-acetylene torch.

Techniques

When metal has been heated to the right temperature in the fire the blacksmith places it on his anvil and strikes it with a hammer. The flattened metal is squeezed out in the other dimensions and so to stretch it one way (for example in length) it must be beaten in the other two dimensions (width and thickness). This is called 'drawing' and the reverse, in which metal is thickened, is called 'upsetting'. 'Bending' is achieved by hammering metal over the horn or sides of the anvil or by inserting one end into a vice or a hole in the anvil and forcing the free end over. To 'weld' two pieces of metal together they are both heated, one placed on the other and beaten until fused together.

The final process, 'tempering', involves cooling the hot metal quickly, usually by dousing it in water. The hotter the metal and the faster it is cooled, the harder but more brittle the metal will be and so this will be adjusted according to the intended use to which the metal will be put.

right: Fanciful door-knocker shaped like a dragon; made by John Christian at the Boquio Iron and Glass works in Cornwall, England.

Working with Stone

The most ancient and imposing surviving artefacts and monuments are made from stone. Carved into the memory and imagination are iconic sites such as Stonehenge, Petra, Angkor Wat, Machu Picchu, the Pyramids of Giza and the Moai of Easter Island. The Crusader castles of the Middle East and the medieval cathedrals of northern Europe are still standing today. Just as important archaeologically are the simple petroglyphs, pecked into a rock face, that provide important clues to ancient and lost cultures such as the Anasazi (Ancient Puebloans) in the American Southwest, the Thamud in Jordan or the Picts in Scotland.

In Europe a considerable amount of stone is carved in relief or has letters incised into it. For thousands of years it has been the first choice for markers, memorials and gravestones.

The Qualities of Stone

The way in which rock is formed dictates its harness and texture. The easiest to carve are metamorphic rocks that have been changed by compression, heat or chemical action over millennia. These include soapstone, alabaster and marble. Sedimentary rock is formed from the build up from plant or animal remains. Suitable for carving are sandstone and limestone. Igneous rocks such as granite, formed in subterranean fire, are the hardest and the most difficult to work.

The Techniques of Shaping Stone

Stone is traditionally removed from quarries and shaped into blocks by driving wedges into holes drilled in a line. The roughly shaped blocks are then transported to the workshop for more careful shaping. The masterful Michelangelo famously travelled to the marble quarries at Carrara to select specific blocks for his projects, observing the individual qualities of each, purity, texture, colour, markings and so on. He said he looked for the form within to reveal itself to him.

left: The slate gravestone of English poet Sir John Betjeman at St Enodoc's Church in Cornwall, England; decorated with calligraphy and curlicues by stone mason Simon Verity.
above: Jordanian mason dressing a stone block to be used in the restoration of the Roman city of Jerash. The modern techniques are the same as those used by the Romans.

In the studio or workshop two techniques are employed to remove waste material from the stone in the 'roughing out' process. 'Pitching' involves striking a broad-headed chisel with a hammer at 90° to the surface to cause shockwaves that split the stone. Tapping gently will remove shallow layers from the surface, but forceful blows can split off large pieces. Next the 'punching' technique is employed, striking a chisel or punch with a cylindrical mallet at an angle to the surface, scoring a series of lines across it. As the desired form becomes clearer progressively smaller chisels and gentler blows are used to refine detail. Further smoothing is carried out with rasps, files and rifflers (small, shaped files) until eventually the surface can be polished with abrasive stones and sandpaper.

Letter Cutting

The cutting of letters is a delicate task demanding confidence and control. Letters must be precisely marked out on the stone before cutting and skilled stone cutters, such as Eric Gill and David Kindersley, have also often been great designers of calligraphy and letter fonts.

Although sometimes the background may be chiselled away to leave letters standing proud, the finest lettering takes the form of a V-shaped groove cut below the surface. This is not achieved with a V-shaped gouge, but by cutting two slopes down to a central line with a flat chisel. While cutting the straight strokes of lettering is hard enough, the ability to produce a flowing curve is a considerable accomplishment.

above: Carved 18th-century gravestones at Kilmartin, Argyll, Scotland.
left: A relief carving in the Celtic style by Ronald Henderson of Bridge of Earn, Perthshire, Scotland.

Willow Basketry

Basketmaking is probably the oldest craft in the world, evidence shows it was practised over 12,000 years ago. The American textile expert Jack Lenor Larson put forward the theory that with the invention of baskets early peoples were able to transport their foraged foods to a gathering place where they could eat together. As a result they were able to develop communication skills and language and lay the foundations of communal living and civilization. Even until the late 20th century many European women carried their baskets to and from the market or shops to carry their daily purchases, but the advent of free plastic bags removed the necessity of providing one's own basket. Today, however, many people have recognized the ecological dangers of the production and disposal of plastic bags and have begun to carry a basket once more.

fertile ground like large parts of the English county of Somerset were once used extensively for the cultivation of willows. Cuttings are pushed into the ground and left for several years to root and thicken before being cut back to a short stump or 'stool'. This encourages the willow to produce a vigorous growth of long straight rods that can be harvested annually.

Harvested rods may be used while 'green' or dried and stripped of their bark to become 'whites' or boiled before stripping to turn them 'buff'. Willow rods are flexible when fresh, but when dried for later use they will need a thorough soaking to make them pliable. Although most baskets use whole willow rods it is possible to make very fine articles by splitting each one into thin 'skeins'. Particularly delicate skeined willow baskets are traditionally made in France.

Withies and Osiers

Many natural fibres are used in the production of baskets, but in France and the British Isles the most common material is the osier or withy rod cut from willow trees. Flat, low lying areas of

Techniques

European willow baskets are most often made using the 'stake and strand' method that involves weaving a rod in and out of a set of upright stakes.

Work begins with the base of the basket. If this is to be round then two sets of thick short rods are laid across each other to form a cross or 'slath' which is bound together with a long rod. Next the rods of the slath are splayed out and secured with a pair of rods that are worked in tandem, crossing each other between each of the slath rods, until the base has reached the desired size and the excess can be cut off. The stakes that are to form the sides are then driven into the base, pricked at the junction to prevent breaking, and bent upright. A strong, dense band is worked around the 'upset' using three or four rods in sequence, passing outside two or three stakes and inside one, binding each other down. This is known as 'waling' and is generally also used to reinforce the top of the basket.

left: French willow openwork shopping basket or panier de jour with fitched stakes.
above: Nineteenth-century English willow basket for collecting eggs worked in English randing.

The walls of the basket are built up by passing a rod in and out around the stakes, spiralling up the basket. This process is known as 'randing'. For English randing one weaver or strand is worked at a time, but for French randing a weaver is begun at every stake and they are worked up the basket simultaneously. For openwork, spaces are left and so for greater strength rods may be worked in pairs twisted clockwise ('pairing') or anti-clockwise ('fitching') between stakes. Every time the basketmaker comes to the end of a rod a new one is begun from the inside of the basket, the ends being tidied up or 'picked off' when the work is complete.

below: Openwork basket made by Norbert Faure in the distinctive style typical of Périgord in southwest France.

above: French oval shopping basket made by David Drew from stripped and unstripped willows to provide a colour contrast.

Slip-trailed Pottery

Around 8,000 years ago potters in the Middle East began to decorate their wares with colour obtained from naturally coloured clays and mineral oxides such as iron and copper. Mineral pigments could be painted directly onto a clay surface or mixed with clay, but most decoration used coloured clays diluted with water to make 'slip' which was then applied to the body of pottery before firing took place. This simple method has been used worldwide and continues to adorn much of the everyday pottery made in Spain and Portugal.

Spanish and Portuguese Earthenware

Pottery from the Iberian Peninsula is traditionally made from locally dug earthenware clays which require firing at temperatures of 950–1150°C (1742–2102°F). Cheap and serviceable, earthenware pots, plates, jugs and bowls have been indispensable as kitchen and table wares in Spanish and Portuguese homes from time immemorial. The addition of tempering made from grog (ground-fired clay), sand or seashells improves the clay's resistance to thermal shock which makes it ideal for use in cookery. While cooking vessels are generally left undecorated, table wares are frequently enhanced by the addition of decoration executed in slip with many variations in local style. In spite of the development of tin-glazed ceramics in the 14th century slipware pottery remains popular in many parts of Iberia to this day.

top: Farthenware plate with sgraffito decoration from North Devon, England.
above: Spanish bowl with patterns trailed with several different-coloured slips.
above, far right: Portuguese plate decorated with trailed flowers in the centre surrounded by patterns of dotted slip.

Slipware Techniques

Great care must be taken in the application of slip as poor timing can cause a clay form to collapse or the slip to crack or flake if it dries faster than its base. The ideal time is generally as the body reaches the leatherhard stage when it has some rigidity but is still damp. By dipping a finger into the slip bucket the experienced potter can tell whether the consistency will provide even coverage of the correct thickness. For an all-over coating slip can be poured over a pot or the pot may be dipped into the slip bucket. This may be left as it is or further decoration may be applied over the top. If the 'sgraffito' technique is chosen then a design is scratched through the layer of slip to reveal the contrasting colour of the clay body beneath.

Slip may also be applied selectively to a surface. If two differently coloured slips are poured onto a surface which is then 'joggled' about a random effect resembling marble can be achieved which is known as 'marbling' or 'marbleizing'. Slip may be painted onto a clay surface or onto a layer of slip using a brush. It may also be trailed onto a surface.

Slip Trailing

Trailing is carried out using a special tool consisting of a reservoir for the slip and a spout or nozzle to direct the flow. Early trailers were made from a cow's horn with a quill or reed for the nozzle, while man-made versions were constructed from clay. Modern trailers consist of a rubber bulb that can be squeezed with varying pressure to control the flow through a plastic nozzle. Controlling the trailer requires considerable expertise. The slip is directed through the nozzle which lightly touches the surface while moving steadily across it. Poor control can cause unwanted variations in the thickness of the line, gaps or the spluttering of slip. With practice, elaborate designs can be drawn in lines or dots, but the limitations of the

technique demand a spontaneous style which may sometimes be delightfully naïve. Another technique involves the trailing of parallel lines across the surface and then drawing a quill through them to create a 'combed' or 'feathered' effect.

above and right: Two plates from Beot in France with patterns trailed onto a base layer of white slip.
below: Portuguese charger decorated with dotted slip. Birds, flowers and flowing foliage are popular design motifs on wares of this type.

Plasterwork

At its simplest, plaster provides a smooth finish for walls far superior to other smeared coatings such as mud or dung. Plaster has been frequently used as a base for paintings, but patterns have also been built up from it or carved or impressed into it.

History

Murals and frescoes have been painted onto plaster for millennia, notably by the Ancient Egyptians, the Minoans, the Romans, the Indians and the Chinese. Many of the masterpieces of the Italian Renaissance were painted onto a plaster surface. This was no mean feat as the paint must be applied to a wet surface and so only a small area can be plastered and worked on at a time.

Three-dimensional effects are also possible, ranging from the modest designs of English folk art pargetting in East Anglia to the bas-relief ceilings and cornices of 17th- and 18th-century Europe which included not only borders of vines and flowers, but also whole tableaux of classical and biblical stories. Particularly fine were the walls and ceilings of Moorish architecture during the 15th and 16th centuries, typified by the carved honeycombs and encrusted stalactites of the Alhambra at Granada in southern Spain.

Composition

Plaster in its basic form is a blend, in varying proportions, of lime, sand and water that can be poured when mixed, but dries to a smooth, hard finish. A greater proportion of water will make the mix more fluid and slow the drying, while the addition of gypsum will accelerate it. A more pliant medium can be produced by adding glue or almond oil and the texture can be altered by adding marble dust for smoothness or brick or stone dust for a rougher effect.

Plaster of Paris was a term introduced in the 15th century to describe a form of fine, dense plaster made with calcined gypsum. It is ideal for making casts and sculptures.

above: Carved stucco decoration on a column in Marrakesh, Morocco. Stucco is a form of lime plaster that gives a dense, hard finish.

above: The plasterwork ceilings of the nave of the Sagrada Família in Barcelona, Spain, designed by Antoni Gaudí.

Modelling, Casting and Carving

For interior and exterior decoration plaster is built up in layers, first with the addition of hair to aid adhesion to the existing surface. Before the top layers are set designs can be impressed with a stamp or drawn freehand with a tool. Another technique is to shape plaster in a mould and then apply it to the surface to produce a pattern in low relief. For fine, hard-edged work, such as calligraphy, it is also possible to carve the plaster when it is dry.

Sculptural work of considerable size has often been made from plaster, sometimes as work in its own right but often, as employed by the English sculptor Henry Moore, as a matrix for casting in metal. The basic form is built up using a wooden or metal armature which is then wrapped in plaster-soaked cloth. The final form is refined by carving and filing before smoothing to a finish as smooth as marble.

While three-dimensional objects are easily made by pouring plaster into a mould made from clay, rubber or metal, plaster is itself also frequently used for making moulds for casting forms from other media such as clay.

In Barcelona in Spain work continues on the Temple de La Sagrada Família eighty years after the death of its extraordinary architect Antoni Gaudí. Today, it is possible to see craftsmen creating huge elements from plaster which are lifted up to become starry forms at the intersections of the vaulting far above.

top left: Plasterwork cornice decoration, Scotland.
top right: Workman applying layers of plaster to a module intended for the ceiling of the Temple de La Sagrada Família in Barcelona, Spain.
above: Stucco panel at the Alhambra in Granada, Spain, carved with an inscription from the Koran.

Wooden Toys and Festive Figures

Tchaikovsky's ballet *The Nutcracker Suite* was based upon the magical adventures of a painted wooden nutcracker doll that comes to life on Christmas Eve. Its inspiration was a brightly painted wooden figure still popular in German homes during the Christmas season. In the densely forested areas of northern Europe the tradition of carving wooden toys and seasonal decorations goes back centuries. From its origins, when delightful objects were created for the amusement of family members, it has evolved into a cottage industry providing a welcome source of income in rural areas. Sometimes the wood is left plain, but often it is painted in bright colours intended to appeal to children and appropriate to festive celebrations. Subjects vary from miniature people and animals to more fanciful constructions, sparking children's imaginations and encouraging creative play.

left: Wooden nutcracker decorated with paint and hair. The lever at the back opens his jaws to crack nuts, Thuringia, Germany.
above: A pair of German painted wooden figures in Dutch costume made from turned components. Figures were made wearing the costumes of many different regions.

Soldiers and Smokermen

In Germany, Sonneberg in Thuringia is home to the production of the famous carved nutcrackers that inspired Tchaikovsky. Carved in the shape of soldiers, kings or knights, they serve a dual purpose at Christmas since they are decorative, but are also fitted with a lever that opens and closes their jaws to crack nuts. They are painted in brightly coloured uniforms. Erzgebirge in Saxony is another famous German toy-making centre where, among other things, 'smokermen' are made. These are human-shaped incense burners traditionally used at Christmas to purge the house of bad influences. The Black Forest area has rich woodcarving traditions that include intricately carved clocks made from lime (linden) or walnut decorated with foliage and animals including bears. Brienz in Switzerland is well known for its life-like carved wooden bears which are very popular with tourists.

Stacking Dolls

Matryoshka dolls, commonly referred to as Babushka dolls, have been made in Russia since the 1890s, a set consisting of a number of brightly painted figures of decreasing sizes that fit one inside another. The name Matryoshka comes from the word 'Matryona' which refers to a comely jolly Russian peasant woman. Nowadays these sets can portray anything from mythical to political figures. They are made from lime wood in Lipyetsk Polkhow and then painted in Semyenov. It is believed that the first set might have been inspired by stacking wooden souvenir dolls from Japan which represented the Seven Gods of Fortune.

Woodturning

Many of the toys and dolls made in Germany, Russia and the regions between are shaped by turning on a lathe. In former times this was powered by tension between a foot pedal and a springy pole, but it is more likely today to be an electric machine. A block of close-grained hardwood is fixed between two centres and rotated at speed on the lathe. The edge of a chisel or gouge is held against the wood, trimming off fine shavings to create variations of a cone or cylinder. Widely used to shape the convolutions of chair legs, turning is ideal for forming the simple, stylized body shapes of dolls and nutcrackers. For turning a hollow form like that of the stacking dolls, it is necessary to fix the piece of wood to the face-plate of the lathe and work inwards from the end. Many dolls and figures consist of little more than a painted skittle, but others may be assembled from a number of turned components, sometimes with articulated arms or legs.

right: Pair of Russian turned dolls in peasant costume.
below: A set of stacking Russian turned-wood Matryoshka dolls; made in Lipyetsk Polkhow and then painted in Semyenov

above: Traditional brightly painted wooden horses or *dalahästen*. Made at Nusnäs in Dalarna, the *dalahästen* is now a treasured Swedish icon.

Blown Glass

Glassmaking was revolutionized by the Phoenicians in Syria during the 1st century AD by the introduction of an innovative technique in which air was blown through a tube to form a bubble inside a 'gather' or 'gob' of molten glass which created a hollow vessel. The Romans adopted and developed this new technology and by the 4th century glassblowing workshops had been established in many countries across the empire including Italy, Spain, Belgium, France, Germany, Switzerland, Croatia and Slovenia. Foremost among glassblowers in the later centuries have been craftsmen on Murano in the Venetian Lagoon and in Bohemia in what is now the Czech Republic.

The Technique

Although the first glass may have been blown using ceramic tubes 30–60 cm (1–2 ft) long, it was only a matter of time before this was superseded by a iron tube about 150 cm (5 ft) long with a bore of 6 mm (¼ in.), almost identical to ones used today.

At the heart of the workshop is a furnace where the glass is melted in a crucible. The first job is to gather the correct amount of molten glass onto a pipe and then to roll it until it is regular and properly centred, a process called 'marvering'. Air is then blown down the tube to create a bubble in the glass, causing it to expand like a balloon. The creative craftsman may then 'free-blow' the glass into a desired shape but, for consistency, at this point it is more often introduced into a mould on the floor over which the blower stands and then blows it into a regular form, the tube being constantly rotated to ensure evenness. Moulds with several sections may be used to create complex forms or to give the surface of the glass texture of relief patterning.

Glass may be cut from the blow pipe and attached to an iron rod called a 'pontil', the same size as the blow pipe, which is given to a man sitting in a chair with long arms. He then rolls the iron backwards and forwards, refining the shape of the glass with a selection of wooden tools and tongs. Additional gobs of molten glass may be attached and drawn out to form handles, stem, feet or for decoration. Finally, the glass form is cut from the blow pipe or pontil and the rim neatened with shears and smoothed by reheating.

left: Blowing air through a pipe to expand the glass into the form dictated by a mould on the floor, Barcelona, Spain.

opposite, above: Refining the glass form using wooden tongs on a table, Barcelona, Spain.

Decoration

Most glass is more or less transparent and colourless, but with the addition of certain minerals, such as cobalt or copper, a varied palette of bright colours becomes possible. Coloured glass may be used at the beginning of the process or used to add detail by applying small gobs as desired or by trailing over the surface. Not so long ago a common sight in a fairground or at the seaside was a booth in which a craftsman sat drawing out gobs of brightly coloured glass and fusing them together into every conceivable animal.

Early glass was opaque and often full of bubbles, but the addition of soda lime or lead to the flux results in a transparent glass referred to as 'crystal'. This can be decorated by engraving designs into the surface (inside or out) or cutting with a wheel. Engraving requires a steady hand, scratching vignettes or calligraphy into the hard surface. For 'cut' glass the design is first marked out and then the glass held against a revolving wheel once edged with silicon carbide, but now with a diamond edge. This edge may be flat, convex or V-shaped, depending on the desired effect. The creation of sharp facets refracts light and causes it to sparkle in the same way as cut diamonds.

above: Glass for drinking spirits made in Transylvania in Romania.

left: Wine glass from Bohemia, a region in the Czech Republic.

Maiolica

In Europe, up until the early 13th century, even polychrome pottery was decorated in a subdued, limited colour range.

However, with the introduction of tin-glazing, pottery entered a new era of bright colours.

Difficulties

Earth pigments painted onto a ground of natural clay or even one coated in slip fire to the subtle, natural colours of most European medieval pottery whereas bright colours could be produced by mixing coloured oxides with the glazes. However, the lead glazes of the time were very fluid and it was difficult to prevent the colours running into each other and blurring.

The Solution

It was eventually discovered that mixing tin oxide (produced by burning tin into ashes) into a lead glaze created a dense white that covered the clay body entirely and fired to a pure white. The tin glaze was applied to biscuit-fired clay and, before a second firing at about 1000°C (1832°F), pigments that were chiefly oxides could be painted on the white ground. Once fired, the wares would be bright and the colours would not have run together. To prevent reduction and smoke damage, tin-glazed wares were enclosed in a clay box or 'saggar' in the kiln. Among the pigments used were manganese purple, cobalt blue, copper green, antimony yellow and iron rust red.

For hundreds of years most of the tin used in European pottery was acquired from Devon and Cornwall in England long before the English acquired the technology for tin glazing their own ceramics.

History

The first tin-glazed pottery was made in the Near East and the technology had spread across North Africa with the Islamic conquest. The Moors set up workshops in Andalusia in Spain from whence the colourful wares were traded all across Europe,

closely followed by craftsmen with an understanding of the techniques. The knowledge spread and had reached France by the end of the 14th century, the Netherlands by the 15th and England and Germany by the 16th.

In Italy, the term 'maiolica' was coined as the first tin-glazed wares had come from Spain via the island of Maiorca; this appelation is recognized all over Europe. Tin glazing has also been known by many other names: as 'faïence' in France, 'fayence' in Germany, 'Delft' in the Netherlands and 'delftware' in England.

Subjects

Today brightly coloured tablewares with bold floral designs are still made and used all over Europe, particularly in the south where they are used for foodstuffs. But early maiolica was an expensive luxury item often reserved for display. The first pieces had been decorated with Islamic-inspired patterns but a European style soon developed in which fabulous beasts and voluptuous vegetation fought for space. Prized pieces were often decorated with painterly executions of scenes from the

above, left: 18th- or 19th-century tin-glazed tiles from Delft, the Netherlands.

Bible and classical mythology in the style referred to as *istoriato*,
a genre that has survived in Italian workshops in many towns
such as Deruta, where work inspired by past glories is still
created. It remains a common event when walking the narrow
streets of Spain, Italy or Malta to come face to face with the
beatific face of the Madonna or a saint looking down from
a large tiled panel on a wall.

above, left: Jug made in Deruta, an Italian
town famous for its maiolica wares.
above, right and right: Contemporary
Maiolica plates from Deruta, Italy, decorated
with motifs that date back to the 16th century.
opposite, right: Maiolica tile panel made
in Lisbon, Portugal, 17th century.

Glass Beads

 'Who would compare a glass bead with a pearl?' asked the Persian mystic Hafiz when comparing the ecstasy of absorption in the divine with the delights of earthly pleasures. Few indeed would compare the unworldly, nacreous sheen of a pearl with a common, industrially produced piece of glass, but it is the very cheapness of materials and the simplicity of manufacture that have made the glass bead one of the most widely traded of all man-made goods. During the 19th century Venetian beads were exported by the ton and by the million for trade with the indigenous peoples of North America and sub-Saharan Africa.

History

Developing from the manufacture of faience, glass-bead making was probably first developed in Egypt about 4,500 years ago using sand, potash and lime. The technique spread throughout the Middle East and was eagerly taken up by the Phoenicians who decorated their beads with superimposed blobs of different colours creating the appearance of eyes, a sure talisman for averting evil. Eye beads have been made ever since, notably in Turkey, the home of the blue bonjuk bead.

During Roman times glass-bead technology was taken to Italy and by the 11th century was firmly established in Venice. In

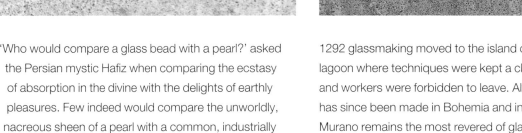

1292 glassmaking moved to the island of Murano in the Venetian lagoon where techniques were kept a closely guarded secret and workers were forbidden to leave. Although beautiful glass has since been made in Bohemia and in the Netherlands, Murano remains the most revered of glassmaking centres.

Making Glass Beads

Glass beads are categorized according to the method used to make the hole. The oldest type is probably the 'wound' bead which is made by winding glass softened by heating around a wire. 'Moulded' beads are pressed into a mould that includes a needle to punch the hole. The most impressive technique is that used to make the 'drawn' bead. A hole can be created in a 'gather' of molten glass by inserting a metal tube into it and then pulling the glass around it or by blowing a bubble into the gather and then stretching the glass out into a long cane, sometimes up to 60 m (200 ft) long. Finally the canes are cut into beads and smoothed.

top left: Selection of beads, from Ghana, made from powdered glass.
top right: An assortment of beads, including imported Venetian chevron and millefiori beads, bought in Africa.
above, left: Twelfth-century Islamic trailed glass bead with dragged tails.
left and above, right: Egyptian glass beads from the Roman period.

Chevron and Mosaic Beads

The surface of a bead may be decorated with added blobs or stripes of coloured glass or lines may be trailed and dragged or feathered with a piece of wire. The popular chevron bead is built up from several layers of glass over a core that has been moulded with longitudinal grooves. When finished and ground, the bead shows stripes along its length, but stars around the hole.

The mosaic bead is assembled from small medallions cut from a length of drawn glass cane built up from several different colours so that in section it is like a flower, eye, star or even a face. Each piece is attached to a hot wound glass core that is finally rolled to fuse the medallions together. The most splendid mosaic beads are known as 'millefiori' which means 'a thousand flowers' in Italian.

Powder Glass Beads

In West Africa beads are made from ground recycled glass. Pressed into a mould and heated, the resulting bead has a grainy, matt finish not dissimilar from the faience beads of Ancient Egypt.

below: Venetian glass millefiori beads made by the ton for export to West Africa during the 19th century.

Polish Paper-cuts

Poland is a land rich in colourful folk arts and crafts where traditional dress is often worn for festivals and special occasions. Costumes, furniture and homes are frequently decorated with embroidery, painting and cut-paper renditions of flowers and rustic scenes. The exodus of Poles fleeing their country during World War II and more recently the diaspora of workers moving abroad have led to the establishment of widespread Polish communities where Polish culture is preserved far from home.

Origins of Paper-cuts

The origins of paper-cuts in Poland remain unsure, but some historians believe that they date back to a time when few people had glass in the windows of their homes. Sheepskins hung over the apertures kept the elements out, but made the interior dark and stuffy so small holes were snipped in them with shears to let in light and air. The patterns produced provided the basis of a design repertoire when conditions improved and the techniques could be applied to working with paper for purely decorative purposes.

Wycinanki

The paper-cut (in Polish *wycinanki*) requires no more than a good sheet of paper, a sharp pair of scissors and dextrous fingers and so this artform is both cheap and easy to produce, making it popular and widespread. In Kurpie a monochrome image of birds and spruce trees is cut, like a silhouette, from a single piece of paper. However, in the centre of Poland, in the vicinity of Lowicz, distinctive works are produced, created by cutting and superimposing layers of differently coloured paper. These may be rectangular *kodri*, usually depicting scenes of everyday life, long thin *tasiemki*, decorated with flowers and hung vertically, or round *gwiozdy*, decorated with colourful flowers and birds.

The Technique

Gwiozdy are usually symmetrical and for accuracy two sheets of paper, or one folded in half, are cut out at the same time. A beginner, sometimes a girl as young as six, may draw out the design first, but the more experienced may produce the design freehand from memory or even make up new ones spontaneously. This first layer, depicting background foliage, is the darkest layer and is often black. Subsequent layers, first of birds or flowers then of finer and finer detail, are cut out using brighter or lighter paper. Once all the layers have been cut they are glued together and finally fixed on a piece of white paper for contrast or attached directly to walls or windows.

Paper-cuts Worldwide

Similar techniques are found worldwide, but the multi-coloured Polish style is unique. Often the use of paper-cuts is closely linked with festivals and celebrations. In China, for instance, auspicious cut-paper 'window flowers' are glued to the windows at New Year, while in Mexico strings of cut-paper banners depicting animals, guitars and skeletons are hung up during festivities such as Independence Day and the Day of the Dead.

Lotte Reiniger

The most successful of all paper-cut artists is the German-born Lotte Reiniger (1899–1981), who became famous for animated films of fairytales which used silhouettes inspired by the shadow puppets of the Far East.

opposite: Circular Polish paper-cut from Lowicz with a design of flowers or peacock feathers.
above: Design of a wolf feeding a cub and a child cut from black paper, Kazakhstan.
right: Square paper-cut with design of birds and flowers, Lowicz, Poland.

Painted Easter Eggs

From the most ancient times eggs have been associated all over the world with the miracle of birth and of life. Readily adopted into Christian iconography, the egg has become a symbol of the tomb and the rebirth of Christ and has therefore become an integral part of the celebration of Easter. In Eastern Europe for the last thousand years Easter eggs have been painted and given to loved ones, while in the West children have become more familiar with the giving of chocolate treats shaped like eggs.

The Story of the Easter Egg

In the Ukraine (where the painted eggs are known as *pysanky*) the story is told that as Christ hung on the cross his blood fell onto the ground and each drop was transformed into a red egg. Mary, his mother, wept and her tears fell, splattering the eggs with beautiful patterns. Another tale popular in the Orthodox Church relates that after Christ's Ascension Mary Magdalene went to the Emperor of Rome and greeted him with the words 'Christ is risen'. The scornful Emperor replied, 'That is about as likely as that egg on the table turning red.' when, surely enough, the egg on the table turned red. Even today the most common colour for decorated Easter eggs is red, the colour of blood and, symbolically, of life.

Easter Customs

In Romania women and children traditionally gather on Good Friday to paint their eggs, a day when no other work should be done. The finished articles are presented by women to their god children and by girls to their sweethearts. All over Europe boiled eggs are tapped together by festive combatants until the winner succeeds in smashing the shell of his opponent's egg. In parts of England 'pace' or 'paste' eggs (named after a corruption of the Latin for 'Easter') are rolled down hills and village streets and then examined to see if any have survived intact.

Charms

Pagan, pre-Christian superstitions have survived in many folk customs such as the widespread belief that painted eggs will protect the home and domestic animals from lightning, fire, illness and accidents. Many eggs were blessed by priests and buried under the cornerstone of a house for protection while others were employed to, hopefully, encourage bees to make honey, to make marriages happy and fertile and to grant protection to travellers. The effectiveness of these charms was generally dependent upon the right choice of colour and pattern, the correct time and place of decoration and often even the selection of an appropriate artist to carry out the painting.

Technique

Eggs for painting may be boiled or blown for longer preservation. This is accomplished by pricking a small hole at each end and blowing gently until white and yolk are expelled. Eggs for sale are generally subjected to rougher treatment and may well be made from turned wood.

The most traditional method of decoration in many regions resembles batik. Patterns are drawn onto the eggshell with beeswax using a special applicator before dipping the egg into dye which is most typically coloured red. Sometimes the designs are picked out after dyeing by scraping with a knife or etching with aqua fortis (nitric acid). Often nowadays images are painted on with a brush using a wide range of colours and motifs which may, or may not, be traditional.

above, left: Painted wooden Easter egg from Poland.
above, centre: Hungarian painted wooden Easter egg.
above, right: Blown egg decorated with raised pattern, Romania.

left: Blown egg decorated with tiny beads set into wax, Romania.

left: Painted wooden Easter egg from Poland.

left: Polish painted wooden egg with the typical red colouring.

right: Painted wooden egg from Russia.

right: Wooden egg painted with a religious icon, Minsk, Belarus.

Chip-carved Spoons

The rich folk tradition of the forested regions of central and Eastern Europe encompasses the decoration of a large range of domestic objects including furniture, pottery, textiles and utensils. In peasant societies all over the region carved spoons can be found lovingly decorated in an elaborate style that far belies their function as utilitarian objects. With a plentiful supply of wood, a basic spoon can be fashioned with minimal tools, just a knife in some cases, in a short space of time for immediate use. Embellishing a spoon takes it to a higher realm.

Folk Art

This craft often perfected in spare time at home or at leisure in the woods or hills gives personal satisfaction to the carvers and is a testament to their skill. For instance, a shepherd may while away the hours carving himself a whistle or a carpenter might decorate a box for his tools. The item may be functional, but the decoration is intended solely to provide pleasure to the maker and user. It is a form of folk art. In Slovenia, Croatia and the Transylvanian region of Romania wooden chip-carved utensils, including yokes, bowls, paddles for beating washing and, particularly, spoons abound. In Wales intricate love spoons are traditionally carved as gifts for sweethearts with chains and rattling balls as well as geometric decoration. A row of beautifully crafted wooden spoons is a frequent sight in many European kitchens. Today, when it is cheaper to buy a mass-produced spoon, the carving of spoons to be sold to tourists has provided an additional source of income all over the world.

Spoon Carving

The spoon is one of the most basic and universal of utensils and similar techniques for their manufacture have developed worldwide. The ideal wood comes from a curved billet split down the middle with the convex outer surface providing the back of the spoon. The handle and shoulders can then be roughed out with a hatchet before refining the shape with a knife. Finally, the inside of the bowl is hollowed out. For this the ideal tools are a spoon-bent gouge with a scooped shape or a special spoon knife with a curving blade.

Chip-carving Techniques

Chip carving is a widely used technique that can achieve a vast array of complicated patterns based on a series of simple triangles, circles and squares. Patterns are precisely measured and marked out on the wood using a pencil, ruler and compasses or scratched into the surface with a metal scriber or a pair of dividers. Then each geometric shape is chipped away in a series of cuts to reveal the pattern. Fine-grained woods, such as sycamore and olive, achieve the best result, enabling a clean cut as well as being free of strong tastes or odours. A stabbing, short-bladed knife or a knife with a one-sided blade are the most commonly used tools. A skew chisel with the cutting edge set at 60° can also achieve a smooth slicing action.

below: Chip-carved, double-ended receptacle with bowls shaped like spoons, Transylvania, Romania.

Distribution

Chip carving is a technique that lends itself well to large or small objects with a flat surface easily accomplishing an interesting surface texture. Because of its simplicity it is extensively used anywhere with a plentiful source of timber, not only in Europe, but as far afield as the Swat Valley in Pakistan and the Solomon Islands in the Pacific Ocean.

left: Transylvanian wooden spoon with a simple chip-carved design on the handle, Romania.

left: Slovenian wooden spoon with chip-carved handle.

left: Transylvanian wooden spoon with large chip-carved splat, Romania.

Khokhloma Ware

In Russia the year is punctuated by a number of festive occasions including religious holidays, weddings and christenings. In addition to birthdays, people traditionally celebrate their 'name days', the special day allocated to the saint after whom they are named. These feast days are enjoyed with generous hospitality accompanied by many speciality dishes. Semenov in Nizhni Novgorod Province east of the Volga is famous for the manufacture of Khokhloma ware including painted wooden bowls, spoons, goblets, plates and other utensils which grace the table on such occasions.

The Origins of Khokhloma Ware

The north of Nizhni Novgorod Province is a richly forested area well known for its rich woodcarving heritage, of both houses and domestic ware. Painted wooden ware has been produced in the area since the 17th century, initially in villages along the Uzola River, particularly those of Khokhloma and Novopokrovskoe. In the 18th century a trading post was established for local craftsmen to sell their goods which became generally known as Khokhloma ware. These light, strong, boldly coloured, patterned and gilded articles are now exported extensively and are part of Russia's rich folk handicraft heritage.

Decorative Techniques

Local craftsmen have become adept at constructing a large range of objects using endemic carving and turning techniques, but it is the painted decoration that makes Khokhloma wares distinctive. The predominant colours used for painting are red, gold and black, colours typically used for decorating monastic vessels, the cinnabar red representing beauty, the gold shimmering to symbolize spiritual light and the black pertaining to the struggle to purge the human soul of wrong doing. The elegant but homely patterns are derived from many sources including manuscripts, icons and brocade fabrics and also motifs inspired by nature. Particularly in modern times, the patterns depict flowers, leaves, raspberries and strawberries encapsulating memories of bountiful summer days. The technique requires fine, skilful brushwork that has been in use on Russian handicrafts since ancient times.

Gilding

The areas to be gilded are primed with a clay solution impregnated with boiled linseed oil and then dusted with aluminium powder. Once the surface has been varnished the object is heated in a special oven causing the varnish to acquire a yellow tint that gives the aluminium the appearance of gilding.

Other Painted Wares

Painted woodwork appears in many parts of Russia and includes stacking Matryoshka dolls and intricately painted boxes made in Kholui that feature episodes from Russian folk tales. Painted and decorated spoons, bowls and containers are ubiquitous in many other forested regions of Europe, transforming simple household objects into something sublime and joyful. In Hungary, Romania and Bulgaria, for example, spoons are gaily painted in bright colours and hung up for decoration when not in use. Bread boards, salt boxes, ladles, drinking goblets, platters and bowls receive similar treatment all across Eastern Europe. This peasant tradition takes advantage of a readily available, cheap local material that, with a little time and patience, produces something that is both functional and beautiful.

opposite, above, left: Old Khokhloma spoon with gold painted bowl, Russia.

opposite, below, right: Two Khokhloma spoons and a beaker decorated with a design of pomegranates and berries. The hanging hook of the larger spoon is clearly visible.

above: The range of colours and motifs used on Khokhloma spoons is limited, but a great variety of subtle effects is possible as shown here with the different background colours.

Embroidered Costume

A wealth of exuberant, richly embroidered textiles are made all across Europe, but the lack of industrial development and the continuance of a rustic 'peasant' lifestyle well into the 20th century has ensured the survival of traditional costume and embroidery styles in Eastern Europe. Worn on important and festive occasions from childhood through to old age, it is still common in peasant societies for someone to be buried in the costume in which they were married.

The Importance of Costume

Traditional Eastern European clothes are made from locally available materials of woven linen or wool and also sheepskin and felt. Cotton has replaced linen in modern times but the traditional style of dress has remained virtually unchanged for generations. The clothes instantly proclaim a person's origins, denoting regional, cultural and national differences and are worn

with pride. They represent hours of dedicated work decorating blouses, shirts, skirts, aprons and trousers. Although some treasured items are inherited from their mothers, it is the custom for girls to start work on their trousseau at an early age, not only sewing their own wedding dress, but also the bridegroom's shirt and the nuptial bed sheets. Their skill at embroidery demonstrates their desirability as a wife.

Colour and Protection

Black, white and particularly red are the most frequently used colours. The colour red plays a significant role in peasant costume. It is the colour of blood and so represents life and fertility and consequently youth and marriage. In Russian

below: A Russian folk song and dance troupe wearing traditional costumes decorated with a variety of embroidery techniques.

left: A heavily embroidered apron is an important accessory in traditional Ukrainian costume as in many parts of Eastern Europe.
below: Bulgarian girls in traditional costume; note their aprons and elaborate headgear.

inspired by flowers and birds. Satin stitch, on the other hand, can be used much more loosely to create striking floral designs of graduated colours. Chain stitch has a more linear quality ideal for edges and borders and for outlining shapes. Whitework, employing white thread against white cloth, has a subtle, restrained beauty enhanced by eyelets and cutouts. Like lace, crochet or needleweaving, drawn and pulled threadwork, in which holes are created by removing threads from the fabric or pulling them together, appears most often near the borders and hems of aprons and bed linen.

costume red predominates on embroidered fabrics. The Russian words for 'red' and 'beautiful' share the same root. In much of Eastern Europe red is considered effective protection against witches and evil spirits and red stitching is used around vulnerable points such as seams, edges and particularly neck openings. Richly embroidered women's aprons are used to protect the sexual organs and ward off evil influences. Dense embroidery is also used around pockets, cuffs and collars to practical effect, ensuring against wear and tear and also guarding against evil.

Motifs and Stitches

Bright, colourful embroidery, employing silk, cotton or wool thread, is very effective on plain white cloth, whether linen or cotton, producing richly embellished work that transcends its humble origins. Skirts, blouses, shirts and trousers are generally full and loose to provide ease of movement, shown off flamboyantly in traditional folk dances.

The most common stitches used on Eastern European embroidery are satin stitch, cross stitch, chain stitch and whitework. Cross stitch is ideal for the counted-thread work made easy by the clear weave of linen and cotton and is used for formally arranged, densely worked motifs that may be abstract but, in the cases of Ukrainian costume, are often

below: Dyed and incised calabash, Burkina Faso.

4 Africa

opposite (background image): Late 19th-century bedding rug made by the Ait Ouaouzguite, High Atlas, Morocco.

opposite, left: Clay beer pot with stamped decoration, Swaziland.

opposite, right: Painted wooden genre figure representing a teacher, Cameroon.

Introduction

Africa is the second largest continent both in terms of its size and its population. It was in Africa that the first humans evolved and one of the earliest and most renowned civilizations, that of Ancient Egypt, was established. Outsiders have often talked of African culture, arts and crafts as if they comprised one single subject whereas the crafts of Morocco and Zululand, for example, are as different as those of Iran and Japan in Asia. There are fifty-three countries in Africa and more than a thousand languages are spoken. The disparate dictates of geography, culture, climate, lifestyle and religion have resulted in a vast variety of skills and techniques using an enormous range of materials.

Improvisation

African crafts reveal an ability to improvise, innovate and adapt, qualities originally developed from survival mechanisms by people often living in harsh conditions with meagre resources. The philosophy behind this even applies to the way children play, making a ball from plastic bags by binding them into a makeshift ball with string. This adaptability can be witnessed in the use of the metal

left: Burnished clay beer pot, Lesotho.
below: Weaving raphia cloth, Cameroon.

left: Carved wooden Ashante stool, Ghana.

from car suspension springs for making swords for the Saharan Tuareg and also in the way Zulu night-watchmen adapted traditional basketmaking skills to create baskets from discarded telephone wire.

Throughout history the availability of materials has dictated architectural style. For instance, in the 13th century, when European cathedrals were being built from

below: Pair of Moroccan carved wooden soup spoons from Marrakesh.

above, left: Carved wooden figure burnished by frequent handling; bought in Ghana.
above, centre: Kenyan carved spoon with twisted handle.
right: Coiled grass basket, Ovambo, Namibia.

Introduction

below: Basketry hat made from grass and strips cut
from plastic rice sacks, Zimbabwe.
right: Ugandan stacking baskets constructed from grass.

stone, the mosques of Mali were being built from mud.
These extraordinary buildings, such as the Great Mosque
in Djenné, seem to be part of the
landscape. They exploit a cheap,
readily available material that
is periodically repaired with
religious devotion by an
army of volunteers. This is a form of architecture that is
efficiently designed and appropriate to its location and
much admired by modern European architects.

African Crafts Today

Outsiders have in the past looked down upon the
craftsmen of Africa, judging with eyes and minds
blinkered by a belief in the superiority of their own world
view and different aesthetic criteria. They failed to see the
sophistication of form or the layers of meaning, functional,
spiritual and symbolic, in even the most practical objects.
Africa is, in fact, home to a large number of different
cultures and crafts, from the woollen weavings
of the Muslim Berbers in the Atlas Mountains to
the basketmaking of aristocratic Tutsi women
in Rwanda or the black spherical pottery of
Zulu women.

above: Fon appliqué banner with a lion, a symbol of royalty, Abomey, Benin.

Berber Rugs

left: Twined patterns on the reverse of a Zaiane cushion, Middle Atlas, Morocco.

Techniques

Berber rugs are seldom made using only one technique, but often combine plainweave, tapestry, twining, pile and even embellishment with sequins.

Pile carpets woven in different parts of Morocco employ various knots. The asymmetric or Persian knot is occasionally found in the Middle Atlas, while the symmetric or Turkish knot is used all over, but particularly in the High Atlas and around

The Berbers, who have lived in Morocco since records began, were called 'barbari', meaning 'bearded ones', by the Romans; northwest Africa was once known as 'Barbary'. Before the Romans, the land was occupied by Phoenicians and Carthaginians and was later invaded or occupied by the Vandals, the Byzantines, the Arabs who brought Islam and then the Spanish, the Portuguese and the French. During these periods of foreign dominance the Berbers, especially in the Atlas Mountains, have remained somewhat apart and have retained a tribal identity that continues to manifest itself in their customs, traditions and crafts. Although they can be found over a large area and use many different techniques and materials, their weavings retain a distinctiveness mainly apparent in the bands of pattern motifs.

above: Cushion woven by the Zemmour, western Middle Atlas, Morocco.

Talismans and Tattoos

The decorative repertoire of the Berbers has a long history and there is a powerful resemblance between motifs on artefacts from Phoenician times (2,600 years ago) and those on pottery and rugs made today. Most of these designs are geometric and many, including diamonds and triangles, are believed to represent eyes that provide protection against evil forces. They are frequently used as tattoos on hands, ankles and faces and these motifs can also be found in the patterning on rugs, tent walls, pillows and bags.

right: Late 19th-century bedding rug made by the Ait Ouaouzguite, High Atlas, Morocco.

Marrakesh. Sometimes it is tied in a modified form with the ends pulled in different directions. Berbers in the Middle Atlas generally use the Berber knot, found only in North Africa, which resembles a clove hitch tied around a single warp. Knotted carpets are predominantly red and designs are sometimes meandering and erratic.

Berber flatweaves are weft faced and dominated by black, white and red with small amounts of detailing in other colours. The pattern is worked in a series of bands across the width.

The larger pattern bands feature the most complex designs and are worked in tapestry weave or with a supplementary weft following the line of pattern thus avoiding the need for long floats on the back. The narrow bands are decorated with designs composed mostly of white diamonds or zigzags on a black ground. These are worked using a combination of plainweave and weft twining.

Weft Twining

The technique of twisting or twining a pair of wefts together between the warps has been employed for working textile patterns for centuries in North Africa and was probably introduced by Arab nomads such as the Bedouin during the early period of Islamic expansion after the 7th century. Bedouin groups can be encountered from Tunisia to Jordan in the Middle East and still incorporate bands of weft-twined pattern into their tent hangings or *saha*. Like the Berber, the Bedouin often employ a number of techniques including warp-faced patterning, twining, tapestry and an unusual form of wrapping worked around pairs of warp bundles.

opposite, below: Zaiane cushion, Middle Atlas, Morocco. Zaiane weavings often feature sequins and tassels; only tufts remain here.

Hands and Crosses

Jewelry is often far more than decorative: its function may be talismanic or amuletic, protecting the wearer from dangerous invisible forces in the world around. For Christians the most powerful amulet worn on the person is a cross or crucifix, for Muslims it is the Hand of Fatima.

The Hand of Fatima

The hand is a powerful, widespread symbol, but is particularly associated with Islam and Fatima who was the daughter of the prophet Mohammed and wife of Ali, the fourth Caliph. *Khamsa* is the Arabic word for both the hand and the number five which has great potency being, among other things, the number of daily prayers and the 'Pillars of Islam' which guide a Muslim's behaviour. The wearing of the Hand of Fatima is considered equivalent to the incantation *khamsa fi ainek* (five in your eye) which averts evil by poking the fingers into its eye. The hand may also appear on textiles, leatherwork or printed onto the walls of a home.

The style of the hands varies from naturalistic to stylized, at its most abstract taking the form of five dots arranged in a group with one in the centre. These dots may be arranged around a cross which is believed to dissipate negativity to the four cardinal points.

Ethiopian Crosses

Christianity reached Aksum in northern Ethiopia in the 4th century, making Ethiopia one of the first countries in the world to embrace Christianity. Here the cross is omnipresent, carried in the hand or on processional staffs held by priests and worn around the neck by a large number of the populace. Processional crosses are large and heavy and personal crosses quite small but all are decorated, sometimes with religious iconography, but often with intricate designs of interlocking crosses.

Representing the crucifixion of Jesus Christ, the cross is a symbol of sacrifice, but also the sign of his resurrection and has therefore become an amulet that gives the wearer hope and averts the powers of darkness.

The Southern Cross

The cross is now seen mainly as a symbol of Christianity, but its mystical use stretches back into the mists of time. The Southern Cross bears little resemblance to the Christian cross, often having several arms and triangles and circles incorporated into the design. It is more reminiscent of the *ankh* of Ancient Egypt, a life and fertility symbol shaped like a cross topped with a loop. Among the Tuareg of the northern Sahara these 'crosses' are highly prized amulets which are often passed down from one generation to the next.

Sheet Metalwork

Some of the larger Ethiopian crosses were once cast using the lost-wax technique, but most amuletic pendants in North Africa are cut from sheets of metal. Discs, crosses and hands are cut out with a file or saw before being decorated. This may involve piercing or the fusing of tiny globules of metal onto the surface, but most patterns involve the incision of lines or stamping of details. In some areas, for instance in Tunisia, filigree work may be added with thin strands of silver.

Working on a larger scale, the souks of Marrakesh and other towns resound with the hammering of sheet metal being made into lamps, lanterns and plaques now destined for the homes of souvenir hunters.

opposite, far left: Silver Christian cross with engraved and pierced decoration, Ethiopia.
opposite, above: Moroccan Hand of Fatima set with small semi-precious stone and wire.
opposite, below: Pair of earrings with engraved designs, Morocco.

left: Plaques cut from sheet metal on display in the souk in Marrakesh, Morocco.
above: Two silver Southern Crosses as worn by the nomadic Tuareg of the northern Sahara.

Tuareg Leatherwork

The Tuareg are a nomadic pastoralist people of west, central and southern Sahara who once controlled the trade routes across the desert. They traditionally traverse Algeria, Libya, Mali, Burkina Faso, Chad, Niger and Nigeria, although today many have settled in towns or taken up agriculture. They are the iconic 'blue men' of the Sahara, characterized by their dark, indigo-dyed long robes or *gandoura*, the colour of which rubs off on their skin. The long blue turban, the *alacho*, is worn by men wrapped around their head and across their face, revealing only the eyes. It protects against sun and sand and also veils the wearer from strangers. They are a proud, independent and superstitious people. Those who remain nomads travel long distances across the Sahara taking everything they need to survive with them. Their all-important camels, who make existence in the desert possible, have distinctive leatherwork saddles and trappings that are displayed in the tent when in camp.

Uses of the Leatherwork

The Tuareg produce exquisite, much sought-after leatherwork made from the skins of their flocks of goats and sheep and, less often, from camel skin. Tanned in urine and worked by high-status Tuareg women known as *temaden*, the leather is used to make the walls of tents, domestic and personal pouches, bags and packs that are elaborately embroidered and appliquéd and dyed in striking, contrasting colours. Bags are usually an elongated shape with a folded over top that forms a flap. Fringes are popular. The Tuareg women's travelling bags are squarer in shape with a narrow top opening.

above: Pair of men's babouche made from dyed leather, bought in the souk in Marrakesh, Morocco.
near right: Tuareg animal trapping of dyed and cut-out leather, southern Morocco.
far right: Bag of dyed and appliquéd leather made by the Tuareg, southern Morocco.

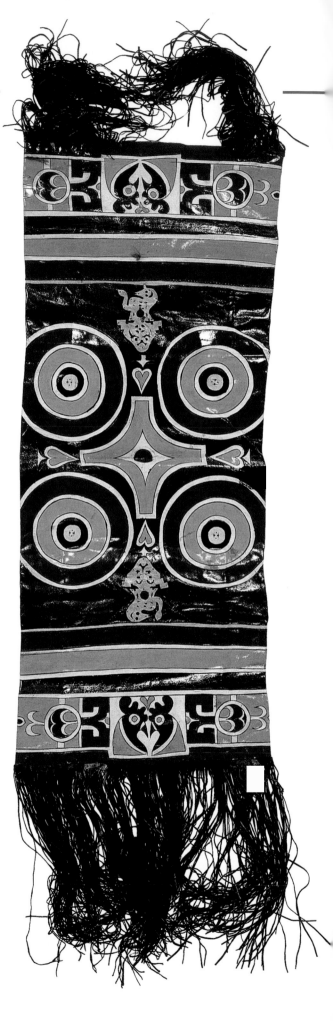

Decoration

All the decoration is geometric, involving various combinations of appliqué, embroidery using a fine leather thread, stamping, painting, incising with a knife and the weaving in of leather strips. Patterns include zigzags, chequerboards, triangles, circles and spirals, the six-pointed star and the famous Tuareg cross, a shape also found in silver jewelry. These are often symbolic and protective in nature. Some of these motifs are based on the calligraphy of the *tifinar* script used to write *tamachea*, the Berber language spoken by the Tuareg, while others are pre-Islamic in origin.

The Tuareg preference is for leather dyed bright colours, red, yellows, greens and blues. The most popular colour is bright green-blue, relating to earth and fertility, in openwork cut-out designs on a contrasting background. In the south backgrounds are typically dark brown or black while in the north they are a mustard yellow. The finish may be matt or polished.

Urban Techniques

Leatherwork in towns is produced almost exclusively by men with additional embroidery or appliqué worked by women. It is made using sheep, horse or goat hide. Goat skin is the best material as it is so soft and can be dyed in brilliant colours. The skins are tanned by immersion in animal urine and then dyed in large vats sunk into the ground. The craftsmen all belong to particular guilds according to their specialist skill. Each region or town has a saint they venerate, but all leatherworkers in Morocco revere and consult Moulay Idris. Leatherwork is a trade that employs huge numbers of people and products are exported extensively.

The *babouche*, a type of Moroccan slipper is probably the best-known article popular with locals and tourists alike. It is traditional footwear worn at home or when visiting the mosque. Some of the finest workmanship is dedicated to Koran bindings of intensely decorated goat or gazelle skin.

below Tuareg leather saddle with dyed and stamped decoration, southern Morocco.

Fulani Hats

According to tribal legend, the Fulani or Peul are descended from the Biblical Tribe of Judah who, upon the exodus of the Israelites from Egypt, did not head north with Moses, but went west, skirting the Sahara into the Sahel. To this day people of Fulani stock are found from the Sudan and Chad to Mali and the Gambia. Some have settled but many remain nomads, wandering the scrubby landscape in search of grazing for their flocks and herds, seldom stop more than a few days in one place. The Fulani are the largest nomadic group in the world today and known by many names in different places, they call themselves 'Fulbe'.

Desert Clothing

To cope with the ferocious heat the Fulani wear loose robes, brightly coloured but sparsely decorated. Like many nomads, they keep property to a minimum for ease of transport and invest their wealth in the enormous gold earrings that the women wear every day. For men, ornamentation may take the form of an unusual hat that keeps off the sun and also serves as a symbol of wealth and status.

Construction of the Hats

The Fulani hat takes the form of a flared cone generally about 20 cm (8 in.) high and 42 cm (17 in.) in diameter. The rim is broad to create shade, while the crown is high to insulate the top of the head. It is made of grass and occasionally raphia or wool. Work begins at the centre of the crown with bundles of grass radiating outwards to form the warp elements. These are woven together using the basketry twining technique which involves weaving a pair of wefts in and out, one over, one under, crossing each other between each pair of warps. As the structure grows wider, the bundles are initially split to provide a greater number of warps until it is necessary to add in extra warps. The twining is tight and dense, forming a rigid structure.

above: Twined grass Fulani hat with leatherwork detailing from the Sahel.

opposite: Fulani hat from northern Nigeria made from a grass base interlaced with wool.

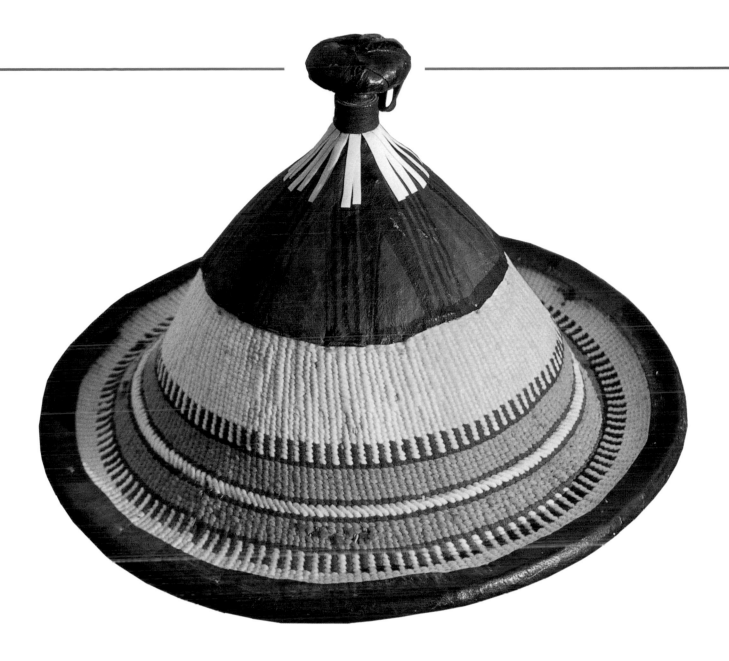

Decoration

A small amount of pattern may be woven into the hat using dyed grasses but the most obvious decoration is the pieces of leather that reinforce the crown and brim, concealing the start and finish of the weaving. The leather is generally dark brown or red and attached in large pieces, while the sides of the crown are often decorated with interlaced strips which are threaded strategically into the structural members of the hat. The latter technique is typical of hats from Burkina Faso while those from Mali are generally plainer.

Extra decoration such as buttons or cowrie shells may be applied. Far from the sea, cowrie shells are widely valued by many peoples as a form of currency and as a fertility charm.

Other Grass Hats

The savannahs and grasslands of Africa provide a plentiful supply of material for basketry and hat making in many regions south of the Sahara. In Ghana naturally coloured grass is twined into flat-crowned, broad-brimmed hats with bands of pattern incorporating dried grass, while in Cameroon grass hats have been made in the shape of trilbies. In Zimbabwe strips of recycled synthetic rice sacks sometimes take the place of grasses in the making of brightly decorated head gear.

Calabashes

Gourds and squashes, members of the *cucurbitaceae* family, are used as containers in many tropical and sub-tropical regions of the world but in sub-Saharan Africa the calabashes, the biggest of the *cucurbitaceae* family, often grow large enough to produce receptacles with the capacity of a bucket. The calabash is the African equivalent of the cornucopia, the horn of plenty of the Greeks and Romans, and, according to the myths of the Fon in Benin, the Creator shaped the world like a giant calabash because it would provide people with everything they needed. When the first man and woman descended from the sky they brought with them a long wand and a calabash. Gourds and calabashes are also found in the religious rites of the Yoruba in Nigeria where they are commonly found on the altar of Shango, the god of thunder.

left and bottom: Calabash discs with designs created with a hot knife, West Africa.

below: Engraved calabash with a leather rim decorated with cowrie shells, Burkina Faso.

Milk Containers

A band of grassland stretches across Africa south of the Sahara from the Atlantic to the Indian Ocean. The semi-nomadic peoples who live here must move with their cattle to find good grazing and have therefore not developed sophisticated ceramics or metal technology, but have remained dependent on trade or the bounty of nature. Calabashes and gourds are so integral to their lives, for the collection and carrying of milk, that a great deal of time is lavished upon their decoration. On her marriage, a Wodaabe girl in Niger is given calabashes that demonstrate her right to fill them with milk from her husband's cows and at tribal gatherings the women display their wealth as a large rack covered with calabashes which issues the claim, 'we own so many cows that I need all these to hold the milk.'

Calabashes are also used as a form of personal adornment and Fulani girls may select an attractive calabash to carry on their heads when they take their milk to market, believing that it will attract more customers.

Gourds are used as milk containers by many African herdsmen including the Maasai in Kenya, a tribe who subsist mainly on milk mixed with blood taken from a living cow. An arrow is shot at close range to open a vessel in the beast's neck and the pumping blood is collected in a gourd before the incision is closed.

In southern Ethiopia the Borana cover their milk gourds with a basket of tightly woven fibre twine. These beautiful bottles take months to make and often incorporate strands of silver.

The many other uses of gourds and calabashes include spoons and ladles, resonators for musical instruments, and moulds for pottery.

opposite, right: Underside of a dyed and incised Fulani calabash, Burkina Faso.

left: Large calabash decorated with animals; made for the tourist market in Kenya.

Techniques

Calabashes may be produced and decorated by the pastoralists themselves or bought from settled people such as the Hausa in Nigeria. Like pumpkins, they contain a pulp that must be allowed to dry and then scraped out, leaving a rind that is hard enough to engrave or even carve. The simplest technique is to scratch out a design with a sharp implement. The pattern may be emphasized by dyeing the surface first to create a contrast with the engraved lines or fat and soot may be rubbed into the scratches afterwards. Another method is to use a hot knife to burn a black line into the surface.

Calabashes from Burkina Faso are often further decorated by the addition of pieces of leather and the attachment of cowrie shells.

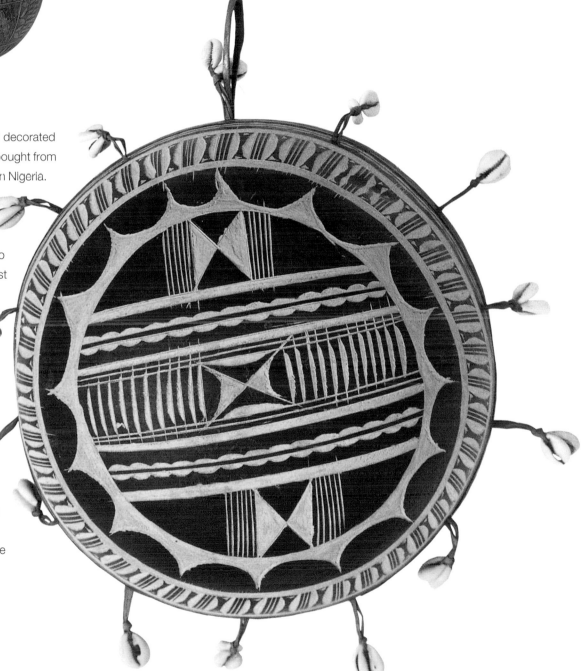

Appliqué Banners and Flags

In Persian myth an army of rebels marched against the tyrant Zohak following a banner made from the leather apron of Kava the smith, Roman legions advanced behind metal eagles and the hordes of Genghis Khan rode behind a banner made from nine yaks' tails. Many have marched behind banners and flags made from cloth, the European armies behind embroidered regimental colours and patchwork flags, the Mahdi's dervishes behind appliqué banners emblazoned with inscriptions from the Koran and British trades unionists behind massive banners elaborately decorated with paint and embroidery. Today, in coastal Ghana, once known as the Gold Coast, Fante men parade ceremonially behind the large appliqué flags of their Asafo companies.

Asafo

The Asafo companies (which literally means 'our people') once served a martial function but now are mainly social, religious and political organizations that provide the common man with a social identity and a voice. They carry out many tasks such as the clearing of tracks to shrines and water sources, but they are most conspicuous at subsequent annual celebrations. For a whole day the rival Asafo companies, divided into subgroups who may be dressed up as policemen, girl guides or boy scouts or wearing brightly coloured matching costumes in the companies' colours, dance, sing and parade exuberantly through the streets. An important individual is the flag bearer who dances while twirling the company flag and throwing it in the air.

Company Flags

An Asafo flag is rectangular and normally measures 152–183 cm (5 or 6 ft) long, although some may be 76 m (300 ft) long. In one corner is a patchwork flag, the British Union flag on older flags and the Ghanaian flag on those made since independence in 1957. Usually motifs are cut out as identical pairs and one is

appliquéd to each face of the flag. Sometimes a shape may be cut out from the ground and a motif sewn, in patchwork fashion, into the hole.

The applied motifs are made to illustrate a traditional, sometimes obscure or arcane, proverb such as 'only the elephant can uproot the palm' or 'when no trees are left birds will perch on a man's head'. In essence all the proverbs can be boiled down to the provocative message that 'our company is better than yours' and so waving and flaunting them is a form of artistic warfare.

Fon Banners

The Fon live in Benin, formerly known as Dahomey and not to be confused with Benin City in Nigeria. The capital, Abomey, was once a thriving centre for cloth workers who produced flags, banners, ceremonial umbrellas and clothing for the royal court. These were decorated with appliquéd images of allegorical creatures and scenes of prowess. Templates used in their creation were saved for making replacements for future generations. Today, these same craftsmen produce 'flags' to be sold to tourists.

The Dervishes

In the 19th century the soldiers of the Mahdi in the Sudan were known as dervishes because of their religious fervour in fighting against the infidel British. Their banners bore appliquéd texts from the Koran and their clothing, known as the *jibbeh*, was covered in patches. Originally a mark of the rejection of materialist values, these patches eventually became formalized into a system that indicated the rank of officers.

above: Contemporary Fon appliqué 'banner' made in Abomey, Benin.
opposite: Three Fante asafo flags, from Coastal Ghana, featuring the Company number and an allegorical message of strength or superiority. The presence of the Union Flag indicates that they date from before independence in 1957.

Kente Cloth

The Ashante and Ewe of Ghana are renowned for their chequered *kente* cloths. They form the traditional costume; men wear a cloth like a toga and women wear two smaller ones wrapped around their bodies. The word *kente* has become synonymous with these textiles, but is actually a Fante word for 'basket' referring to the distinctive pattern of squares. While the Ashante display a taste for bright colours, blues, greens and yellows, the Ewe are more inclined to favour subtle, subdued colour schemes.

Stripweaves

Kente cloth is woven by men in extremely long narrow strips measuring 102–279 mm (4–11 in.) in width. These are cut to length after weaving and 16 to 24 strips are sewn together side by side to make a large piece of cloth. Today, most *kente* cloth is woven from synthetic fibres but in the past Ashante nobility preferred silk while the common people wore cotton. Ewe cloth was usually woven from cotton.

The Loom

Weavers of *kente* cloth use a drag loom in which the warps are tensioned by being attached to a heavy stone that is gradually drawn towards the weaver as work progresses and completed sections are rolled onto a bar at the weaver's waist. A double-heddle system is operated by the feet using pedals made from calabashes. This system pulls up one set of warps to form a shed while the alternate set is pulled down.

Warp-faced and Weft-faced Cloth

Each strip of *kente* cloth is patterned by weaving a band dominated by the warps and then a band dominated by the wefts. The warp-faced sections often feature warps of several colours to produce longitudinal stripes. For the weft-faced sections an extra pair of heddles is employed, raising the warps in groups of six before packing the weft down tightly so that it hides the warps. When the completed strips are sewn together, the warp-faced and weft-faced sections are staggered to create the distinctive chequer.

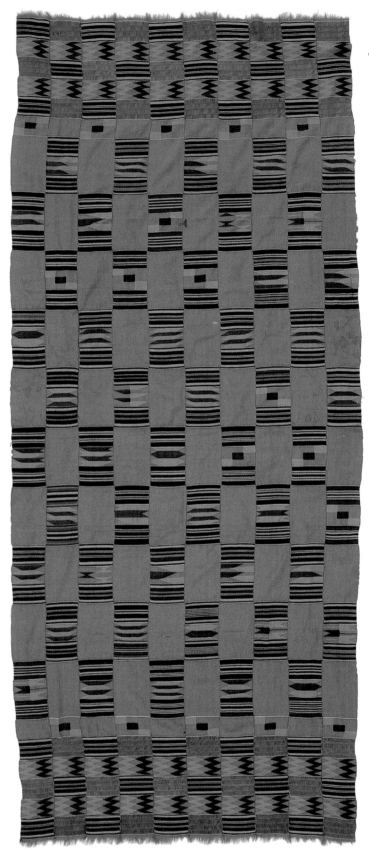

left: Detail of an Ashante stripweave woven with silk yarn, Ghana.
above: Ashante stripweave cloth woven from rayon yarn, Ghana.

Supplementary Weft Motifs

Pattern motifs may be woven into the warp-faced rectangles using the supplementary-weft technique in which extra wefts are introduced floating strategically over the surface. While Ashante weavings incorporate geometric or abstract patterns, such as stripes, lozenges and zigzags, in supplementary weft Ewe cloth can be distinguished by the use of figurative motifs representing symbolic objects such as drums, hands and combs.

Stripweaves Made Elsewhere

Fabric made from several pieces sewn together is not uncommon in the rest of the world but the construction of a large textile from such narrow strips is virtually exclusive to West Africa. The technique is used by, among others, the Mende in Sierra Leone, the Fulani and Bamana in Mali, the Djerma in Niger and the Yoruba in Nigeria.

The Fulani weave blankets called *khasa* which are traded in large quantities, both new and secondhand, at the market in Mopti from whence they may be traded to far-flung places. The *khasa* is made from six strips of narrow cloth woven from the wool of sheep with the background usually retaining its natural off-white. Decoration is carried out in supplementary weft with such precision that when the strips are sewn together the bands of pattern stretch continuously right across the blanket.

below: Ewe stripweave cloth from Agobzumbe in southeast Ghana. Ewe weavings typically display a preference for subtle, muted colouring.

Woodcarving

Whether for domestic, ceremonial, spiritual or magical use, crafts in Africa such as woodcarving have always been functional, but during the 19th and 20th centuries these same works began to be appreciated in the developed world purely for aesthetic reasons and were collected as works of art. In West Africa, in particular, there are many different styles of sculpture reflecting localized customs and beliefs, but in most traditional work the world of spirits and ancestors manifests itself in exaggerated, stylized or angular forms alien to the mindset of the outside, self-consciously sophisticated world. In Europe, these striking images were at the heart of new movements in painting and sculpture that broke with the conventional representation of the everyday world.

African Woodwork

Wood is a major resource in much of West and Central Africa although humidity and voracious insects have ensured that most carvings by previous generations have only survived when collected and preserved in a museum. The techniques employed, however, seem to have changed little and modern craftsmen continue to rough out their work with an adze and refine the detail with a knife. Decorative details are generally in low relief while patterns are likely to have been created by carving out small chips of wood. The human form has always been the most common subject although there is now a thriving trade selling carved animals to tourists in many places.

Famous Craftsmen

Woodcarving was of such importance to the rulers of West Africa, providing ceremonial paraphernalia and imposing settings for the courts of kings, that skilled craftsmen were highly valued and became

far left: In Ghana Ashante girls tuck dolls like this into their waistbands.
near left: Fante doll from Ghana. Dolls are used by a number of West African tribes as a magical aid to fertility.

attached to royal courts. The names of craftsmen are frequently forgotten, but some of these courtly carvers were so valued by their patrons that some pieces can be attributed to a specific hand. Among those whose names we know are the Ashante carver of courtly regalia and figural groups, Osei Bonsu (1900–76) and from Nigeria the great Yoruba carver, Olowe of Ise (1873?–1938), famous for monumental work such as the doors and houseposts of the palace at Ikere.

Wooden Objects

In both royal compounds and the most remote villages skilfully carved objects made by local craftsmen have been produced for daily use. Notable examples are spoons, indispensable for the preparation, serving and consumption of food, which are often

right: Four-part screen probably carved by a Yoruba craftsman, but depicts people in Hausa costume, Nigeria.

above: Nigerian carved Yoruba mirror frame.

below: Elaborate comb carved by an Ashante man for his sweetheart, Ghana.

elaborately decorated. Those of the Dan of Liberia and the Côte d'Ivoire, among whom a respected woman is known as 'the spoon holder', are carved with the handles in the shape of heads or legs. Combs, too, may be elaborately carved, like those made by Ashante youths for their sweethearts.

Furniture in most of Africa is limited to stools or headrests carved from a single block of wood and so there is no joinery. In Ghana such stools, carved from a rectangular block, are carved and pieced into striking forms and sometimes, as is the case with the paraphernalia of Ashante kings, covered in gold.

Small figural carvings or 'dolls' are common and sometimes associated with fertility, but in Nigeria the Yoruba carve *ere ibeji*, a poignant reminder of a twin who has died. These are loved, fed and rubbed with indigo or cosmetics to ensure their happiness and goodwill.

Masks

Masks play an important part in the spiritual and cultural life of traditionally animist societies in Africa. Sometimes tribal masks are a realistic representation of the human or animal head but more often they are carved in an exaggerated or distorted way designed to suggest an unworldly, supernatural presence. So compelling is the carving of some of these masks that people believe they are imbued with a spirit that takes possession of the wearer, bringing a community into contact with the power of the otherworld. Among the most controversial of Pablo Picasso's paintings was *Les Demoiselles d'Avignon*, completed in 1907, for which he admitted his source of inspiration had been African tribal masks. The response of Parisian observers disturbed by such unfamiliar faces was perhaps similar to that of Africans feeling the presence of the dangerous forces.

Masks and Masquerades

It has been suggested that the most important of African artforms is performance. The combination of music, dance and costume combine to create a powerful, sometimes hypnotic, experience that accompanies the ceremonies in many parts of Africa (and indeed other continents), including the celebration of the passing of the year and rites of passage.

The main focus is frequently a dancer, or dancers, in masquerade costume, disguised by a mask, a costume completely concealing the body and posturing or whirling movements so that they no longer appear human but rather the emissaries of another world. The body shape may be exaggerated with stilts and arm extensions or the wearing of voluminous garments or straw capes and sometimes the whole ensemble is embellished with fur, feathers, shells, beads and vegetation. Lanky Igbo 'maiden-spirit' dancers from the Niger River Delta wear a one-piece outfit of appliqué cloth with tiny artificial breasts while, among the Fon in Benin, the Zangbeto spirit is enacted by a dancer in a raphia costume who whirls around like a frenzied haystack. The variety of the disguises is immense, but the whole costume is almost always crowned by a mask boldly carved from wood.

right: Helmet mask surmounted by an equestrian figure used by the Yoruba during ceremonies of the Elefon or Epa cult, Nigeria.

left: Wooden helmet mask acquired in Mali.
below: Life-like Kuba helmet mask from the Democratic Republic of the Congo. When worn, a straw cape could be attached to the holes along the jawline.

Types of Mask

The form of the mask is dictated by the features of the entity represented and also by the level of mobility needed by the dancer. The simplest style of mask, and the least restricting, covers only the face but may be of unnatural size, covering the chest or rising high into the air. This is also the easiest type to carve as it is more or less flat and can be carved from a flat piece of wood. Masks of this type include the simple face masks worn by the Igbo as well as the towering bush spirit masks of the Bobo people in Burkina Faso which are several metres high and painted with geometric patterns.

The carving of 'helmet' masks, which cover the entire head, require a greater level of skill. It demands the hollowing out of a block of wood as well as the carving of the features. Masks of this type include those worn by the Kuba people in the Democratic Republic of the Congo. Some helmet masks support tall, carved superstructures. Yoruba masks of the Epa cult incorporate equestrian figures, while the *Awo* masks of the Gelede cult may feature figural groups representing cautionary proverbs.

A third type of mask is worn on the crown of the head, giving the wearer extra stature. While some of these are shaped like a head, others project horizontally to represent *otoji*, water spirits who inhabit the world where human beings live before they are born into this world.

Indigo

Blue is one of the rarest colours that can be achieved by dyers using natural sources. The truest of blues is obtained from indigo, a substance so highly prized that in the 1850s the indigo trade in India alone was worth two million pounds a year. Colourfast cloth is produced in an alchemical process without the need for the mordants that allow other dyes to 'bite' and prevent fading. In West Africa indigo dyeing is widespread but particularly fine cloth is produced by the Yoruba in Nigeria.

The Raw Material

Indigo dye is obtained from the leaves of many plants around the world, mainly but not exclusively tropical. They all have indican in their chemical constitution. The study of indican in the 19th century led to the invention of industrial aniline dyes (after *an-nil* which is Arabic for indigo). The most widespread source globally is plants of the *indigofera* family, in Japan and China the native

source is *polygonum tinctorium*, while in Europe the source was woad, isatis tinctoria. In West Africa one major source is *lonchocarpus cyanescens*, a local legume, which is also known as 'Yoruba indigo' and called *elu* by the Yoruba.

Indigo Production and Dyeing

The methods of dye extraction vary according to the source plant but to obtain a good batch of dye always demands great skill and experience as well as constant vigilance at each stage of the process. It is an art rather than a science. Among the Hausa in northern Nigeria indigo dyeing is considered a man's

below, left: Indigo-dyed textile with stitched resist pattern, Mossi tribe, Burkina Faso.
below, right: Indigo-dyed cloth, from Gambia, with folded and stitched resist pattern.

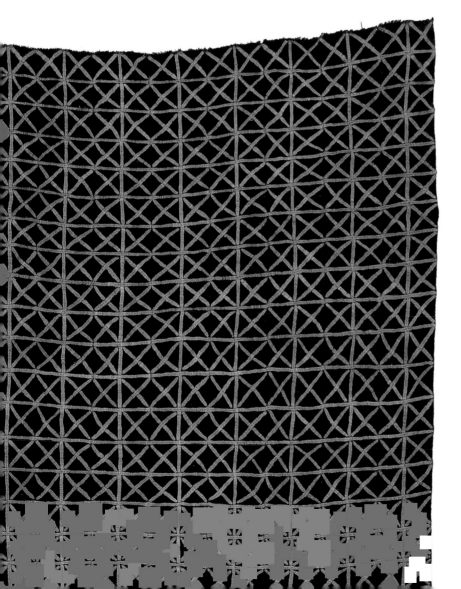

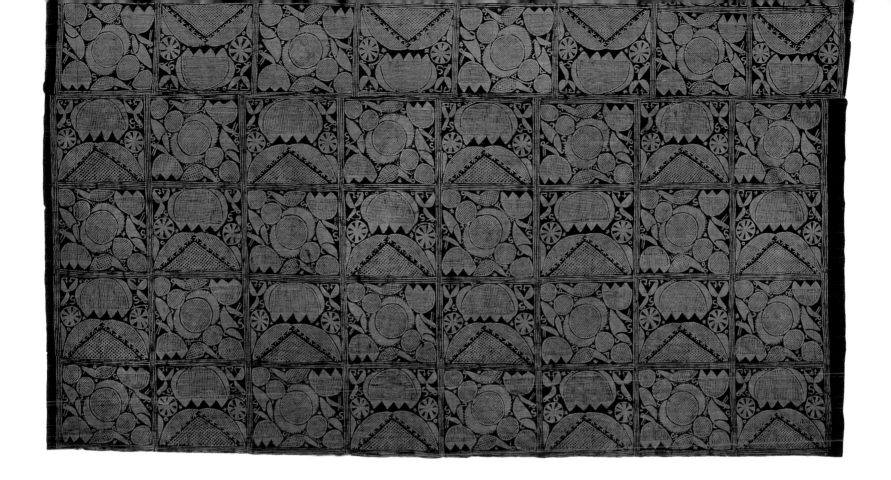

task, but the Yoruba consider it the domain of women and the presence of men is considered unlucky. This female dominance is widespread globally as the vat is associated with the womb. It is also frequently described as sulky and unpredictable. In some parts of Asia, including Indonesia, dyeing is reserved for women who have passed childbearing age.

In many countries indigo leaves are fermented in a tank, but in West Africa the traditional method involves pounding the leaves in a mortar and then moulding the mush into balls which are dried in the sun. Fermentation, which starts during the mushing of the leaves, continues in the dye vat where the leaves are mixed with paste from an old vat of lye made from plant ash. Spring water is filtered in and the vat is then left to ferment in the sun for about ten days.

The most magical part of the process occurs after the cloth has been immersed into the dye vat for a couple of minutes. It remains white once removed, but on exposure to the air the indigo oxidizes and a chemical reaction occurs causing the cloth magically to turn blue before your eyes. Dipping may be repeated again and again until the desired intensity of colour has been achieved.

above: Yoruba *adire eleko* textile, resist dyed using cassava starch, Nigeria.

Yoruba Dyeing Techniques

Most of the indigo dyeing in Nigeria employs resist techniques, collectively known as *adire*, which prevent dye reaching the cloth. Cassava starch is applied with a chicken feather or through a metal stencil to create *adire eliko*. Folding and tying with raphia produces *adire oniko* and patterns created by stitching the cloth tight are known as *adire alabere*. With all these techniques, once the resist material has been removed the fabric is normally dipped once more so the final effect is dark blue and light blue, a combination the Yoruba consider more attractive than blue and white.

The main centres of indigo dyeing in Yorubaland are at Ibadan, Ilorin, Owo, Oshogbo and Abeokuta, the latter being noted for its stencilled cloth.

Hausa and Nupe Embroidery

Techniques

In many parts of the world openings in garments are often decorated with embroidery intended to prevent the entry of bad spirits and the neck of the *babban riga* is both reinforced and protected by dense needlework. The patterns embroidered on the body of the robes probably developed from this reinforcement of seams and edges as can be deduced from the way in which buttonhole stitch, universally employed for edging, is employed to work the hems and the bulk of the pattern. Some robes, with extensive embroidery across the chest, may take several months to complete.

There are few places in the world where embroidery is considered suitable work for men. In northern Nigeria, however, among the Hausa and Nupe, the loose-sleeved robe and baggy trousers worn by men of substance are exclusively the product of male craftsmanship. Embroidery on women's clothes, however, is almost never carried out by men.

Hausa and Nupe Costume

Robe, trousers and embroidered cap are the typical attire of Muslim men in much of sub-Saharan Africa. The robe is a voluminous, virtually square garment with openings at the side which are hitched up onto the shoulders. In French-speaking areas it is called the *boubou*, the Yoruba in southwest Nigeria call it *agbada* and the Hausa know it as *babban riga*. The Hausa and Nupe usually use cotton cloth embroidered with designs in cotton or wild silk thread using a single colour. This is particularly effective when white thread is used on an indigo-dyed ground.

The trousers are enormously baggy with a drawstring to pull in a waist that may be over 5 m (16 ft) in circumference. The ankles, however, are very narrow. The embroidery on these, in contrast to the robe, is generally brightly coloured and worked in wool, but is normally concealed under the long robe.

top: Pair of Hausa drawstring trousers with silk floss embroidery, northern Nigeria.

opposite, below, right: Panel from a Hausa or Nupe 'eight knives' shirt embroidered mainly in buttonhole stitch over a ground of indigo-dyed cotton, Nigeria.

Although patterns are still frequently hand sewn, it is increasingly common for the process of making the garment to have been speeded up by the use of a sewing machine.

Traditional Designs

The patterns on Hausa and Nupe robes are drawn on by a *malaam*, a 'teacher' or 'master', and are considered to have magical and protective powers. They show a fusion of Islamic patterns which are apparent, for example, in the interweaving of lines, and more ancient angular elements and spirals that can also be seen on the pottery and basketry of the region. The repertoire of motifs is, however, quite limited and includes a block of five squares known as 'five houses', a pair of interlaced figures of eight known as a 'knot' or 'tortoise' and a triangular 'knife'. Most of the embroidery is carried out on a large

pocket, sewn on at the end to complete the garment, positioned below the neck on the left of the wearer's chest.

Knives

The knife motif is one of the most popular in this region probably because of the obvious protection provided by a sharp blade. On the 'two knives' shirt, *aska biyu*, the triangles are positioned below the neck while on the 'eight knives' version, *aska takwas*, three more are added on the left breast and another three at the side of the neck opening. Between and around the knives other designs are worked, including a band ending in arrowhead-like chevrons. Sometimes the stitches are so extensive and intense that they cover most of the left side of the garment.

below: Nupe *babban riga* with embroidery over a striped ground, Nigeria.

Kuba Raphia Cloth

left: Square of Kuba raphia cloth, from the Democratic Republic of the Congo, embroidered by women on a ground woven by men.

Working with Raphia

Raphia fibres are woven by men on a diagonal loom into pieces of cloth about 60 cm (2 ft) square, a size dictated by the length of the strands. Some individual squares were woven so finely that they were once used as currency. For longer textiles such as dance skirts a number of these squares are sewn together. Some of these long, wrapped garments may need as many as 30 panels.

Skirts are often decorated in appliqué using angular patches stitched down with brown or black stitching. Designs may be enhanced with the use of a limited range of natural dyes providing yellow, orange, brown, red, black and occasionally purple.

Animal and plant fibres such as bark, banana and orchid fibre, nettles, hemp and palm fronds can be used to make traditional textiles. In the Kasai River region of the Democratic Republic of the Congo the Kuba people developed the skills of making cloth from raphia. According to legend, they were initially educated in the techniques 400 years ago by the ruler and culture hero, Shyam a-Mbul a-Ngong, who also introduced weaving and embroidery, and so valued is this fabric that even today raphia textiles are still used at ceremonies and, in particular, funerals.

Raphia

The raphia palm grows around the tropical forests of Central and West Africa and produces fronds up to 15 m (50 ft) long. Leaflets up to 1.8 m (6 ft) long are cut from the fronds and stripped of their fleshy coating to reveal the inner fibrous layers which are then dried in the sun. They are bleached to a pale, translucent ochre colour and shrink. Splitting the fibres into fine strands is accomplished with the fingers, a comb or a snail shell. These silky strands, not unlike linen, are then used for both weaving and sewing.

right: Embroidered Kuba raphia cloth from the Democratic Republic of the Congo. The designs often follow a precise logic at the beginning, before fragmenting.
opposite, top: Kuba dance skirt with appliqué motifs.

Kasai Velvet

Probably the best-known Kuba textiles are the cut-pile embroidered pieces known as Kasai Velvet. These are the work of women embroidering raphia squares woven by men. An iron needle is used, threaded with a strand of raphia fibre, twisted for ease of threading. The embroidery stitch consists of no more than passing the thread down through the cloth, under a warp and back up again before the thread is cut with a sharp knife leaving just a few millimetres exposed. The stitches are packed closely together in blocks of contrasting colour to build up a pattern.

Patterns

Embroidery is carried out from memory and features a number of motifs which take their names from their incidental resemblance to familiar items such as *molamba*, 'the finger', *bisha kota*, 'the crocodile's back' and *mikope ngoma*, 'the drums of Nikope'; they are not, however, an attempt to depict these objects. Like the designs on Kuba woodwork and body decoration, these patterns are composed of geometric elements that abut or interlace. Although they seem logical at first glance, closer scrutiny generally reveals that the embroiderer has indulged in a number of variations on the theme, sometimes achieving a level of complexity bewildering to the eye of the beholder.

above: Girls' raphia waist ornaments or 'cache fesse' made before 1900 by the Mongo tribe in the Congo.

Tutsi Basketry

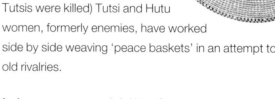

The Tutsi inhabit parts of central Africa. According to local tradition, they are descended from Ethiopian ancestors who moved south about 600 years ago, but their distinctive looks caused German colonists to postulate theories of their origins being European or their even coming from the lost continent of Atlantis. Before the inter-tribal conflicts of the late 20th century, the Tutsi constituted the ruling elite of Rwanda and Burundi. As a privileged minority, they enjoyed leisure time and this enabled aristocratic women to develop refined basketmaking skills.

Agaseki and Agakoko

The *agaseki* is the typical form of a Tutsi basket; it is pot shaped with a conical lid and rather resembles a straw hut. The workmanship is often exquisitely fine, especially with the smaller baskets that may be only a few centimetres high. The technique used is bundle coiling using bundles of rush or papyrus stems twisted into a spiral and sewn together with strands of raphia or sisal. Patterns may be created by changing the colour of the fibre in the coiled bundle or the stitching. Very fine double-skinned baskets are also made in which the pattern is created from strands sewn in coils onto an inner form built using the stake and strand technique.

These delightful baskets are presented as wedding gifts and may subsequently be used for storing or transporting grains, beans or valuables. The flat discs known as *agakoko*, on the other hand, are purely decorative and made for presentation.

Colours and Patterns

The colours of Tutsi baskets are dominated by the mellow natural colouring of local plants. The most common manufactured colour used in designs is black which is achieved with *inzero* dye made from the sap of banana flowers. The other traditional colour is red which may be produced in a number of ways including using colouring from powdered stone, dyeing using a concoction made with the roots and seeds of the *urukamgi* plant or with pigment obtained from the blood of cattle tics. The geometric patterns swirl elegantly around the walls of the basket in triangles or spirals that look like lightning flashes. The lids of baskets from Burundi are also sometimes patterned, but those from Rwanda are always plain.

Modern baskets often incorporate a wider palette using imported dyes and more figurative designs. Since the bloodshed of the 1990s (during which it is estimated 77 per cent of Tutsis were killed) Tutsi and Hutu women, formerly enemies, have worked side by side weaving 'peace baskets' in an attempt to set aside old rivalries.

Inkangara and Milk Screens

Larger baskets called *inkangara* are used for the storage of bulkier items such as clothes. These are double-walled baskets with designs built up from lengths of plant stem sewn diagonally onto the inner base layer. The same designs are traditionally used to decorate the posts at the entrance to the home.

The Tutsi are a people who traditionally measure their wealth in cattle and milk is not only an important part of their diet, but is also used in many ceremonies. To keep it cool it is stored in wooden pots with fine basketry lids and placed upon a special platform shaded behind screens called *inzugi zigize insika*.

above: Presentation discs or *agakoko* made by aristocratic Tutsi women in Uganda.

These are made using similar techniques to the *inkangara* and a number of these screens placed together, all with different patterns of triangles, chevrons and zigzags, create a grass hut with dynamic decoration as well as providing fresh milk and cream.

below: Tutsi *agaseki*: the three in the centre are from Rwanda, while the two either side are from Burundi; they have distinctive decorated lids.

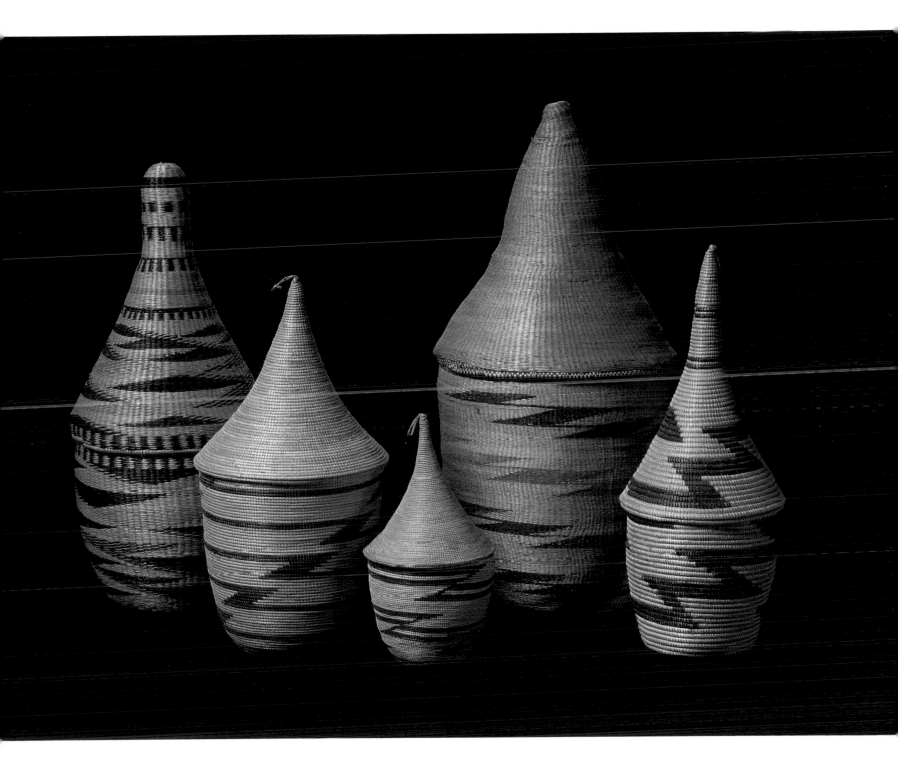

Maasai Beadwork

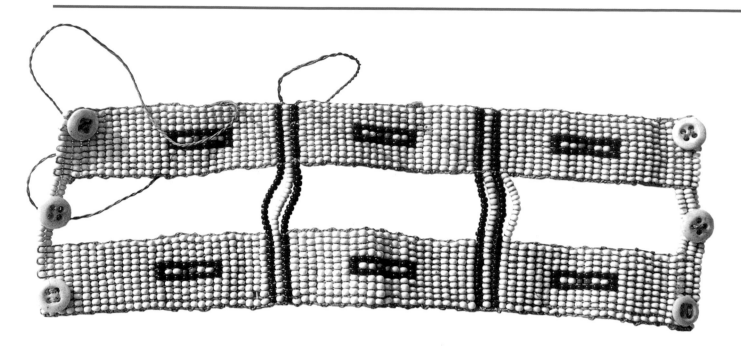

All over Africa both men and women decorate themselves and their clothes with beads. Once beads were made from clay, stone, shell or bone and other animal materials, but with the arrival of European traders in the 19th century coloured glass beads became available and with them a far greater range of design possibilities. Zulu and Xhosa women in South Africa, for instance, became adept at weaving patterns that conveyed allegorical messages of love to their sweethearts. Among the most distinctive African beadwork is that worn by the Maasai which creates a striking contrast with their hide clothing and ochre-stained bodies.

The Maasai

The Maasai are a cattle-herding people who occupy an area of the Great Rift Valley in East Africa on the borders of Kenya and Tanzania. It is their traditional belief that the god Engai placed all the cattle in the world into their care and even today, when their culture is threatened, they measure their wealth and happiness by the size of their herds. Diet is dominated by milk and blood supplemented by honey and occasionally meat; their festive costume is made from hide and their homes are insulated with the dung of their cattle.

Maasai life is delineated by age groups, the most iconic of which for men is the period between the ages of roughly 16 and 35 when, after circumcision, they serve as *ilmoran* (warriors). They dress flamboyantly in a profusion of beads with their long hair dressed in an elaborate coiffure reddened with ochre.

top: Maasai bracelet of 'woven' glass beads and plant fibre.
left: Ornament worn by Maasai women through a hole in the upper ear.
opposite: Maasai collar with glass beads threaded on wires with wooden spacers.

Maasai Beadwork

After the day's chores are completed, Maasai women often gather and chat while working on their beadwork. Young girls may work on ornaments for their warrior boyfriends or, like the older women, on objects to beautify themselves.

All Maasai, both men and women, but with the exception of uncircumcised boys, adorn themselves with a variety of beaded items, many of which are specific to their age or gender. Both sexes wear belts, armbands, bracelets and anklets and a number of necklaces and earrings are worn through the upper ear and the lobe. Women, however, also wear beaded 'diadems' and distinctive large, flat, circular collars often worn three or four at a time.

Although daily attire is generally a cotton wrap, a woman's festive clothing is made of softened hides decorated with rows of beads strung onto sinew and attached with lazy stitch.

Techniques

The colours chosen for Maasai beadwork vary from one geographic group to another. The Ikisongo of Tanzania, for example, have a preference for designs incorporating dark red and dark blue. The simplest ornaments consist of a single row of glass and seed beads strung onto sinew, but collars, head gear and the other stiff ornaments are constructed by stringing a sequence of beads onto parallel wires which are threaded at intervals through spacers to keep them in shape. Broad flexible items, such as armbands, are constructed using a 'weaving' technique. Warp threads are doubled over a cord at the end and a pair of wefts passed across them at right angles, one in front and one behind. They do not actually interweave but are secured in place by passing through the beads which are placed between the warps. Without the beads, the structure would fall apart. This simple technique is used to create bold designs composed within a grid system.

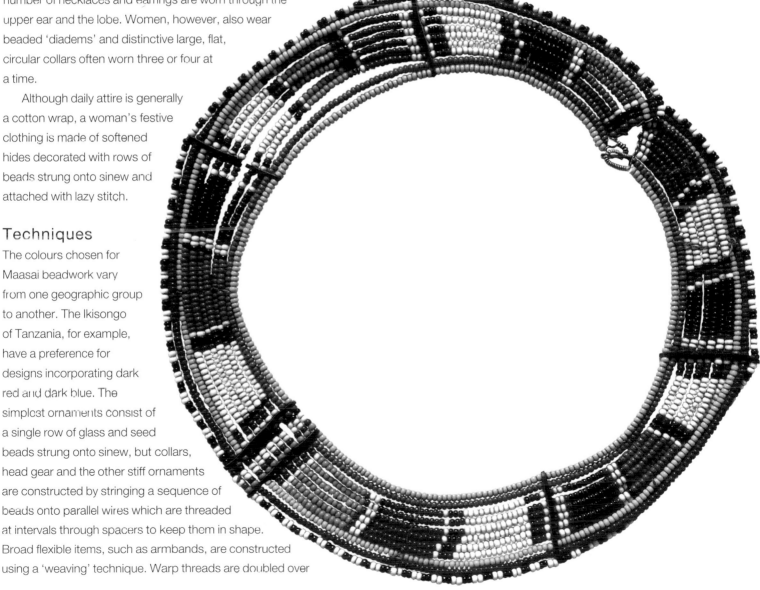

Zulu Beer Pots

above: Zulu women in traditional costume drinking beer from clay pots.

According to Zulu mythology, sorghum beer was invented by Nokhubwane, the goddess of rain, the rainbow and agriculture. Associated with the ancestors, to whom libations are poured when it is drunk, beer occupies an important place in Zulu culture in KwaZulu-Natal, South Africa and, traditionally, special clay vessels are employed in all the stages of its brewing and consumption.

Types of Beer Pot

The brewing of beer takes place on a platform in a dark part of the house preferred by the ancestors. A large vessel, from 40 to 60 cm (16–23 in.) in height, known as an *imbiza*, is used; made from terracotta, which is porous, some evaporation takes place which keeps the beer cool. Unlike other beer pots, this one retains the red-brown colour of clay fired in an oxygen-rich atmosphere. To prevent dust or insects falling in the pot it is covered with an inverted basket called an *imbenge*. Beer is transported in a vessel called an *uphiso* or *ingcazi* which is about 40 cm (16 in.) high. This has a standing rim to prevent spillage. For the storage and actual drinking of the beer a smaller spherical pot called an *ukhamba* is used. These range from 15–40 cm (6–16 in.), the size employed for drinking varying according to the status of the drinker. Like the *uphiso*, the *ukhamba* has a black finish. In neighbouring regions beer is also drunk from clay pots, those from Lesotho being distinguished by their goblet shape and those from Swaziland by their fine impressed designs.

Although in the past pottery was generally made by families for their own use, modern Zulu potters have recognized a market for their wares and have developed individual styles using less traditional forms.

Making and Firing Traditional Pots

Traditionally Zulu beer pots are made by women employing the coiling technique using sausages of rolled out clay. Although no wheel is used, experienced Zulu potters are able to produce near perfect spherical vessels by eye. Once smoothed, the pots are burnished and left to dry.

Symbolism and Decoration

Because of their shape and the fermentation that takes place inside them, beer pots are associated with a woman's belly, menstruation and pregnancy. The designs used to decorate them were once commonly found on the bodies of women in the form of raised scars or cicatrices. On pottery the designs are created by either pressing small balls of clay onto the surface or by making impressions into strings of clay winding over the surface. The lumps are known as *amasumpa* or 'warts' and may be arranged in a variety of patterns, but are believed to represent the cattle that are given as part of a bride's dowry.

above: Zulu pot, from KwaZulu-Natal in South Africa, for drinking beer decorated with clay pellets known as *amasumpa*. The black coloration is the result of reduction during firing.
right: High-rimmed vessel used for transporting beer, KwaZulu-Natal, South Africa.

For firing, the dried pots are placed in a shallow pit and covered with combustible material. This rapidly reaches about 800°C (1472°F) and is allowed to burn for only an hour or so before being left to cool slowly. The black colour of the *uphiso* and the *ukhambo* is the result of reduction achieved by covering the hot pots with dung which absorbs all the oxygen present in the clay as it burns. This black finish may be enhanced by exposing the vessels to the smoke of a fire fuelled with grass, tambooti wood or even car tyres before polishing with beef fat.

Because of the rapid increase in temperature, many vessels crack from thermal shock when this bonfire method is used and sometimes as many as two or three may be lost.

Shona Stone Carving

On its official recognition as an independent nation in 1980, Rhodesia was renamed Zimbabwe. This was a reference to the greatness of the past when, from their capital at Dzimba dza mabwe which means 'the great stone house' (usually known as Great Zimbabwe), the Shona people ruled an empire which reached its peak in the 15th century. Eight boldly carved stone birds were discovered in the ruins of this granite city and have become a potent symbol of the power of the Zimbabwean nation. The tradition of stone carving continues among the Shona today and, since the championing of their skills in the mid-20th century by Frank McEwen (first Director of the National Gallery of Zimbabwe), many sculptors have gained international acclaim for their work.

Stone

The birds found at Great Zimbabwe were carved from soapstone (steatite). This is a soft but very dense material that can be carved with great precision and is therefore often used for small, detailed work. Zimbabwe is, however, blessed with a great number of other types of stone suitable for carving which vary in both hardness and colour including blacks, greens, yellows and reds as well as being plain or striated. The most commonly used stone is serpentine which can be found in large blocks suitable for work of monumental size. It is hard and durable and can be polished to a lustrous green-black sheen.

Hard stone is much more difficult to work than soft stone. It takes longer to carve and makes tools blunt more quickly. For this reason a piece fashioned from a material as hard as verdite will be much more expensive than work carved from soapstone.

Techniques

Great craftsmen such as Michelangelo and Henry Moore talked about the search for the form hidden inside a lump of stone. This is the case with most Shona carvers who tend to begin without a fixed idea of the outcome. Allowing the shape, striations and imperfections present in the raw material to dictate progress, their work has the strength and vitality that often accompanies spontaneity. On a metaphysical level, the Shona believe that there is a spiritual presence in each piece of stone and this attitude too will affect the final form revealed.

below: Chameleons on a branch carved from soapstone by John Phiri, Zimbabwe. Colour has been introduced by polishing some areas and leaving others matt.

Subject Matter

Many modern carvings intended for export are now made in a style reminiscent of Henry Moore and Barbara Hepworth with sketchy human forms pierced with holes. These pieces lack originality or conviction as they pay lip service to the tastes of the developed world. Far more compelling is work inspired by the wild life of the region such as birds, rhinos, elephants and chameleons. These are sometimes stylized but are nonetheless life like and well observed. The most powerful images are those truest to the Shona psyche. Often inspired by myth, folklore and traditional culture, these feature robust, compact forms of characters, both legendary and domestic, who seem to thrust their way forcibly out of the stone.

right: 'Stories from the Past', a larger than life sculpture carved from springstone by Sylvester Mubayi, Zimbabwe.

Apart from verdite, most of the stone used in Zimbabwe for carving is quarried only with hand tools. The sculptor too uses only hand tools, roughing out with a hammer and chisel before refining the work with files and smoothing with sandpaper. Once finished, the carving is heated and polished with clear wax. Often a contrast in colour and texture is created by leaving 'background' areas matt.

above: 'The Beadmaker', a life-sized sculpture carved from springstone by Colleen Madamombe from Zimbabwe.

Recycled Metal

Those of us who live in the developed world have become profligate in our use of packaging and our disposal of waste materials, but fears for the well being of our planet have prompted many of us to attempt to reduce environmental damage by recycling as much as we can. In the poorer communities of southern Africa where people have little as much as possible is reused or turned into something else. From an early age the pattern is established, bottle tops are used for counters on draught boards, dolls are made from discarded clothing. Waste materials can, however, be an opportunity for indigenous communities to equip themselves with necessary utensils and to make some money. Recycled artwork is now often destined for collections thousands of miles from the place it was made.

Uses of Scrap Metal

Metal sheet would be an expensive commodity to buy but an abundant stock is available in the tins used for liquids of all kinds from Coca-Cola to cooking oil. With a little welding an oil can can be given a handle and spout and turned into a jug or a watering can or have wires stretched across it to make a guitar. For more delicate items the ideal material is the aluminium drinks cans easily cut with scissors and bent with pliers or even fingers. On the streets of Cape Town and Johannesburg in South Africa today a common sight is the craftsman cutting and bending cans into cars and aeroplanes or threading bottle tops onto wires to make handbags and radio cases.

In Zimbabwe scraps of heavier metals salvaged from the industrial areas of Harare are worked with nothing more than tin-snips, pliers and hammers. One collective of enterprising brothers formed the Improved Arts Metal Sculpture Project in 1986. Now they make life-like versions of the wild animals of the bush: lions, zebras, warthogs and so on by ingeniously folding them from a sheet of metal. These lively animals are painted in bright colours and patterns that are unrealistic but dynamic.

Pattern and Colour

Rather than use paint, many craftsmen would prefer to exploit the shiny colours and designs already printed on a can. The vast majority of models are bright red since they are constructed from the ubiquitous Coca-Cola can. An inventive craftsman will carefully select and arrange pieces with different colours and patterns to create the best effect.

Telephone Wire

The *imbenge*, a traditional Zulu basket made from grass, is used to keep the dust out of large beer pots. In the early 1990s

top left: Aeroplane made from recycled bottle tops and a beer can by Michael Callaghan, Cape Town, South Africa.
above: Wire bottle top handbag by Michael Callaghan, Cape Town, South Africa.
opposite, below: Painted scrap metal baboon, from Harare, Zimbabwe, made in one piece.

night watchmen with time on their hands began experimenting with scrap telephone wire to make a modern interpretation of the *imbenge*. Although new basketry techniques were required to work with wire, the pattern opportunities provided by the colours available has led to the development of one of the most successful of modern crafts with huge numbers of baskets in vivid colours and a kaleidoscope of patterns now on sale at South African airports.

Other Materials and Other Places

Craftsmen and women the world over are ready to exploit all manner of cheap or free recycled materials. Rubber car tyres can be seen in the souks of Marrakesh, Morocco, turned into buckets or in Pakistan converted into stools. In India as well as South Africa miles of wire are bent and coiled into lizards or bicycles. Recycled craft is often skilful and sometimes inspired.

above: Telephone-wire basket inspired by boer pot covers, Cape Town, South Africa.

below (background image):
Large medallion *susani*,
Bukhara, Uzbekistan, *c.* 1800.

below, centre: Indigo-dyed jacket
with wax-resist patterns, Pojao,
Guizhou, China.

opposite, right: Figure of the rice
goddess, Dewi Sri, made from palm
leaves, Bali.

5 Asia

Introduction

far left: Prayer board used by Muslim women praying at home, Swat Valley. Pakistan.
near left: Snake-like *nagas* covered with mirror tiles at a Buddhist temple in Chiang Mai, Thailand.
below: Carved wooden figure of the Hindu god, Krishna, Udaipur, Rajasthan, India.

The continent of Asia is vast and diverse. Its topography and climate have resulted in an enormous range of natural materials and therefore a vast range of appropriate skills tailored to the manufacture of crafts catering for the daily needs of people leading equally varied lifestyles. Styles and decorative forms have been influenced by some of the world's greatest civilizations and the philosophy behind the use, construction and decoration of craftwork is saturated with not only local belief systems, but also the world's major religions disseminated by evangelists and conquerors from one end of the continent to the other.

Topography and Climate

Topography and climate are inextricably linked. While mountains stimulate the fall of rain and plains create pressure systems, the resulting rains and winds scour and shape the landscape, drop life-giving moisture or leave it arid and desolate. People have adapted their lifestyles and survival techniques to the restrictions and opportunities of disparate regions. For example, on the grass-covered plains and plateaus of Mongolia, Tibet and Turkestan life

is traditionally nomadic, constantly following herds and flocks to better grazing. Craftsmanship here is predominantly based on wool and leather. Elsewhere in the damp jungles and forests of Borneo the main materials are wood, bamboo and vines which are exploited to make weapons, traps and all manner of utensils. The great civilizations of Mesopotamia and of the Indus Valley were strategically located where the rivers provided water for irrigation and the alluvial deposits were rich enough to grow food for thousands of people. Here the sedentary lifestyle allowed the development of ceramic and metalworking technology.

Religion

Asia is the birth place of many religions, the oldest of which is

left: Indian appliqué quilt made by Meghwal women from Rajasthan.
below: Felted woollen cloth embroidered boots, Tibet.

Hinduism. The extensive pantheon of gods, the wealth of stories and the ecstatic practices of mystics have made it probably the most colourful of all faiths, inspiring a profusion of art and architecture, but in spite of this there are only small pockets of Hindus outside the Indian subcontinent. Buddhism, however, has spread much further, reaching as far north as Tibet and as far east as Japan, while the number of devotees continues to swell in the Western world.

Introduction

right: Double-walled storage basket bought in Chiang Mai, Thailand.
opposite: Mirrorwork backless blouse, or *choli*, from Sind, Pakistan.

Judaism, Christianity and Islam all began in the Middle East. A realm of influence stretching from Turkey to Indonesia, probably accelerated by the nomadic origins of its earliest adherents, was built in the name of Islam. Christianity has many representations of the human form, whether man, saint, angel or God himself, Islam has developed a refined vocabulary of tessellating geometric forms and swirling arabesques which appear with local variations from one end of the continent to the other. In remote, inaccessible regions, particularly in the once impenetrable forests, the great faiths were unknown and here, even today, many folk still retain vestiges of old animist beliefs, placing their faith in the bounty of the natural world and the goodwill of ancestors. It is here that some of the most distinctive and haunting arts and crafts are produced, little affected by global styles and fashions but true to their function and resonating with powerful symbolism.

above: Labijar Uzbek kilim woven in slitweave and double interlock, Northwest Afghanistan.

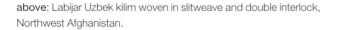

above: Detail of a Samarkand *susani* worked largely in *basma* stitch.

Inlay and Marquetry

left: Inlaid Koran stand, King Hussein Mosque, Amman, Jordan.
below: Wooden tray inlaid with brass wire, Bahrain.

The 'Death Pits' of Ur, in what is now Iraq, were the burial chambers of Sumerian royalty who died about four and a half thousand years ago. In the 1920s archaeologists discovered, among the sacrificed bodies of a host of retainers, opulent grave goods including the fabulous 'Standard of Ur', a box-shaped object lavishly decorated with lapis lazuli, shell and red limestone glued on with bitumen. The quality of workmanship suggests that this technique of overlaid decoration must already have been in use for a considerable length of time. In Old Kingdom Egypt (c. 2650–2150 BC) craftsmen were producing work, inlaid with ebony and ivory, to be placed in the tombs of pharaohs for use in the next life. Both Sumerians and Egyptians controlled the Levant at times during the second millennium, presumably taking craftsmen or their work with them. It is perhaps not surprising that today Syria is a prolific producer of fine marquetry and inlay.

Materials

If the finished surface is to be flat, the craftsman must use materials that can be cut into thin sheets or pieces. Wood veneers are ideal and many beautifully coloured hardwoods are available, the black of ebony being particularly useful, but other materials such as mother of pearl, ivory or bone and even metal are often employed. Today it is quite common to find white plastic used as a cheap substitute for ivory. The inlay technique can also be used for setting stone in stone as can be seen, famously, on the façade of the Taj Mahal in India.

Techniques

Although similar in appearance, the techniques of marquetry and inlay are different. The former is constructed from cut shapes glued directly onto a surface while inlay demands

that the shapes be sunk into a shallow recess in the surface. This is precision work demanding a sharp knife and a steady hand.

As Islamic pattern is composed of a great many repeated modules; the painstaking process of cutting pieces can be speeded up by a technique of end-grain cutting developed in Syria in the 9th century AD. This involves taking a number of 80 cm (31 in.) rods of different colours and tessellating shapes and gluing them into a bundle, rather like a stick of seaside rock. Dozens of identical slices can then be sawn off the end and quickly assembled into a composite design.

Decorative Woodwork and the Spread of Islam

From AD 661 to 750 Damascus was the seat of the Omayyad Caliphate, effectively the administrative centre of the Islamic world. Islamic art is not representative, but depicts colour and pattern. This could take many forms including tilework but here it found expression in the decorative possibilities of marquetry,

right: Iranian pen box with painted ivory lid and sides decorated with end-grain marquetry.
below: Marquetry box with wood veneer, bone and mother of pearl, made in Damascus, Syria.

covering a surface with complex patterns of tessellating shapes. Objects decorated in this way were both spiritual and worldly, ranging from Koran stands to jewelry boxes and backgammon sets appreciated by locals and visitors alike and exported in great quantities to neighbouring countries.

Islam travelled west across North Africa to Morocco and then up into Spain, east into Persia, Central Asia and India, taking ideas and skills that blended with local ideas to produce distinctive regional variations in science, literature and craft. The surface of a wooden artefact in Arabia might be inlaid with brass wire, a box in Morocco might be decorated with bone and mother of pearl set in resin and an Iranian pen box might be covered in intricate end-grain marquetry.

Kilims

In Anatolia (the Asian part of Turkey once known as Asia Minor) 'kilim' is the name for a flatweave rug, one woven on a loom rather than knotted. In Afghanistan the term is 'kelim', in the Ukraine 'kylym' and in Iran 'gelim'. For affluent collectors in the Western world the knotted carpet has always been the aristocrat of the carpet world and the kilim its poor country cousin. Although tying the thousands of knots required to create the complex swirling arabesques of a Persian carpet is time consuming, it only requires the knowledge of a single knot. To produce the bold designs of a woven rug, on the other hand, requires familiarity with a variety of techniques and a sensitivity to tension. This is particularly crucial if the loom is dismantled by a nomad weaver while weaving is in progress.

Uses

The techniques employed when weaving flatweaves are not restricted to the making of floor coverings. For nomads, in particular, the wool of a family's sheep and goats may be woven into tent doors and dividers, seating and bags. These goods are traditionally displayed in the tent or home as a sign of wealth and once made up an important part of a bride's dowry. Although made by the women for domestic use, weavings could also provide a potential source of cash during times of hardship.

Pattern and Technique

For thousands of years traders, invaders and settlers have crossed the plains of Anatolia leaving the footprints of their culture woven into the local rugs; today villagers and nomads continue to weave the same motifs and patterns on their looms. Although these days intermarriage between tribes and communities and the commissioning of particular patterns by collectors and dealers has blurred the boundaries, many designs, colour schemes or fibre combinations remain typical of one social group testifying to their origins and identity. Solving the problem of structural integrity caused by colour changes in a pattern has dictated the designs chosen by a weaver. Most kilims are weft faced and the warps are hidden behind the tightly packed wefts. If two blocks of colour abut each other then a slit is produced where the wefts are turned back. In this technique, known as 'dovetailing' or 'slitweave', it is essential that vertical lines are kept short and this dictates

'steps' at the edges of colour blocks. Alternately wefts may overlap and 'interlock' around the warps, a technique that produces a slightly fuzzy edge. 'Double interlock' involves the wefts interlocking with each other. This creates a clean join but the join shows on the back of the weaving and so, unlike the other methods, it is not reversible. By sticking to diagonal colour divisions the problem is side stepped and for this reason flatweaves all over the world are found with patterns constructed from triangles.

Weft and Warp Patterning

By manipulating the weft (weft-faced patterning) it is possible to create more delicate designs such as the intricate patterning on the Balouch rugs of Iran, Pakistan and Afghanistan. Wefts can

above: Slit-weave kilim, *c.* 1800, Konya district, Turkey.
opposite, right: Slit-weave kilim from the Kayseri area of Anatolia, Turkey.

above: Kurdish slit-weave kilim from the Bijar area in northwest Iran. The slit-weave technique is easy to execute and therefore widespread, but rugs woven in this way lack the structural strength of those where the weaver has employed an interlocking method at the point where blocks of colour join.

be woven in, appearing on the front only when required and floating across the reverse. Non-structural supplementary wefts may be introduced for this purpose.

In warp-faced weavings, such as narrow yurt bands, patterns can be created in the same way by manipulating the warp, causing it to appear in the design or float across the back as required.

Metal Beating

Bazaars and towns throughout Asia and North Africa once resounded with the ringing of hammers beating sheets of metal into water pots, ewers, jugs, coffee pots, bowls and drinking vessels. Although more expensive than clay, metal is lighter and more resilient, qualities that endeared metal vessels to townsfolk and nomads alike, unrivalled until the introduction of plastic buckets and containers in the 20th century.

Copper and its Alloys

As copper can be 'won' from ore by smelting at a fairly low temperature it was probably the first metal in common usage, hard enough to take an edge while soft enough to be beaten into shape. Bronze, a much harder metal more easily shaped by casting, is produced by mixing tin with copper, a technological breakthrough of sufficient importance that it gave its name to a period of history, the 'Bronze Age'. The addition of zinc to copper, on the other hand, produces a metal

which is malleable but has a colour and lustre similar to gold. Copper and brass, and variations with additions of small quantities of other minerals, are the metals most widely shaped by beating with a hammer.

Until the 18th century many domestic utensils in Europe were made from pewter, a softer metal than copper which, unfortunately, is easily dented. Both copper and pewter were popular among craftsmen during the Arts and Crafts movement in the British Isles during the late 19th century.

Shaping Techniques

When a sheet of metal is struck a dent is created which reveals on observation that a curved surface has been produced by compressing and stretching the metal. Controlled use of this principle by skilled hands can turn a flat sheet into a container, a process most effective when the metal has first been softened by heating.

above: Beaten copper and brass vessels. The two beakers at the back are from India and the tea kettle is from Thailand. In the centre is a Middle Eastern coffee pot and in the front on the left is a Thai kettle and on the right a Japanese tea kettle.
right: Beaten brass vessel for carrying water, Rajasthan, India.

The most basic beating technique involves placing the sheet over a hollow in a hard piece of wood and tapping away with a convex-headed hammer, stretching the metal until it fits the recess. This is known as 'sinking' or 'hollowing' and is ideal for forming bowl shapes.

'Raising' is more skilled: the metal, which is repeatedly heated, is beaten on the outside while supported by a special anvil called a 'stake' on the inside. The metal is revolved slightly with each hammer blow and the work progresses in concentric circles until the required cylindrical form is achieved.

'Spinning' is a technique in which pressure is applied against a piece of flat metal attached to a form on a lathe. This method has been in use, independently or in combination with hammering techniques, since Roman times and has the advantages of speed and achieving a smooth, regular surface.

above, left: Turkish beaten copper pot from Istanbul.
above, right: Beaten metal beakers from India except for the one second from left which is from Afghanistan.

Complex Forms

To achieve spherical and more complex forms an item may be assembled from several separately made components, most typically a curved or conical neck, a waist and a concave base. The waist is often made from a strip of metal curved into a cylinder with limited beating. The sections may be riveted together but better quality work is assembled by brazing over heat and 'glueing' together with a metallic solder with a lower melting point than the parent metal. The vessel is then ground and polished to make the joint invisible. To perfect the illusion many items, such as those used in Afghanistan and Central Asia, are given a coating of silvery tin which may then be decorated with chasing or stamping.

above: Brass samovar made in Russia for the Afghan market.

Persian Carpets

A Persian carpet with its knotted pile holds a mysterious fascination. Not only are they beautiful and evocative, but even the following of a design can be magical. While some designs might be remembered by the weaver and complex patterns might be copied from a drawing or an older masterpiece, the patterns of hundreds of knotted rugs were once retained in the memory of a blind *ma'allem*, the 'carpet conductor' who could sing the sequence of knots row after row.

History

Although cotton, silk and even linen have been used to make knotted pile textiles, the most commonly used fibre is wool and it is among the herdsmen of Central Asia with their flocks of long-haired sheep that we must look for the origins of the technique. It was at the tombs in Pazyryk in the Siberian Altai Mountains, among the felts and appliqués, that the oldest known knotted textiles, a rug from the 5th century BC and a saddle cover from the 6th century, were discovered frozen in the permafrost.

The techniques spread to both east and west and a number of different knots were developed. The most prized came from Iran and the term Persian carpets is still used to describe carpets from Iran and some of the neighbouring regions.

Knots

The 'knots' used for creating pile are not truly knots but loops and are held in place by the weft. Most are wrapped around two warps with the exception of the Spanish knot which is wrapped around just one.

The most widely used knot is the Turkish, Smyrna or Ghiordes knot (the last two names referring to towns in northern Iraq). It is symmetrical, very secure and ideal for long piles and was used to make the Pazyryk carpet.

The Persian or Sehna knot (named after a town in western Iran) is asymmetrical and used less than it once was, now being mostly confined to parts of Iran. It is, however, excellent for fine work as a yarn end appears between every pair of warps, giving an evenly textured surface. It was used to make the Pazyryk saddle bag.

The Berber knot, which resembles a clove hitch tied around one or two warps, is used by the Berbers of the Atlas Mountains in Morocco.

Technique

Whether on a horizontal or a vertical loom, knotting is carried out on the warps only and wefts are woven in between rows of knots to bind the work lightly together. The weaver may tie the knots using pre-cut lengths of yarn or tie them from the end of a hank before cutting them off. The average number of knots to the square inch is between fifty and one hundred, but a particularly fine carpet may be as dense as one thousand.

Because each knot is independent, colours may be changed frequently without complex joins and so it is simple to produce intricate, convoluted designs.

After a carpet is completed, the pile may be trimmed to an even length with a large pair of scissors. While the pile of most carpets is cut fairly short, sometimes it is deliberately made very long for insulation rather than aesthetics. Among these are the Uzbek *dschulchir* (bearskin) rugs and the *ryas* of Finland and Sweden.

opposite, left: Kurdish wool pile carpet woven in the *mina khani* (five flower) pattern, 19th century, northwest Iran. Although the Persian empire no longer exists, the term 'Persian' is still used to describe pile carpets from the lands that were once part of the empire.

opposite, centre: Balouch bag with flatweave weft patterning and areas of pile, southwest Afghanistan. The nomadic Balouch typically employ a combination of different techniques in one weaving.

opposite, right: From southwest Afghanistan, this Balouch bag has pile patterning and bands of flatweave weft patterning.

above: An intricately patterned Qashqai wool pile carpet from the Fars district of southwest Iran.

Weft Wrapping

left: A large bag with extensive weft wrapping made by Kazakh people in northern Afghanistan where rugs of this type are known as *lakai*.

Weft wrapping is used in combination with kilim weaving techniques to produce a dense, strong, tightly patterned rug. Archaeological evidence has shown that the technique has been used to weave textiles for thousands of years in regions as diverse as Switzerland, Peru, Persia and Egypt, but it is now mostly associated with the rug-making of semi-nomadic tribespeople in Afghanistan, Persia and the Caucasus.

Shemakha or Soumak is a Caucasian town in Azerbaijan which is famous for its weft-wrapped rugs. Thinking the technique exclusive to this area, early kilim collectors dubbed it *soumak* after the name of the town and subsequently, by association, referred to all weft-wrapped rugs as *soumaks* no matter where they were made. However, weavers in other regions do not recognize the term and it should be used with care.

The Technique

At its most basic, weft wrapping consists of passing the weft across several warps, wrapping round the back and then passing across the front of several more warps. The numbers vary according to tribe or location, but the diagram shows a sequence of over four, round two, over four, round two. Because of this difference between the number of wefts appearing on back and front, rugs woven with this technique are not reversible.

When rows of wrapping are built up without the use of a ground weft to secure them it is known as 'plain' weft wrapping. Ground wefts may be woven in between rows of wrapping which gives greater strength and also prevents slits when patterns are built up in blocks of colour with a vertical join. When this 'compound' weft-wrapping method is used the ground weft is hidden by the wrapping.

The most obvious quality of this technique is the texture it produces. When all the rows are wrapped in the same direction the surface to some extent resembles embroidery and has occasionally been mislabelled as *suzani* (Persian for 'needlework'). In contrast, when rows of wrapping alternate in direction the result is a herringbone effect very like knitting.

It is most common to wrap wefts horizontally but they can also be wrapped vertically or diagonally and used to reinforce slitweave or act as an outline. This variation is a common feature of Iranian kilims from Bijar and Garmsar.

Patterns

Rugs made by the Taimani Aimaq in western Afghanistan, Kazakhs in Kazakhstan and northern Afghanistan and the Bakhtiari in southwest Iran are almost entirely covered in delicate patterning worked in weft wrapping. However the technique is often used, as by the Balouch in Iran, Pakistan and Afghanistan, as part of an overall design in combination with weft-faced patterning and pile.

By altering the direction of the wrapping or by changing the colour it is possible to work quite intricate designs. Many weft-wrapped rugs feature geometric patterns or abstract renditions of stars but the rugs made by the Shahsavan in northwest Iran and the Bakhtiari in the southeast are often intensely decorated with fields full of camels or horses.

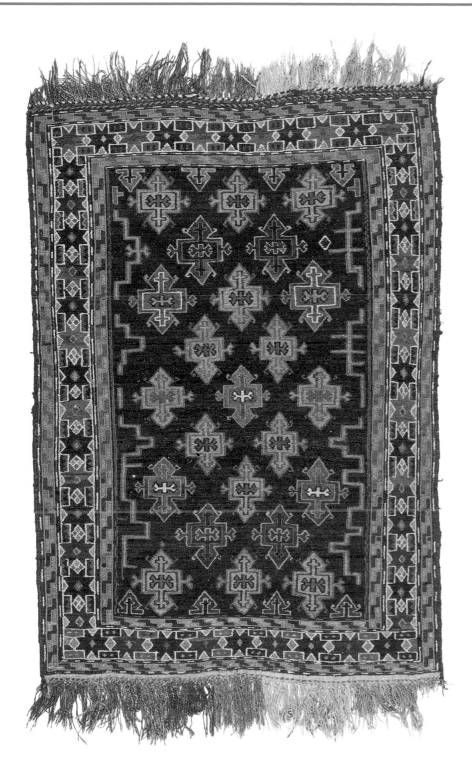

above: Taimani weft-wrapped rug from west central Afghanistan.
right: A Balouch Malaki rug woven in two strips using a combination
of flatweave, weft-faced patterning, weft wrapping and knotted pile,
western Afghanistan.

The Jewelry of Turkestan

The arid region once known as West Turkestan lies in a vast basin stretching from the Caspian Sea in the west to the foothills of the Tien Shan in the east and from the Hindu Kush in the south to the Aral Sea in the north. Among the peoples who live here, particularly the Uzbeks, Tadjiks, Kazakhs and Turkomen, rich distinctive styles of jewelry-making have developed. In particular, the nomadic Turkomen, famed for their horses and carpets, have always invested their wealth in jewelry rather than property as favoured by townsfolk and their women are traditionally bedecked from head to toe in all manner of silver ornamentation.

Types of Jewelry

Silver jewelry is an integral part of Turkomen costume, worn on the body as well as being sewn onto the clothing and head gear of women and children. A diadem is worn across the forehead with pendants at the temples. These may be separate or attached in a combination piece to a pair of earrings. Ornaments are also attached to pigtails. Bracelets are worn on the wrist and rings on the fingers, and sometimes the two are connected together by chains to form a 'hand rose'. From the neck, necklaces and pendants may hang down the front of the body or down the back. Men reserve their ornamentation for weapons and horse trappings.

Decoration may be abstract but often features floral scrollwork, birds and rams' horns. Many motifs have magical significance.

Amulets

Much jewelry has an amuletic function, some pieces designed to hold a Koranic text while others bear symbols of pre-Islamic origin. Triangles and circles are widely used, the former invoking the aid of the ancient goddess while the latter calls on the power of the sun. Boys may wear a pendant shaped like a bow and arrow to protect them from wounds. Semi-precious stones are also valued for their magical power. A red cornelian, for instance, is believed to stop bleeding and miscarriages while blue stones such as turquoise or lapis lazuli are considered proof against the evil eye.

Fire Gilding

A diagnostic feature of Tekke Turkomen jewelry is fire gilding, a technique requiring only small amounts of gold. Designs are engraved into the surface to act like a reservoir and then these areas are painted with an amalgam of gold dust and mercury. When heat is applied the mercury evaporates leaving the gold fused to the surface.

Other Techniques

The linear designs on Turkomen jewelry may be incised with a graver but are as likely to have been worked by stamping a series of tiny dents. This may often be seen in work by Tekke craftsmen.

Raised designs may be hammered from the back using repoussé or chasing but many small items are made using a matrix or bottom swage. A piece of silver plate is placed over a matrix worked with the desired motif and covered with a piece of sheet lead before hammering into shape.

Appliqué techniques include the superimposition of cut-out shapes and the addition of wiggling lines of 'gallery wire' generally used as a band or border. Granulation is the fusing of tiny globules of metal onto the surface, a technique that can be simulated by stamping. Granulation is a common feature of Kazakh jewelry.

opposite, top left: Kazakh-style earrings, from Uzbekistan, with granulations and inset carnelians (left); fire-gilded Turkomen earrings, northern Afghanistan or Uzbekistan (right).
opposite, centre: Yomut Turkomen earrings with appliqué stamped details, Turkmenistan.
opposite, right: Fire-gilded Turkomen amulet case, from Afghanistan, used to carry Koranic verses.

above: Tekke Turkomen fire-gilded pectoral ornament set with carnelians and hung with stamped pendants, northern Afghanistan.
right: Woman from northern Afghanistan in traditional Tekke Turkomen costume pre-1890.
right, inset: Fire-gilded bracelet with granulations and set with lapis lazuli; probably Ersari or Saryk, northern Afghanistan.

Felt

Felt is made and used in many countries, but for thousands of years it has been at the heart of the lives of the nomadic herdsmen of the vast steppes of Central Asia, even to such an extent that in the 4th century BC the Chinese referred to the region as 'the land of felt'. This unwoven wool textile is used for floor coverings and bags, for clothes and the coverings of collapsible homes called *yurts* or *gers*, and even for the images of the spirit who guards over the home.

The Origins of Felt

In Persia the story was that it was Solomon's son who first discovered how to make felt. Convinced he could make a waterproof fabric from wool, he tried again and again to make the fibres join together with no avail until, shedding tears of frustration, he began to jump up and down on a pile of fleece. By the time his passion was exhausted the fibres of the wool had become knitted together into felt. In truth, carefully watching his troublesome flocks, so prone to illness and vulnerable to the attacks of wild beasts, any responsible shepherd would observe how damp fleece becomes matted into dense lumps when under friction.

above and right: Turkomen camel harnesses and an *okbash* (bag for the ends of roof poles) made from felt and decorated with appliqué and embroidery, from Uzbekistan or northern Afghanistan.

Although wool perishes over time, making evidence hard to find, felt may be the oldest of textiles. The oldest known felt articles, including carpets, clothes and saddle blankets, were found preserved in the Siberian permafrost at Pazyryk dating from the 7th century BC and at Noin Ula in Mongolia dating to the 4th century BC.

Colour

The hair of goats, camels and other animals may be used in felt making (Canadian beaver fur was widely used for making hats popular in Europe during the 18th and 19th centuries), but sheep's wool is the most widely used. Sheep's wool is available in white, light brown and dark brown, sometimes one animal may have wool in all these colours as in the case of the Jacob sheep. Striking but simple monochrome patterns may be made using a combination of these natural colours but the wool is often dyed, either before or after felting. A great many plants are traditionally used for making dyes varying according to local availability but today the use of synthetic dyes has become common.

Making Felt

To make a large felt rug requires the fleece of four or five sheep. It is first separated into fibres by carding, vibrating with a bow or simply beating with sticks. The wool is then laid out on a reed mat in several layers, each in a different direction. Hot, generally

above: Kirghiz *numdah* (felt floor cover) with patterns made by laying dyed wool onto a base of natural wool before rolling and fulling, northern Afghanistan.

above: *Mapramach,* a felt rug with patterns embroidered in wool using chain stitch, *c.* 1900, Tajikistan.

above: Turkomen felt rug with a counterchange pattern made by overlaying and cutting out several layers of felt and then reassembling them in different combinations, Uzbekistan or Afghanistan.

soapy, water is sprinkled over the wool and the mat is then rolled up in a bundle and tied tightly. The bundle is then rolled back and forth for several hours, during which time the bundle may be undone and the woolly mass re-rolled in a different direction. Finally, the bundle is unwrapped and the finished felt is rinsed, dried and smoothed with wood or stone implements.

Making Patterns

Patterns may be created by laying out different colours on the mat before the felting, or fulling, process which produces a fuzzy, organic design. Alternately, motifs may be cut from felt of different colours and sewn together as patchwork or appliqué. Elaborate counterchange patterns are created by cutting motifs from layers of differently coloured felt and then assembling the positive and negative elements.

Woodcarving in the Hindu Kush

left: A Nuristani 'six plank' chest made from cedar wood intensely decorated with chip-carved designs, Afghanistan.
below: Carved wooden panel from a chest or door decorated with a typical motif representing the horns of the markhor, a species of mountain goat, Nuristan, Afghanistan.

High in the mountains of the Hindu Kush, north of the Kyber Pass between Afghanistan and Pakistan, lies the land once called Kafiristan ('the land of the unbelievers'), an inaccessible region virtually unknown to the Western world except as the destination of the two fortune-seeking sergeants in Rudyard Kipling's story *The Man Who Would Be King*. In this part of Afghanistan and in the neighbouring valley of Swat in Pakistan lived fiercely independent people with their own customs and pagan beliefs. It was not until 1895 that Abdur Rahman, the Amir of Kabul, subjugated Kafiristan, forcibly converting its people to Islam and changing its name to Nuristan ('the land of light').

Geography and Culture

Even today this region is difficult to penetrate. It is a land of precipitous mountainsides, deep valleys and fast-flowing streams cut off by snow for several months a year. In this enforced geographic isolation the inhabitants developed a system of distinctive animist beliefs unlike those of surrounding regions placing their faith in household gods, propitiating the minor deities of the environment and worshipping the war god Gish who inspired their martial resistance to the incursion of Islam.

In the forested valleys the main material was wood and until the modern invasion of plastic and concrete local craftsmen converted wood into buildings, furniture (notably chests and low chairs), spoons, yokes, racks, idols and even tombs and the cabs of lorries. Woodwork involves turning, an extensive repertoire of joinery techniques and distinctive relief carving.

Beliefs and Motifs

Whether it be a ladle or the prayer board upon which women prayed at home, virtually every wooden object was extensively carved with flowing floral or geometric patterns. Centrally placed on panels are symbolic motifs often peculiar to the area. One such is the neck ring worn by brides which resembles the torque of Iron Age Europe. Another is a Y- or V-shaped device representing the horns of the markhor, a large mountain goat with magnificent horns. Particularly common are designs symbolizing the tree of life or 'world tree' that connects the realms of heaven, the earth and the underworld. It may resemble a real tree with branches, but frequently takes the form of a column. An alternative is a large triangle representing the 'cosmic mountain', a device serving the same symbolic function.

Materials and Techniques

The forests provide a useful range of woods including oak and walnut, which are favoured for turning plates, bowls and chair legs, but the most popular is the Himalayan cedar or deodar, a softwood with a delightful resinous fragrance. Today visitors to the region favour walnut where cedar was once the traditional choice.

Carving appears most often on panels set into grooves in a frame. This can be clearly seen in the distinctive low-seated chairs where the grooves are cut into the turned elements that form the legs and frame the back. The design is then marked out and the background cut away to an even depth, a technique known as flat-pattern carving. The raised designs may then be enhanced with incised lines and chip carving that give an added impression of depth. On many of the larger panelled chests, used for storing clothes, jewelry or grain, there may be a number of panels decorated with different patterns.

right: Wooden chair from the Swat Valley, Pakistan. Although now a Muslim region, pre-Islamic motifs are common on textiles and woodwork from this area. On the back panel is a large solar disc, while the central pillar represents the 'world tree'.

Papier Mâché

Legend tells us that Babur, the founder of the Mughal dynasty, first introduced the art of paper-making to India, although it is possible that it was introduced from Central Asia prior to this. He set up paper factories in Rajasthan and Kashmir in the 1520s and the industry has been dominated by Shiah Muslims ever since.

Paper was made mainly from cotton waste and used for miniature painting and calligraphy. Offcuts were turned into papier mâché. The earliest items constructed were boxes for pens and brushes, but patronage by the Mughals led to the making of many objects from trinket boxes to doors, bed frames and architectural fittings. Foreign trade began in the 17th century with the arrival of Europeans and papier mâché became a major export item in the 19th century under the British Raj. Most papier mâché today is made for export with the emphasis on smaller, less complicated items. Although the technique is used in other parts of India, it is in Kashmir that the most beautiful pieces are made.

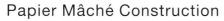

above: Papier mâché box painted with a courtly scene from Mughal times, Kashmir.
left: A Mexican papier mâché doll.

Papier Mâché Construction

The construction process, known as *sakhtasazi*, may be carried out using strips of paper or, for cheaper items, pulp made from paper offcuts, cotton waste, wood or straw and copper sulphate. The desired form is built up over a mould and, once dry, is sawn apart and removed. It is coated with a mixture of chalk and glue before sanding and burnishing.

Decoration

Decoration, known as *naqashi,* is executed by a different hand. Although the background of expensive wares may be of metal foil, in Kashmir most papier mâché

right: Papier mâché platter, from Rajasthan, India, decorated in the style typical of the region.

left: A trinket box, an egg cup and a napkin ring from Kashmir where papier mâché has been used for centuries in the manufacture of a vast range of items.

is given a base coat of black. Other colours are applied one at a time, finishing with the detail painted with a fine animal-hair brush. The finished painting is given several coats of varnish that not only protect the surface, but also add to the warmth of the colours and give an impression of depth.

The subjects hark back to Mughal times when miniature painting thrived in the Kashmir valley. Fields of delicate flowers called *hazara* (which means a thousand) may cover the surface, but often the artist chooses intricate scenes of life at court or noblemen hunting wild beasts among the woods.

Papier Mâché around the World

The fact that papier mâché is such a cheap material and so easy to use has ensured its use in many lands. One of the widest uses is in the making of brightly painted masks often worn at festivals. Among these the most impressive are the giant heads, or *capgrossos*, worn at festivals in Catalonia, Spain and Oaxaca, Mexico. In Lecce, in the Italian region of Perugia, the shortage of wood has encouraged the manufacture of large religious statuary out of papier mâché while, at the other end of the scale, articulated dolls are made in the town of Celaya in the Mexican state of Guanajuato.

In Japan, where it is known as *hariko*, papier mâché is built up from strips of paper glued together with a rice-paste solution. Models may be built up over a mould or formed spontaneously and pinched into shape while damp. *Hariko* is frequently used

above. Papier mâché platter from Rajasthan, India.

for the construction of children's toys and good luck dolls, many of which tumble or have moving parts. Among these are the red, wobbling *daruma* of Gumma prefecture, bought in the hope that they will grant a wish, and the *hariko-no-tora*, a nodding tiger toy from Shimane.

Tibetan Tiger Rugs

The Chinese occupation of Tibet in 1951 saw the suppression of many aspects of Tibetan culture and the destruction or desecration of monasteries and religious artefacts. Since the exodus of H.H. the Dalai Lama and his court in 1959 and the iconoclastic Cultural Revolution during the 1970s, fleeing Tibetans have carried many previously unknown objects into the outside world. Among the most enigmatic of these are the tiger rugs of which only a few hundred are believed to exist.

The Symbolism of the Tiger

The tiger is the leading Asian predator and even in lands where living tigers have never prowled their reputation has established them in myth and symbolism. They have come to represent anger, ferocity, power and kingship and so to sit upon a tiger, or at least its skin, represents superiority over the tiger and therefore authority over other people or one's own base nature. Many paintings and woodcuts depict ascetics performing austerities or meditating upon a tiger skin and Tibetan dignitaries once officiated while seated upon a skin or a rug resembling one.

The Tiger Rug

The expense and rarity of authentic pelts led to the weaving of woollen substitutes around 1 x 1.5 m (3 x 5 ft) in area. Many of these took the form of a rectangular mat with the likeness of a flayed tiger portrayed on them. Another type was an image of one or two tigers depicted formally in profile, often in a clump of bamboo. The third type consisted of a realistic or

left: Tibetan woodblock print of a Buddhist deity riding a tiger.
below: Tibetan meditation rug or *khaden* with a design of stylized tiger pelt markings worked with knotted pile.

abstracted design based on a tiger's stripes that completely covered the surface of the mat.

Technique

It is likely that the first tiger rugs were made in northeast Tibet and were originally woven completely with sheep's wool although at some point cotton warps became common. Although the knot count is not high, being anywhere between 18 and 88 knots per sq. in., the compacted thickly spun fibres produce a dense pile. This is eminently suitable for the bold simplicity of the design; the delicate, flowing arabesques of knotted Persian carpets, for instance, demand a much higher density of knots.

Weaving is carried out on a vertical loom around which a continuous warp is wound. Wefts are woven into the same shed in pairs, one from each side and are inserted and beaten down between each row of pile.

The distinctive feature of the weaving is the unusual method used for knotting the pile with the Tibetan knot. This is similar to the Senneh or Turkish knot except that each knot is tied not only around the warp but also around a rod held against the surface of the work, a technique similar to that used in making velvet. When a whole row is complete, the weaver cuts the loops created with a sharp knife and beats the pile down with a hammer before securing it with the next pair of weft threads and beating it all down with a heavy metal comb.

The ends of the rug are often secured with rows of tri-axial weaving

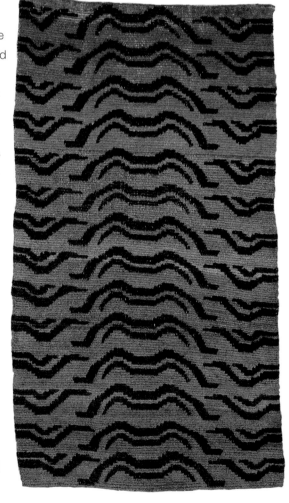

in which the weft passes between warps that cross each other diagonally.

Modern Tiger Rugs

Tiger rugs are now woven for sale by expatriated Tibetans in Nepal and at Dharamsala, India, home of the Tibetan Government in Exile. Often these modern rugs have the background cut away to produce a rug shaped like a real pelt.

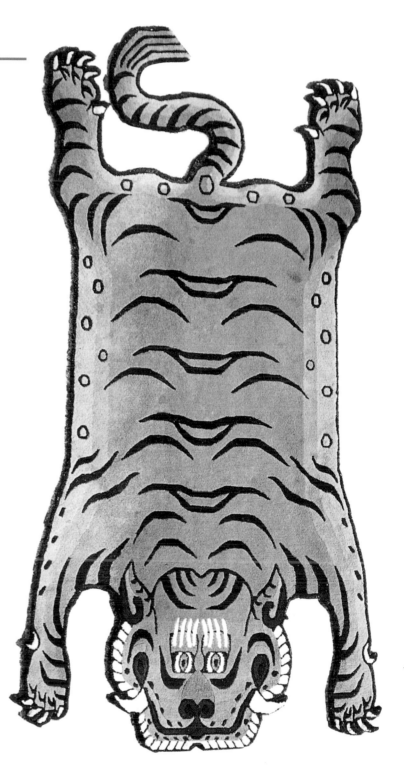

left: Meditation rug with pattern of simplified tiger pelt markings, Tibet, c. 1900.
above: Contemporary, pelt-shaped tiger rug woven by Tibetan refugees living near Kanchenjunga in eastern Nepal.

Metal Casting

Early man was able to hammer naturally occurring metals such as copper into crude shapes, but when the technology to convert ore into metal with heat was developed in the Near East about 6,500 years ago this led to a huge shift. The ability to turn metal into swords and ploughshares meant that man was able to pursue the arts of both war and agriculture with a vengeance.

Pyrotechnology

Metallurgy was the direct result of the skills acquired in the development of efficient firing techniques for pottery. The extraction of copper from ore requires a temperature of 1083°C (1981°F) and with the use of charcoal and controlled draughts created with a bellows this could now be achieved fairly simply although it required great physical effort. However, smelting is more complex than simply melting the raw materials: they must be placed in a furnace separated from the fire or a crucible with a lid so that the ore, in an atmosphere of reduced oxygen, will be converted into metal rather than oxide.

left: Sand-cast brass door knocker acquired in Guangxi, China.

Once in a liquid form, metal can be cast into shape in a number of ways. The earliest known moulds were open and hollowed out of a soft stone such as sandstone. This stone had to be heated before the molten metal was poured in to prevent cracking from thermodynamic shock. Open moulds produced items that were flat on the upper surface, but later more sophisticated moulds were fashioned from stone or clay in two pieces, making a more rounded form possible. With the addition of a core section, often of fired clay, it was possible to cast a hollow object such as a socketed axe.

Whatever form the mould might take, it must be open at one end to allow the pouring in of molten metal. Complex forms need to be fitted with runners and risers forming passageways for air and gasses to escape from the mould.

Sand Casting

An efficient method of forming a mould is to create an impression in damp sand. For a two-part mould two boxes are required which are filled with damp, hard-packed sand. The impression is made with a matrix generally in the form of a three-dimensional wooden pattern. Once impressions are made and the wood removed, the two sections may be carefully aligned and fitted together ready for the metal to be poured in.

left: Brass animals, from Orissa, India, cast using the lost-wax technique which is particularly obvious in the open latticework.

left: Chinese bronze sand-cast tea kettle.

In India styles vary enormously from the elegantly proportioned gods of Tamil Nadu to the folk art animals and toys of Orissa and the eccentrically crafted deities of Bastar in Madhya Pradesh. In Africa masterpieces of metalwork were the kingly heads of Benin City in Nigeria (known as 'bronzes' although actually cast from brass).

When the metal has cooled the sand may be knocked off. The finished cast may be somewhat rough and will require filing and burnishing and possibly detailing using a chisel or graver. The wooden pattern may be used again to create another, identical object. In China bronze objects were first cast in sand about 4,000 years ago.

The Lost-wax Technique

Some of the finest pieces of metal casting have been made using the lost-wax, or cire perdue, method. The craftsman first constructs a model from wax built over a clay core and the mould is then formed with a clay coating over the surface of the model. The mould is heated to melt and remove the wax before the molten metal is poured in. When cool, the mould is knocked away to reveal a metal copy of the wax original. As both wax and mould are destroyed in the process each piece is unique.

right: Brass lost-wax statuette of the Hindu god Shiva carrying Ganesh on his shoulders, Bastar, Madhya Pradesh, India.

Lacquer

The production of a piece of lacquer ware is a painstakingly slow process. For the apprentice this pain is very real as the liquid sap employed causes an allergic reaction on the skin. Fortunately many craftsmen have persisted until they have built up a tolerance to the toxins: a finished piece of lacquerwork has a lustrous translucent sheen that rivals the finest porcelains.

Lacquerwork in Burma

Pagan was the capital of Burma from the 11th to the 13th centuries and here lacquer wares were admired as much as porcelain was admired elsewhere. The begging bowls of monks were lacquered as were many prestige objects at the royal court and a tradition of lacquerwork continues today. The base used for lacquerwork in Burma and northern Thailand is as likely to be of basketry made from thin slivers of bamboo as it is of wood but the technique is the same. The lacquer is obtained by tapping a tree (*melanorrhoea usitata*), making a diagonal cut in the trunk and collecting the sap that bleeds out into a cup. The sap is refined by heating and straining and is then painted over the base and allowed to dry before coating again and again until all dents are filled and the surface is smooth. Drying is slow and best achieved when the atmosphere is humid. Finally, sometimes after several months of repeated painting and drying, the surface is rubbed with sesame oil and polished. The sap dries black but dye is often added to make a red. Many of the designs that are painted on the

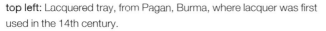

top left: Lacquered tray, from Pagan, Burma, where lacquer was first used in the 14th century.
above: Japanese lacquered plate showing the grain of the wooden base.

top right: Pot made of lacquer over a bamboo base decorated with traditional designs, Pagan, Burma (left) and a Karen stacking pot for betel nut (right) made with lacquer over a basketry base, northern Thailand.

left: Soup bowl made of lacquer over finely turned wood, Ishikawa Province, Japan.

surface of Burmese lacquerwork today, mostly floral designs and Buddhist iconography, date back to the time of the prominence of the city of Pagan.

Lacquerwork in Japan

Lacquerwork is practised all over Indochina and the Far East but astonishing delicacy has been achieved in Japan where it is has been used for coating anything from soup bowls to pill boxes and from furniture to armour. Lacquerwork is so important in traditional Japanese dining, especially for the serving of miso soup or soba noodles, that today many tablewares are made from plastic cunningly contrived to imitate the real thing right down to the vagaries of the wood grain.

Japanese Techniques

Urushi is the Japanese word for 'lacquer' and *shikki* is Japanese for 'lacquerware'. Derived from the sap of a sumac tree, *rhus verniciflua*, the lacquer is itself transparent but is generally tinted red with vermilion or black with iron oxide. Sometimes a red layer may be applied over black so that with wear, or distressing, black is revealed through the red.

In Japan the base for lacquerwork is most often wood, frequently shaped by turning or carving, the preferred wood being icho or ginko which are both light and strong. In Yamanaka and Wajima soup bowls are turned so that they

are so thin that light can be seen through them. Even with a dozen coats of lacquer they may remain no more than two or three millimetres thick.

Although lacquer wares are frequently left plain, especially when intended for use in the tea ceremony, it is not uncommon for some form of surface decoration to be applied. This may take the form of gold dust scattered into the lacquer while wet or gold leaf applied to the surface. The most opulent work might include not only gold leaf, but also pieces of inlaid mother of pearl. Generally, however, Japanese lacquer wares for daily use are of one colour or decorated with a simple contrasting band of red on black.

above: The painted and gilded design on the underside of the lid of a soup bowl from Ishikawa Province, Japan.

Tied and Stitched Resist Dyeing

To ensure the even colouring of cloth when using dyes, it is essential that penetration is not restricted by foreign matter or by constriction of the fabric. In ancient times dyers were aware of this and exploited their knowledge to find ways of deliberately preventing dye soaking into cloth. One simple way of achieving this resistance is to tie threads or fibres around selected pieces of cloth or to pull them tight with stitching.

Tie and Dye

The best known of resist techniques is tie and dye, also referred to as 'tie dye', an incredibly simple technique. It is known as *plangi* ('rainbow') in Indonesia, *bandhani* in India (from which we get the word 'bandanna' for a spotted neckerchief) and *adire oniko* in Nigeria. Although the technique is simple, the results are striking in their bold simplicity.

If fabric is pinched between finger and thumb into a peak it is quite easy to bind a thread tightly around it. When placed in the dye bath, the tight thread and the constricted material both prevent the penetration of the dye so that upon removal and untying an undyed area shaped like a circle is revealed.

Laying Out the Pattern

By tying a piece of cloth in many places a variety of patterns can be produced. The simplest is to pinch the fabric into one peak and then tie thread around it several times at intervals. When untied, this reveals a series of concentric circles. Alternatively the cloth can be pulled up and tied in a number of different places to create an arrangement of circles.

above: *Shibori* (tie and dye) silk jacket with a pattern created by tying resist threads around grains of rice, Japan.

opposite, left: Indigo textile with stitched resist patterns revealed in white. Some details have been picked out in white stitching after dyeing, Guangxi, China.

Folded Patterns

By folding or rolling the material a whole new repertoire of patterns can be created. Tying up bunches of folded fabric will produce a symmetrical arrangement of dots and circles but if the cloth is folded or rolled into a long bundle and thread is tied around it before dyeing the result will be a pattern of stripes or checks.

Colour

Another dimension can be introduced by adding colour. For this a resist is tied and the cloth is dipped in dye and then tied and dipped again a number of times in dye vats containing different colours, each new tie preserving the last colour. Further variations are possible if some ties are undone and overdyed or even if the cloth is dipped in a bleach to remove any exposed dye colour.

Today, when industrial printing imitates traditional hand craftsmanship, dyers in India and Pakistan often leave the resist ties in place to prove to the purchaser that it is the real thing.

Stitched Resist

Resisting the dye with stitches is also a widespread technique found particularly in Indochina, Indonesia and West Africa. In Sumatra it is called *tritik* and in Nigeria *adire alabere*. Stitches

may be sewn tightly to create a precise line after dyeing or sewn loosely and pulled tight so that the fabric bunches up, resulting in a fuzzier effect. Traditionally work is carried out by hand but increasingly sewing machines are used because they have the advantage of tight, regular stitches and, of course, speed.

Stitched resist, notably at Palembang in Sumatra, may be combined with tie and dye, adding further to the possible variations in pattern and texture.

above, right: Silk tie and dye shawl from Tajikistan. Squares are produced by pleating and then tying pinched up fabric.

Ikat

Ikat is the most arcane and demanding of all the techniques of resist dyeing textiles because, although the process is in essence tie and dye, it is yarn and not cloth that is treated. Many ikat cloths have a distinctive fuzziness which is the result of the problems of registering the pattern accurately.

Historical Ties

Although fine examples of this technique are found in Indochina, India, Japan, Central Asia, Yemen, Majorca and even South America, ikat is particularly associated with the cultural traditions of Malaysia and Indonesia where it takes its name from a corruption of the Malay word *mengikat* which means to tie or bind. The name ikat is universally used for the process even though many regional names are more descriptive. In Central Asia, for example, it is known as *abr* (cloud) cloth and in Majorca as *roba de llengues* (cloth of tongues).

It is believed that the first ikats were probably woven in Indochina and the technique was subsequently introduced to the Malay Archipelago by members of the Dong-Son culture emigrating from northern Vietnam between the 8th and 2nd century BC.

Warp Ikat

The process of creating a pattern by dyeing yarn before it is woven is a very specialized art. The simplest and most used technique for making ikat cloth is the dyeing of the warps, although the technique is far from simple. First the yarn that will serve as the warps (running the length of the cloth) is wound

above: Warps, already resist dyed by tying with thread, set up for weaving *kasuri* on a Japanese loom.
right: Japanese double-ikat indigo man's jacket woven using warps and wefts that have been resist dyed prior to weaving.

onto a frame and then thread is wrapped around bunches of yarn at specific points. When the yarn is subsequently submerged in the dye bath the ties resist the dye in just the same way as those on tie and dye cloth and when they are untied they reveal undyed yarn. This tie and dye process may be repeated a number of times before the unbound cloth is attached on a loom arranged as it was on the tying frame. The wefts are then woven in across the width, binding the warps together and fixing the pattern in place. As it is very difficult to align the warps precisely there is usually a slight blurring of motifs, a quality exploited in many Central Asian silk *abr* cloths.

above, left: Silk weft ikat textile from Siem Reep, Cambodia, woven with wefts resist dyed before weaving.
above, right: Warp ikat silk *chapan* showing the designs and colours typical of *abr* from Bokhara and Samarkand, Uzbekistan.

Weft Ikat

The making of weft ikat is even more demanding than warp ikat, but the results are often very beautiful, frequently being made from silk or fine cotton. Particularly intricate examples are produced in Thailand, Laos, Cambodia and Orissa in India. The tye and dye process is essentially the same as for warp ikat, but the dyed weft must be woven back and forth through the warps on the loom, painstakingly lining up the pattern with each new pass of the shuttle.

This technique was probably developed in the Yemen and introduced to India and the East by Muslim traders and settlers.

Double Ikat

It is possible to weave one piece of cloth incorporating patterns created by wefts and warps independently, a process known as compound ikat but it is also possible to coordinate both elements so that they combine to create symmetrical, usually geometric motifs. Cloth produced using this complex, time-consuming method is not surprisingly highly prized. Among these prestigious fabrics are Indian *patola* cloth from Gujarat, Balinese *geringseng* and *kasuri* from Japan.

Rush Shoes

Even the most flimsy of materials such as grass, straw, reeds and rushes can be used in an astonishing variety of ways. It is their length and thinness that makes them useful, as they are flexible and, when bundled together or interwoven, surprisingly strong. Around the world they have proved useful in the manufacture of not only mats and baskets, but also hats, boats and even shoes.

left: Rush sandals with thongs; acquired in northern Thailand.

Materials

Long, thin materials lend themselves to weaving and basketry techniques. The abundant grasses of the savannahs and prairies of Africa and the Americas have been used in the construction of many baskets and hats. In China and Japan the straw remaining after the rice harvest was used in the making of everyday sandals. These were tough enough for daily use, but did need replacing frequently when making a long journey. On Lake Titicaca in the High Andes the plentiful *totora* rushes are still used for building large boats, mistakenly known as 'reed' boats.

The most obvious difference between these materials is that while grasses, straw and reeds are hollow, rushes are filled with soft, pithy vesicles. This means that rushes are spongy, a quality that makes them ideal for use underfoot as mats or as the soles of shoes.

Fibre Footwear around the World

As they are both cheap and comfortable, rush shoes can be found in many regions where lakes or rivers provide enough materials. They are widespread in Indochina, but can also be

right: Plaited rush shoes from Denmark. The thick spongy soles make rush footwear very comfortable when walking.

encountered as far west as Russia, Romania and Scandinavia. In essence the same techniques have been used to make shoes from grass or straw and also, in Nepal, from hemp stalks. Considerable quantities of plant-fibre sandals were also discovered in the cliff dwellings of the American Southwest, the home of the Ancient Puebloan peoples known to the Navajo as the Anasazi and to archaeologists as the 'Basketmakers' because of their fibre-working skills.

Techniques

Grass, straw and reeds become more brittle as they dry and are therefore best worked with while fresh or, if they have been stored, after a period of soaking in water. Rushes, with their pithy structure, are

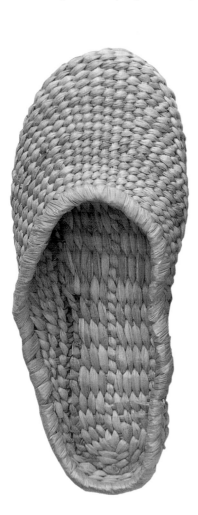

particularly pliable but still benefit from soaking. The method of construction of a rush shoe or slipper is a fine example of the way in which the qualities and limitations of a material dictate the process, resulting in examples from far-flung places looking remarkably similar.

With only a few exceptions, such as certain Chinese rush footwear which is started at the top and worked down towards the sole, the construction of a shoe begins with the sole. A sequence of 'warp' elements is laid out, running most often from side to side but occasionally lengthwise. The 'wefts' are then introduced in pairs twining around the 'warps' from toe to heel. Twining begins in the centre and proceeds to the sides reducing the number of warps around which the weft is twined to create curvature. A tight band is twined around the edge and here the warps may be cut at the heel of a slipper or bent up and over the front of the foot. This area is often given special treatment as it is the most visible, incorporating openwork by spacing out the weft elements or by twining both warps and wefts.

Open sandals are also common where the twining is employed to construct a simple flat sole which is held on the foot by straps also made from rush.

above, right: Openwork slippers made from twined rush, Thailand.
left: Twined rush slippers from Romania. Rushes, straw and grass may not be hard wearing, but they are cheap and have therefore been exploited for footwear in many parts of Asia and Europe.

Stoneware Pottery

It was in China during the Zhou dynasty (10th–3rd centuries BC) that the first stonewares were produced. Potters had discovered that if a sufficient draught was created, with chimneys or a series of chambers ascending a slope, temperatures in excess of 1200°C (2192°F) could be reached causing clays with a high silica or alumina content to vitrify into dense, hard stone-like material. The technique spread quickly throughout the Far East, but it was not until the 14th century that potteries in Europe acquired the technology. Even then, though, earthenware remained the medium of vernacular potters because of the lower fuel costs and the availability of suitable clays. It was the opinion of Bernard Leach, founding father of the modern British craftsman-potter movement, that the most beautiful pottery ever produced was the stonewares of the Chinese Song dynasty (960–1279) and the celadon wares of the Korean Koryu dynasty (918–1392).

above: A pair of Korean celadon bowls used for making and drinking tea.

Glazes

The first stoneware glazes were the result of wood ash falling on pottery in the kiln during firing. The lime in the ash melted and flowed over the surface producing random dribbles and encrustations. Potters realized that by mixing wood ash with other materials such as oxides for colour, silica for glassiness and alumina for viscosity and stability, they could make a glaze that could be deliberately applied to the surface and controlled. Because of the high temperatures involved, stoneware glazes have a subdued 'natural' colour range. Random ash-glazed pottery remains popular in Japan where it is often used for utensils employed in the tea ceremony.

left: Korean celadon chopstick rests in the shape of ducks.

Oxidation and Reduction

Just as blue-grey iron turns into red rust when exposed to the air and orange-coloured copper turns into green verdigris, the colours produced by mineral oxides can be altered by controlling the amount of oxygen present in the atmosphere of the kiln. Iron oxide is red in an oxygen-rich firing, but when the atmosphere in the kiln is altered by closing air vents, reducing the amount of oxygen, it becomes blue-grey and similarly copper oxide is changed from green to red.

Celadon

The technique of celadon glazing was introduced to Korea from China in the 9th or 10th century, probably by migrant potters. Early examples were strongly influenced by Chinese models, but in the next 200 years, during the Koryu dynasty after which modern Korea is named, a distinctive style developed that surpassed its origins. Many pieces relied for effect purely on their elegant forms while others were engraved, inlaid or sparingly painted with motifs of flowers or birds. The distinguishing common

feature, however, is without doubt the subtle green colour of the glaze. Large quantities of celadon-glazed wares are still produced in present-day Korea for both home use and the export market.

The clay body of Korean celadon fires to a light grey. This is coated with an ash-based lime glaze and heated to temperatures of around 1250ºC (2282ºF) in a reduced atmosphere. The small quantities of iron oxide turn blue which combines with the yellowish tint of titanium particles to create green. Combinations of varying quantities of the ingredients of the glaze can produce anything from yellow to light blue but it is the general opinion that the most beautiful celadon-glazed wares were those produced between the mid-12th and 13th centuries when master potters achieved soft glazes with the exquisite translucent green of fine jade.

above, left: Celadon vase decorated with flying cranes painted under the glaze, Korea.
below: Two delicately thrown Vietnamese stoneware bowls with subtle ash glaze.

Mingei: Japanese Folk Art

Mingei is an abbreviation of the Japanese *minshu-teki kogei* which roughly means 'crafts or arts made by the people to be used daily by the people'. Mingei is inexpensive, handmade work made by mostly anonymous craftsmen and can be anything from a paper kite to a bentwood lunch box. The appreciation of Japanese folk art led Soetsu Yanagi (1889–1961), who had coined the word 'mingei', to set up, with other enthusiasts, the Mingeikan or Japan Folk Crafts Museum in Tokyo. The museum is dedicated to the preservation of these much-loved traditional objects in an age of industrial production.

Some have indeed been lost but others remain popular: shops and stalls, for example, are loaded with turned wooden *kokeshi* dolls and good luck papier mâché Daruma dolls by the hundred.

Local Crafts

Many pieces of folk art are specific to one town or region of Japan as a result of the diversity of the topography, climate and local resources. In Fukui, for example, smiths are celebrated for their finely forged scythes used for cutting grass or rice while the people of coastal Tottori make delightful *nagashi-bina*, two figures set in a straw plaque, which are bought in March and placed on the family altar until the following year when they are set afloat, taking bad luck away with them. Other items such as rain capes were once used in every prefecture. They varied locally according to the type of material used, whether straw, hemp or bark, and the techniques employed to secure the fibres.

Luck Bringers

Like the Daruma dolls and the *nagashi-bina*, many mingei items are made specifically to celebrate a particular festival or to bring good luck for the year. These are known as *engi* or luck bringers. Kites shaped like carp are flown from rooftops to celebrate the Boys' Festival on 5 May. Just as the carp swims determinedly upstream, it is hoped the boys will have the strength of character to overcome obstacles in their path. In Fukushima a popular *engi* toy is the *aka-beko*, a red lacquered papier mâché cow with a nodding head that is believed to protect a child from smallpox. And a Tokyo shop proprietor is likely to encourage good trade by installing a *maneki-neko*, a ceramic cat with a wobbling arm that beckons good luck.

Ito-mari

Toys such as dolls, articulated snakes, spinning tops and fighting sumo wrestlers are often made by local craftsmen or by a child's relatives. The *ito-mari* or 'thread ball' was originally

left: *Zaru-Kaburi-Inu*, a papier mâché dog made in Asakusa in Tokyo, a charm presented to babies when they make their first trip to the family shrine, Japan.

used by girls playing catch but has evolved into a beautiful object now more likely to be hung up for decoration. Many are made by mothers and grandmothers to be given to girls on New Year's Day. At the core is a bag of chaff around which yarn is wound. The surface is then decorated in brightly coloured thread worked into astoundingly precise patterns by wrapping around guide threads. An incredible range of designs can be seen.

Origami

The origins of the Japanese art of paper folding are probably the paper streamers hung outside Shinto shrines, but origami is now a hugely popular pastime worldwide. The skill lies in folding a square of paper, without cutting or gluing, into the likeness of birds, butterflies, masks or frogs, the limits being only the skill or imagination of the maker.

below: A group of *ito-mari* balls showing just a few of the innumerable designs possible with wrapped thread.

above: *Senbazuru,* strings of a thousand folded paper cranes, displayed as offerings outside a shrine in Tokyo.

205

Painted and Gilded Wood

In Bali the tradition of local girls carrying hand-woven palm leaf trays loaded with offerings of flowers and incense and placing them on the ground at strategic places in the streets and shops is still very much alive. Bali is a Hindu island although most Indonesians are followers of Islam or are adherents of older animist beliefs. Hinduism, especially in tropical Bali, is an exuberant religion, colouring the lives and crafts of those who live under its influence.

Woodcarving in Bali

Traditional Balinese architecture takes the form of compounds surrounded by masonry walls. Both stonework and woodwork may be carved, but the dwellings of the rich are predictably the most heavily ornamented with encrustations of stone carving and wood that has been not only carved, but also painted and

below, left: The carved and gilded façade of a temple building at the Royal Palace in Bangkok, Thailand.
below, right: Relief carved door and surround at the Neka Art Museum in Ubud, Bali.

gilded. Some, like the Neka Art Museum in the Balinese cultural centre Ubud, positively sparkle in the bright tropical light.

Gateways and doors are given the most attention as it is important to provide protection from malevolent forces at those points. The leering, fanged face of the protective spirit Bhoma can often be seen among the scrolling floral patterns. On the wall panels depicting scenes from the Hindu epics of the *Mahabharata* and the *Ramayana* intricately carved in high relief are frequently found.

Carvers were formerly attached to a court or community producing almost exclusively religious work, but when the country was under Dutch colonial control in the early 20th century the system went into decline. Craftsmen were forced to find other markets and now there are thriving ateliers of

woodworkers in centres such as Mas, outside Ubud, where they create work for the tourist and export market. Carved wood was traditionally painted and gilded, but today the preference is for the natural colouring of the wood. Traditional buildings, however, are often painted in the old way.

Tools and Techniques

Cheap work may be turned out in softwood, but carving of good quality demands hardwoods such as local kulkul and jackfruit or ebony imported from Borneo and teak from Java. A large project is begun by blocking out the form, chopping the waste away with a hatchet, before refining the wood with a mallet and chisel. As greater care is demanded the chisel may be controlled by hand or a special knife, the *pongutik*. Finally texture may be added by hammering with a stamp. Today the finest work is left unpainted but cheaper, cruder items are often brightly painted.

Woodcarving in Indochina

Opulent architecture can be found throughout the Buddhist countries of Indochina. Temples, in particular, are lavishly decorated with carving, painting, gilding and glass mosaics, from the finials on the sweeping roof to the snake-shaped balustrades of the entrance steps. These temples, visited daily by a throng of devout worshippers, are usually kept in pristine condition.

Iconography in Thailand generally takes the form of gilded Buddhas, often gigantic in size, accompanied by deities and saints carved in the round, rather than in relief. The walls, however, are likely to be extensively painted with murals of narrative scenes from the lives of the Buddha. Frequently doors are particularly striking, comprising sophisticatedly simple figures gilded on a plain, usually red, background.

above, left: Carved and gilded doorway at the Neka Art Museum, Ubud, Bali. Above the door is the face of the guardian spirit Bhoma.
above, right: Carved and gilded building in a temple complex in Chiang Mai, Thailand.

Batik

Batik is a process of resist dyeing in which hot wax or rice starch or another kind of paste is applied to the surface of a fabric to resist the dye and form areas of pattern. It is a technique widely practised around the globe from India to China and Southeast Asia to West Africa. Undoubtedly it is at its most glorious on the Indonesian island of Java where the finest quality batik is produced. Known as *tulis*, a Javanese word meaning literally 'writing', the intricate hand-drawn motifs and patterns, produced with dexterity and skill, transform a humble length of cloth into a work of art.

Wax Resist

The word 'batik' is now used to describe all kinds of applied resists but was originally a Javanese term specifically referring to wax. The wax-resist technique involves the trailing of hot wax across fine cotton cloth using a tool called a *canting* which has a wooden or bamboo handle attached to a copper reservoir

with one or more spouts through which the wax is applied. After immersion in the dye vat, the wax is removed by boiling or scraping off, so revealing the pattern.

Quicker than the *canting* method is *cap* printing which uses a copper block (*cap*) loaded with wax and stamped onto the cloth in a series of repeat patterns. This technique has enabled the mass production of handmade batik cloth. Nowadays much imitation batik is machine printed in the Netherlands for export all over the world.

In southwest China ethnic minority groups employ a *lado* knife to apply the wax. This 'knife' has a bamboo handle with triangular layers of copper attached onto it. The wax flows onto cotton or hemp cloth between the layers of copper marking out complex patterns. When the wax is cool and has set the cloth is dyed in a cold vat of indigo. After dyeing, the wax is removed by boiling which leaves white patterns on deep blue.

Starch Resist

This process is commonly used in Japan and West Africa. Rice, bean or cassava paste is applied to the cloth with either a piece of wood, a palm leaf stem or a feather. After dyeing, the starch is scraped off the dry cloth to show the pattern. The Yoruba people of Nigeria famously produce wonderful indigo-dyed *adire eleko* textiles using this method. Resists can also be

above, left: Indigo dyed fabric with resist patterns executed with a *lado* knife made by the Blue Hmong people of northern Thailand.
above, right: Japanese indigo dyed textile with stencilled starch resist patterns.

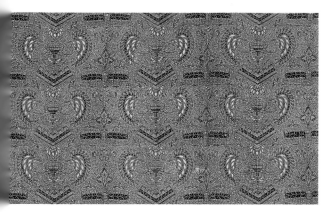

above: 'Garuda wing' batik motifs created by printing wax resist onto the fabric with a copper block, Surakarta, Java.

right: Batik sarong with designs hand drawn in hot wax using a *canting*. Different parts of the work were carried out in Lasem and Pekalongan in northern Java.

turned out swiftly by application through a stencil, in Japan made from paper and in West Africa from a sheet of thin metal.

Patterns and Motifs

The designs executed on *kain panjang* ('long cloth') and sarongs (a tube of sewn up cloth) in Java are multifarious and complex. The wearing of batik cloths was originally promoted by the highly sophisticated *kraton* (court) culture of central Java at Yogyakarta and Surakarta. At one time only batik cloth was worn in the palace confines and designs worn there were proscribed elsewhere. They were characterized by the colours cream, indigo-blue and a brown derived from the bark of the soga tree.

Patterns include wavy *parang rusak* (broken knife) and crescents symbolizing the wings of the mythical Garuda.

On the north coast, influenced by trade and settlement from India, Arabia and particularly China, batiks feature flowing designs of clouds, lions and garden designs with copious amounts of bright red. Pekalongan is famous for its floral *tulis* designs made by Indo-European women and popularized by

Dutch colonial women in the 19th century. A clever innovation, showing economy of style, is the *pagi-sore* (literally 'morning-evening'), a *kain* with a distinct pattern at each end, one to be worn in the morning, the other in the evening.

Bamboo and Rattan Baskets

The island of Borneo comprising Kalimantan, Sarawak, Brunei and Sabah, straddling Malaysia and Indonesia, was once covered with a vast forest that provided the inhabitants with everything they needed including the bamboo and rattan with which they made a range of basketry. The basketry was used for carrying everyday tools and equipment, and for transportation, building and clothing. The traditional way of life is changing as the forest is cut down for timber and vast tracts of land are cleared for the cultivation of oil palms, but baskets are still used today. Many are now made from synthetic or recycled materials using time-honoured techniques but beautiful baskets are still made from bamboo and rattan in isolated pockets in the forest or to sell to the growing number of tourists.

Bamboo

Bamboo is one of the most useful of all plants. Its tubular structure is exploited for containers and pipes while its tough outer skin, when split into skeins or splints, is a wonderful material for making baskets as it is both strong and flexible with a tensile strength comparable with steel. Large carrying baskets often employ bamboo and the *wakid*, a backpack made by the Kadazandusun of Sabah, is an interesting example. At the base a number of splints are arranged in a circle and are linked at intervals by a ring of twining to keep them in place. Higher up the basket the splints are split and secured by more twining

before being split again and again, producing a tall tube that splays out towards the top.

Rattan

The gathering of rattan vines is a painstaking process; it is covered with vicious thorns that must be stripped off, but it yields a pliable material of great length. It may be employed as it is but is often split into finer lengths which are easier than bamboo to

above, left: Iban plaited basket for harvesting rice with a distinctive motif representing the deity Singalong Burong, Sarawak, Malaysian Borneo.
above, right: Kadazandusun *wakid*, a backpack basket made from bamboo splints split more and more finely to create a flared top, Sabah, Malaysian Borneo.

manipulate and, using a combination of natural and dyed elements, are frequently employed in weaving patterns. It is not uncommon for basketmakers to display their finesse by weaving tiny patterns from the finest slivers of rattan.

Pattern and Motifs

Baskets are made in many other parts of Southeast Asia and South America using the same techniques, but those made in Borneo have a distinctive design repertoire that is executed with very fine twilled plaiting. As well as the natural colour of the fibres, red and black are often made by dyeing with vegetable and mineral dyes such as red derived from rattan berries and dark pigment from indigo. Many designs are geometric and are often symbolic like the 'curved snake' that appears on Penan mats and backpacks in Sarawak, while others are more pictorial like the recognizable representations of the bird-like Singalong Burong.

Plaiting is essentially a simple process in which two sets of elements cross and interlace with each other, generally at right angles with the work laid out on the diagonal. For plain or basket weave the sequence is over one under one, over one under one. If the two elements are of contrasting colour the appearance will be chequered. For twilling, one element might cross two or more others and by varying this, making one element appear only where required, more complex designs can be achieved.

In Kalimantan, the Indonesian part of Borneo, basket weavers sometimes cheat by plaiting a plain basket and then tucking short lengths of dyed splints into the structure to create the pattern, a process which does not require the planning and careful manipulation necessary to make a pattern by authentic twilling.

above, right: Large floor mat of plaited split rattan made by the Penan people of Sarawak, Malaysian Borneo.

below: Woodcarving of an ancestor figure from the Lower Sepik region of Papua New Guinea.

bottom: Ceiling of a Maori meeting house showing the painted designs known as *kowhaiwhai*.

Australasia and Oceania

below: Painted barkcloth from the Finistere Mountains, Madang Province, Papua New Guinea, early 20th century.

Introduction

In ancient times early peoples began the long journey from Southeast Asia east towards the rising sun. The lands that they settled in are now collectively treated as a continent and are referred to as Australasia and Oceania or even, simply, the Pacific. This is the largest 'region' on the planet but is home to the least number of people who live on more than 20,000 islands scattered across vast stretches of open sea.

The Geography of the Pacific

This region stretches from New Guinea and Australia in the west to Easter Island in the east and from Hawaii in the north to New Zealand in the south, covering more than a third of the Earth's surface of which only a tiny proportion is land. To the west lies Melanesia ('the black islands'), which consists of New Guinea, and the southwestern islands stretching out to Fiji. To the south of here is the landmass of Australia ('the southern land') and its inshore islands, which are solid land but nonetheless mostly arid and sparsely populated. To the north and east of New Guinea lies Micronesia ('the tiny

islands') and in the central Pacific lies Polynesia ('many islands') which also includes Hawaii to the far north and New Zealand to the southwest. With the exception of New Zealand, Easter Island and a large part of Australia, all these islands are situated between the Tropic of Cancer and the Tropic of Capricorn, ensuring the warm, wet weather that encourages the growth of luxuriant vegetation.

Migration and Settlement

The earliest settlers travelled across Indonesia into New Guinea and down into Australia over 40,000 years ago, travelling mostly over land revealed during the Ice Age or making short boat crossings from island to island. The settlers developed survival strategies so well suited to their environment that their lifestyle changed little until the arrival of European explorers, settlers and missionaries in the 17th and 18th centuries.

It is not known why colonizers made the journey to the islands further out into the Pacific Ocean, but to set sail across uncharted waters in search of unknown

opposite, left: Village headman preparing *kava* for a welcoming ceremony, Wayalailai, Fiji. The distinctive wooden bowl is reserved for this purpose.

opposite, right: Barkcloth made from the banyan tree, Fatu Hiva, Marquesas Islands.

above, left: *Upeti*, a wooden board used for rubbing patterns onto barkcloth in Samoa.

above, right: Girls from Pago Pago in Samoa wearing pandanus mats and ornaments made from flowers and shells in the early 20th century.

Introduction

lands was obviously a decision not taken lightly. One factor was the development of the outrigger canoe that made vessels much more stable and, therefore, made travel across open water much safer. Ocean voyages probably reached Fiji about 3,500 years ago, the Marquesas Islands about 2,150 years ago and Hawaii about 1,500 years ago. The final voyages of exploration and settlement reached New Zealand from Polynesia only 1,200 years ago. The Polynesians accomplished such epic feats of navigation in open boats without the sophisticated mathematical instruments of European sailors, relying on their far superior knowledge of tidal swells, the flight of birds, weather phenomenon and the movement of the stars.

Cultural Similarities and Differences

Cargo space was limited on an ocean-going canoe and the voyagers took little more than pigs, chickens, taro plants and their cultural heritage with them. With the natural resources available on most Pacific Islands communities evolved on isolated islands in very similar ways, but with many subtle differences. The coconut frond and pandanus baskets of most islands, for

instance, are used for the same purposes and are constructed using the same techniques although there are many varieties of the form. The greatest differences occurred in New Zealand where the climate dictated a different lifestyle and the utilization of natural materials such as phormium fibre for basketry and also for clothing as there were no trees that could provide suitable bark for cloth.

right: Turtle design painted on barkcloth made from the paper mulberry tree, Fatu Hiva, Marquesas Islands.

opposite, above: Slit drum with chip-carved patterns, I ali, Cook Islands.

right: The carved underside of a wooden ceremonial bowl from the Lake Sentani area, Papua New Guinea, early 20th century.

Aboriginal Art

During the late 18th century European explorers and early settlers in Australia saw the indigenous inhabitants as belonging to a primitive Stone Age society. In fact over the 40,000 years or more that the Aborigines had occupied the land they had developed an efficient system of hunter gathering which was sustainable and caused minimal environmental damage, an example from which we can learn much today. Many retain an encyclopaedic knowledge of plants and animals and an extensive memory of where and when to find them. Their lives were uncluttered by material goods and they were therefore able to travel light when they needed to move to new hunting grounds.

Culture

In pre-contact Australia, in spite of the existence of 500 tribal groups and at least 250 languages, an extensive network of trade routes covered Australia from one end to the other. Trade items included microlith tools made of flakes of stone, greenstone for axes, spinifex gum for glue, ochre and shells. The interdependence of tribal areas was also evident in the existence of the 'Songlines', a form of mythological map which records the travels of ancestor figures in the Dreamtime or *altjeringa*, a kind of parallel universe in which the origins of things can be found. As stories, dances and paintings, each region has its own local 'dreamings' which are separate but link with the dreamings of their neighbours. These are popular subjects for artists today.

Materials, Tools and Pigments

Contrary to popular thought, stone tools can be very sharp and today in the hospitals of the developed world obsidian blades are employed in some of the most delicate surgical procedures, the American Medical Association reporting them 500 times sharper than steel. Heavier chopping and shaping work may be accomplished with tools made from stones with ground edges, but with a flaked blade delicate patterns can easily be engraved into a wooden surface. The most common wooden equipment used by men includes spears, shields, boomerangs, clubs and spear throwers, all of which may be decorated with incised patterns

left: Painting on bark of Mimi spirit men by Curly Barrgupu, Ginwinggu tribe, western Arnhem Land, Northern Territory, Australia, 1965.

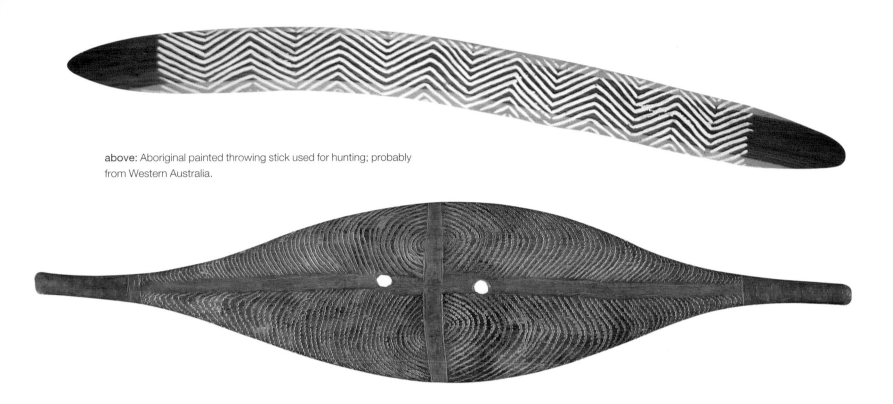

above: Aboriginal painted throwing stick used for hunting; probably from Western Australia.

above: Finely carved wooden shield from the northern Murray River region, New South Wales, c. 1850.

below: Wooden *wunda* (shield) with painted zig-zag patterns made by Aboriginal people in the Western Desert during the early 20th century.

or by painting with earth pigments mixed with a fluid such as the fat of emus or witchetty grubs. Smaller sacred objects of wood and stone were also decorated with carved lines and carried on the person.

Design and Pattern

The choice of carved or painted decoration varies over the country and so too does the repertoire of motifs. In some places the motifs are abstract or symbolic while in others they are figurative. Some designs are linear while others are composed entirely of dots. In Arnhem Land the *raark* style, distinguished by its cross-hatching, is popular while in Oenpelli pictures in the 'X ray' style depict the internal organs of the subject.

Aborigine Art Today

The Aboriginal art tradition is possibly the oldest art tradition in the world. Rock paintings originating from thousands of years ago have been retouched and reworked right up to the present. Smaller scale work is often carried out on sheets of bark but today, encouraged by the increasing fascination with Aboriginal painting, artists are as likely to work on canvas or board and use acrylic paints rather than earth pigments. Ironically, after 200 years of degradation as a primitive people, it is their 'Stone Age' artform which provides many Aborigines with a means of survival in the modern world.

Bilums: Bags from New Guinea

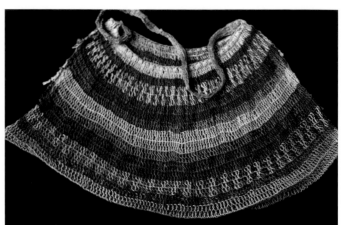

The interior of the large Melanesian island of New Guinea is one of the least charted regions of the planet and the lack of roads, the vast, dense forests and the inaccessible valleys have left many isolated groups virtually untouched by the modern world. Over 700 languages and dialects are spoken and neighbours in even the closest valleys may not be able to understand each other. Some tribal groups still maintain elements of a Stone Age lifestyle, hunting and gathering in the same way as their distant ancestors and fighting inter-tribal wars; headhunting and cannibalism are a living memory. Isolation and the minimal impact of the culture of the outside world have ensured the preservation of indigenous lifestyles and their traditional crafts and artforms. Wood, bone and plant fibres are the most commonly used materials worked into domestic or spiritual objects decorated with intricate carving or embellished with shells, feathers and boars' tusks. Nowadays the hunter-gatherer's opportunism may manifest itself in the way objects imported from outside are recycled because of their bright colouring.

The Bilum

Hunting and gathering from a settled base are made possible by the possession of bags and baskets in which the day's finds can be carried home to be shared with other members of the family or community. Throughout New Guinea the most essential piece of a woman's equipment is the bilum, a stretchy fibre bag worn with a strap across the forehead taking the weight and the load suspended down the back. They are a standard part of daily costume, and since they are light and collapsible, a woman can carry several at a time for use when needed to carry fruit, vegetables, piglets or even babies.

Construction

Bilums are traditionally sewn with a needle using the vegetal fibres of plants such as the wild orchid, but today may be made using cotton or even wool. Beginning at the base and working one circuit at a time, the fibres are interconnected in a series of figure-of-eight (or hourglass) loops with a wide gauge. By changing the colour of fibre at the beginning of a new circuit a pattern of stripes can be achieved but by beginning several differently coloured strands at the same time and looping them in a predetermined sequence, more complex geometric or abstract designs can be created.

Similar string bags can be seen in the Amazon Basin in South America and are made by ethnic minorities in the hills of southwest China.

Dilly Bags

The Aboriginal tribes of neighbouring Australia, particularly those of Arnhem Land in the Northern Territory, have often been studied by anthropologists wishing to learn about their own ancient hunter-gatherer forebears. It is a culture that has not forgotten the ways and wisdom of a traditional lifestyle.

The gathering bag of aboriginal women is the dilly bag. Materials and construction methods vary regionally and they may be knotted from flexible pandanus fibre or twined into a more rigid tube. This later technique produces a container almost identical to the kishie, a gathering bag woven on Scotland's Shetland Islands from oat straw, dock stalks and rushes.

below: Densely constructed bilum from the Western Highlands, Papua New Guinea.

opposite, above, left: Bilum made from wool and cotton yarn, Mount Hagen, Western Highlands, Papua New Guinea. In modern times commercial yarn is often employed instead of traditional plant fibres.
opposite, above, right: Loosely constructed bilum made from plant fibre, Western Highlands, Papua New Guinea.
opposite, below, right: Australian knotted pandanus fibre dilly bag from Maningrida, Arnhem Land, Northern Territory.

Shellwork

A necklace or a pair of earrings can be fashioned with ease from shells and the appeal of shell jewelry is as great in modern society as it was in ancient times. In the Pacific the conch shell is traditionally still blown to summon people to a gathering. Cowrie shells were once traded far inland and much valued as fertility symbols and as protection against misfortune. They continue to be used for jewelry and are sewn onto everyday apparel all over Asia, Africa and the Pacific. With its beautifully opalescent sheen, mother of pearl is widely used for inlay on wooden objects, particularly in the Middle East. During the 1890s the Torres Strait Islanders off the north of Australia produced the bulk of the world's supply of pearl shell, used for buttons, hair combs, buckles, wood inlay and other objects before the advent of plastic.

Ornamentation

On small islands in the Pacific pearl and turtle shell were important trade resources. These and other shells, such as nautilus, are used to decorate all manner of objects and clothing including flamboyant festival headdresses used on dance costumes on Samoa and other islands. Ownership of rare shells imparts prestige, status and good fortune to the owner. In Fiji the *civa vono vono* is a pectoral ornament worn only by the chief made from pearl shell and plates cut from the larger teeth of the sperm whale. In New Ireland, the *kapkap* is another

above: Headband of tightly linked plant fibres decorated with cowrie shells, Western Highlands, Papua New Guinea.
right: *Wafu*, a shield-shaped wooden panel decorated with nassa shells used as dowry currency and also in healing ceremonies as a symbolic womb, Lumi area, West Sepik, Papua New Guinea, first half of the 20th century.

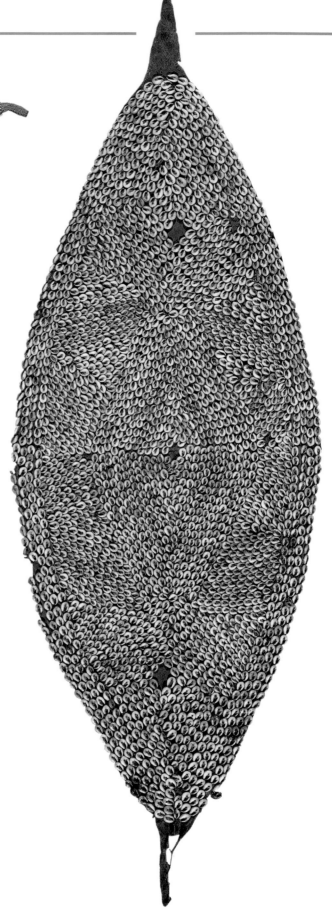

pectoral made from discs of giant clam shell overlaid with turtle shell fretwork and is only worn by initiated men. These are also made in the Solomon Islands where they are worn on the forehead; on Santa Cruz they are called tema and on Santa Cruz the nelo is a nautilus shell nose ornament worn during initiation ceremonies. In Papua New Guinea shell discs were traditionally attached to ornamental sceptres called gobaela as currency and in the Sepik River region shell nose rings were worn as status symbols by warriors. Shells were also mounted on shields and pectoral ornaments to display wealth and were given as part of a girl's dowry. On the northwest coast part of the bride price, or talipun in Pidgin, is a spiral, woven cane disc with sea snail shells attached. Shell belts were commonly used as currency on many islands including Malaita in the Solomon Islands.

In New Zealand paua shells are set into wooden panels and lintels in Maori meeting houses to represent the eyes of ancestral figures as well as add decorative detail. The ancestor figure Kahungunu is associated with the gathering of paua shell because when he first dived for the shell he surfaced with one stuck to his head which, as a ritual first catch, was given to atua Tangaroa, god of the sea. According to Polynesian creation myths, Tangaroa made the world from his body. The top half of the shell in which he lived became the sky and the bottom half the rocks and sand.

Other Uses

In the Cook Islands large cowrie shells are used to scrape and smooth pandanus leaves to remove excess fibrous material when making mats. With the lack of hard stone on volcanic islands, giant clam shells were used to make axe heads, chisels and hoes. They are also used to collect rainwater and as cooking vessels and containers. Special 'balor' shells are used to bale out canoes. In the Solomon Islands shells are set into resin-covered wickerwork in intricate designs. Another craft in Manihiki in the Cook Islands and in the Solomon Islands features wooden dishes and bowls with shell inlay, some in the shapes of animals such as fish and frigate birds, which are used at feasts.

right: Large ceremonial mask portraying a clan ancestor decorated with hair and cowrie shells, Korogo village, Middle Sepik, Papua New Guinea.

Palm Frond Baskets

The Samoans tell the story of how Sina fell in love with Tuna, but Tuna was a Fijian and Sina's brothers would not stand for it and in their rage they struck him down. With his dying breath, Tuna turned to Sina and told her that he would always be with her for from his grave would come the most useful of all things. From his grave grew the coconut palm, a tree with a huge range of uses. Its milk can be drunk, its flesh eaten and its oil applied to the skin medicinally. The husk of the coconut can be used for lighting fires or twisted into sinnet, a coarse string. The shell of the nut is used for making spoons, cups, jewelry and buttons, while the wood of the trunk is used for building or is carved into utensils. The enormous leaves or fronds are a handy material for the construction of many articles, both temporary and permanent.

Coconut Fronds

Fronds grow from the crown of the coconut palm and may reach 6 m (20 ft) in length. Down the centre of the frond is a woody rib or 'rachis' from which grow around 100 leaflets, each between 4 and 6 cm (1½–2¼ in.) wide. The leaflets can easily be split down the middle if required. The great advantage of the coconut frond for plaited basketry is that, uniquely, all the elements (the leaflets) are already connected which gives the work stability during construction and greater strength when complete.

The coconut palm is ubiquitous in the Pacific and is therefore generally at hand when a makeshift basket is required, for instance when transporting freshly gathered foodstuffs such as root vegetables or even coconuts. Fronds are collected for plaiting into many styles of basket, hats, fans, plates and even cooking containers buried in an earth oven, a traditional cooking technique still popular. Fronds are also plaited into mats, wall dividers and the thatch for buildings.

While the leaves of the pandanus are employed for the finest, most intricate work, the coconut frond is at the heart of daily life in the islands of Polynesia.

above: Plaited palm frond hat; work starts at the rim and continues up towards the crown. Hats like this are made spontaneously as needed in many parts of Polynesia.

Techniques

The improvised temporary basket is made on the spot from a freshly cut frond when required by both men and women and discarded after use. Permanent baskets are only made by women and may utilize fresh fronds or those that have been wilted, boiled or drawn through a fire to make them tough and supple.

To make the temporary basket a frond is laid out flat on the ground so that the leaflets on each side of the midrib all lie in one direction forming the first set of elements for plaiting. Alternate leaflets are then bent back to form a second set of elements crossing the first set diagonally. Plaiting over and under then begins, sometimes with twilled patterns created by crossing over more than one element at a time. When the edges are approached the two sides are bent up and joined together with a French plait which may be extended to form a handle. Generally this type of basket is constructed around its burden which is released at its destination by splitting the rib open with a machete. Other baskets are made that begin with a frond cut into two pieces along the rib.

Hats can also be made from fresh fronds. For these, however, a strip of leaflets is pulled from the rib and curled around to form the hat's rim before plaiting inwards towards the crown. At the top leaflets may be bent over and woven in back down to the rim and allowed to project like a fringe. A similar technique may be used to construct more permanent cylindrical storage baskets.

above, left: Weaving a basket from freshly cut coconut frond, Wayalailai, Fiji.

above, right: Constructing a palm frond hat in Fiji; it is similar to the one shown opposite.

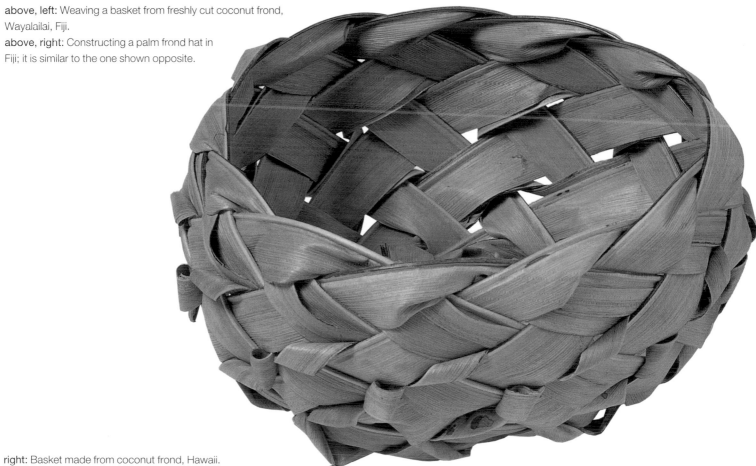

right: Basket made from coconut frond, Hawaii.

Barkcloth

is the paper mulberry (*broussonetia papyrifera*) which was introduced from China during the early Pacific voyages of the Polynesians' ancestors. The outer bark is stripped off the tree and separated from the softer inner bark which is then cleaned and softened by soaking in water.

Making Barkcloth

The strip of inner bark is placed over an 'anvil' made from a tree trunk and beaten with a regular, repetitive action using wooden mallets. During this beating the fibres of the bark become inseparably meshed together like felt so providing a strong 'cloth'. At the same time the beating compresses and stretches the 'cloth' until it reaches as much as four times its original size. Holes are mended with patches glued on with sap and by further beating. As the paper mulberry tree can only yield cloth 50 cm (20 in.) wide several pieces of barkcloth may be joined together to make larger wraps or mats which may on occasion be several hundred metres long.

Although barkcloth may be left plain it is often boldly decorated with designs and techniques diagnostic of their origins. One method (most encountered in Melanesia and New Guinea) is to paint designs on using natural pigments (or today sometimes commercial dyes). Another method, at which the Samoans excel, is to lay the cloth over a wooden board (*upeti*) with patterns carved into it and then rub over the top with dye until the pattern shows. A third method employs a set of stencils which may be used in different combinations to create an all-over pattern. This technique is used to great effect in Fiji where motifs are mostly geometric but may include flowers or even crustaceans.

Sometimes a combination of decorative techniques is used, for example the Tongans often use extensive painting, but may also first rub designs over a board and then pick out details by hand.

Barkcloth in Other Parts of the Tropics

Barkcloth is made in many places lying more or less within the belt of the tropics. In Southeast Asia loincloths, jackets and paper were once made from banyan barkcloth. In Africa painted barkcloth was made by the pygmies of the northeast Congo

With the exception of the Santa Cruz Islands and the Carolines, there is no tradition of weaving in Oceania partly because of the lack of long-haired animals. Instead the inhabitants of Polynesia and the other island groups have come to rely on 'textiles' made from the felted inner bark or 'bast' of certain trees. This 'barkcloth' is known in Samoa as *siapo*, in Fiji as *masi*, in Tonga as *ngatu*, and in the Marquesas as *hiapo*. Around the world it is often erroneously referred to as *tapa* which is actually a Tongan and Samoa term for an undecorated edge. Barkcloth is used in the same way as woven textiles and provides clothing, bedding, matting (both domestic and ceremonial), interior wall decoration and tourist souvenirs.

Materials

A number of different trees are exploited in the Pacific for the making of barkcloth including the breadfruit (*artocarpus altilis*) and the banyan (*ficus bengalensis*), however the most important which had spidery linear decoration while the Ganda of Uganda created bolder designs applied with lake mud. In Mesoamerica barkcloth has been made since ancient times and there has been a resurgence of its use in Mexico among the Otomi and Nahua peoples who paint *amate* barkcloth paper with colourful scenes for sale to tourists. Unfortunately excessive demand is now depleting stocks of the source trees.

below, left and below, right: Barkcloth decorated by rubbing over a carved wooden block, Samoa.
bottom right: Fijian piece of barkcloth with stencilled patterns.

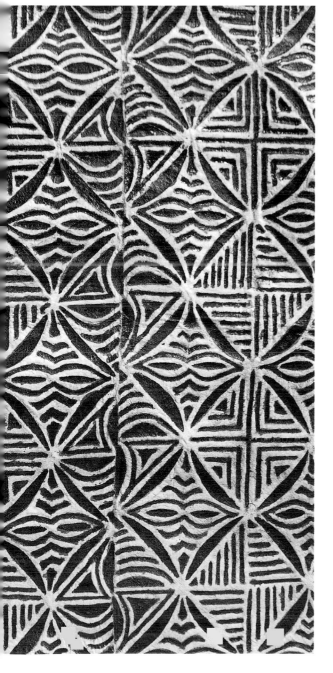

Maori Pendants

left: Maori carved double-twist greenstone pendant.
below: Maori greenstone pendant in the spiral *koru* style.

Hei-matau

The literal meaning of the Maori *hei-matau* is a neck pendant in the shape of a fish hook. It is a popular form of ornament in New Zealand, made in a number of curlicues inspired by the shape of hooks designed to catch a variety of fish. Associated with the story of Maui, the *hei-matau* represents strength and determination, important qualities in the Maori ethos, and is thought to bring peace, prosperity and good health as well as providing protection when travelling over water.

Other Forms

One form of relatively modern design is the koropepe which has a spiral shape representing a coiled eel-like creature with a bird-like head. To some extent it resembles the simple spiral *koru*. Any small item of value might be pierced or notched and hung from the ear. Worn singly by men, the *kapeu* is a long, straight piece of nephrite with a curved lower end that was also used as a teething ring for babies. Another pendant, long, straight and slightly wedge shaped, is based on the *whao*, the Maori greenstone chisel, once hung from the ear by woodcarvers to keep them safe when not in use.

Maui-tikitiki is the great superhero of Polynesia. Using strength and guile, he accomplished many feats; he slowed the course of the sun to provide more daylight for mankind and stole fire from the gods. He failed only once and that was in his attempt to defeat Hine-nui-te-po, the goddess of death. One day Maui went fishing with his five older brothers but because they were tired of his mischievous ways they refused to give him a fishhook. Maui had tricked his grandmother out of a magic jawbone and from it he made the fishhook *manai-a-ka-lani*, which means 'come from the heavens'. Chanting incantations he cast the hook into the sea and hooked a gigantic fish called Te Ika a Maui, 'the Fish of Maui'. This creature was so vast that he could not pull it completely from the water and it broke the surface in many places so forming the islands of Polynesia. Maui's brothers started cutting up the largest piece, the North Island of New Zealand, making the fish writhe and wrinkle its skin and that is why, to this day, the island is covered in hills and valleys.

Hei-tiki

The *hei-tiki* pendant is in the shape of a stylized squatting figure with a large head leaning to one side and represents human rather than divine ancestors. Although the *hei-tiki* is a symbol of Maori identity worn by both men and women, it is shown as either sexless or female and is believed to aid fertility and ease childbirth. Many *hei-tiki* are family heirlooms that have accumulated spiritual power (*mana*) over the generations and have been given their own names.

Materials

Traditionally Maori pendants are made from whale or human bone or from *pounamu*, the Maori name for greenstone or nephrite, a form of jade, however modern versions may be fashioned from plastic or resin. Occasionally the eyes of *hei tiki* are inlaid with discs of paua, an iridescent shell of the haliotis species. The cord from which pendants hang was usually made from the twisted fibre of the New Zealand flax plant, *phormium tenax*, known to the Maori as *harakeke*.

above: Three Maori bone *hei-matau* pendants in which the hook shape has been exaggerated almost beyond recognition.
far left: Drawing after a Maori woodcarving depicting Maui hauling up the islands of New Zealand.
near left: Maori bone *hei-matau* pendant decorated with a stylized head.

Te Whare Runanga

left: The Meeting House at Waitangi with carved *maihi* (bargeboards) and a *tekoteko* figure standing on the apex of the roof, North Island, New Zealand.
opposite, left: Ancestor figure carved on the *poutokomanawa* (a pillar supporting the ridge) inside the Meeting House at Waitangi.
opposite, right: Ancestor figure carved on a *poupou* in the Meeting House at Waitangi. The panels of woven reeds on either side are called *tukutuku*.

According to Maori tradition, the legendary Polynesian explorer Kupe landed in the northeast of New Zealand in 925 and then returned to his mythical homeland, Hawaiki, after which settlers made many voyages; the tribes that spread over the islands took their names from these settlers. The centre of the life of the tribal community is the *marae*, a cleared piece of enclosed land dominated by an ancestral meeting house.

The Meeting House

Te Whare Runanga, as the meeting house is called in the Maori language, has become the focus of Maori pride and identity, a position once held by the war canoe and the storehouse. It is here that funerals and religious and political meetings take place. It is where community matters are discussed, weddings planned and visitors entertained. The finest meeting houses are decorated throughout with panels of carved wood.

The visitor to the *marae* is met by a warrior performing a threatening, postural dance before being greeted with the *hongi*, the pressing together of noses. In front of the meeting house he may watch as the assembled warriors perform the *haka*, with its intimidating staring, stamping, body-slapping and sticking out of tongues, which reminds him of the pride and strength of his hosts.

The Symbolism of the Meeting House

The structure of the building is identified with the body of the community's main ancestor: the ridge pole equates to his backbone. On the apex of the bargeboards above the entrance is carved the *tekoteko* which represents the founding ancestor. The lintel over the entrance may be carved with female figures representing Mother Earth giving birth to the gods or the goddess of death defeating Maui. Alternately it may feature the male figures of Tane and his brothers pushing apart the bodies of their parents, the Earth and the Sky, to allow light to enter the world.

Inside the visitor is confronted by a column supporting the ridge pole, *poutokomanawa*, carved with the likeness of an important ancestor and around the walls are panels, *poupou*, which also depict specific ancestors with their attributes.

Woodcarving is the work of men but other decorative features are created by women such as the *tukutuku*, panels of woven reeds with symbolic patterns which are positioned between the *poupou*. Women may also be responsible for the swirling *kowhaiwhai* patterns that are painted on the rafters, connecting the ancestor panels to the ridge pole.

Techniques

New Zealand is blessed with many densely grained woods such as *mere*, *totara* and *kauri* which are ideal for carving. Prior to the 18th century, tools were predominantly made of stone, adzes

and chisels were of basalt and greenstone, while smoothing was carried out with a piece of sharkskin. The introduction of metal allowed finer carving and therefore a greater variety of regional styles. One particular feature is the *haehae* line which is a groove cut with a veiner (a V-shaped gouge). These grooves, flowing over the carved bodies like tattoos, may be further embellished with a variety of chip-carved notches following the curves with mathematical precision.

Finished carvings on the outside of a building are painted red, once red ochre pigment mixed with shark-liver oil was used. Carvings inside are often simply polished, giving the meeting house a feeling of warmth and intimacy.

Bibliography

Adams, Barbara, *Traditional Bhutanese Textiles*, Bangkok, 1984

Adler, Peter, and Nicholas Barnard, *African Majesty, The Textile Art of the Ashanti and Ewe*, 1992

———, *Asafo! African Flags of the Fante*, London and New York, 1992

Amsden, Charles, *Navaho Weaving, Its Technic and History*, London and New York, 1991

Anton, F., *Ancient Andean Textiles*, London and New York, 1987

Arbeit, Wendy, *Baskets in Polynesia*, University of Hawaii Press, Honolulu, 1990

Archey, Gilbert, *The Art Forms of Polynesia,* Auckland, 1974

L'Art populaire de Hongrie: Collections du Musée d'Ethnographie de Budapest, Woodcarving Magazine, Budapest, 1972

Askari, Nasreen, and Rosemary Crill, *Colours of the Indus, Costume and Textiles of Pakistan*, exh. cat., Victoria and Albert Museum, London, 1997

Bacquart, Jean-Batiste, *The Tribal Arts of Africa*, London and New York, 1998

Bahn, Paul G., ed., *The Atlas of World Archaeology*, London and New York, 2000

Bahti, Tom and Mark, *Southwestern Indian Arts and Crafts*, rev. edn, Las Vegas, 1997

Baines, P., *Linen Hand Spinning and Weaving*, London, 1989

Baker, Patricia, *Islamic Textiles*, London, 1995

Balfour-Paul, Jenny, *Indigo*, London, 1998

———, *Indigo in the Arab World*, Richmond, Surrey, 1992, 1997

Bankes, Georges, *Moche Pottery from Peru*, London, 1980

———, *Peruvian Pottery*, Princes Risborough, 1989

Barley, Nigel, *Smashing Pots, Feats of Clay from Africa*, London, Washington, D.C., 1994

Barnard, Nicholas, *Arts and Crafts of India,* London and New York, 1993

Barratt, Olivia Elton, *Basket Making*, London, 1990 and New York, 1993

Beckwith, Carol and Angela Fisher, *African Ceremonies*, New York, 1999

Benjamin, Betsy, *The World of Rozome, Wax-Resist Textiles of Japan*, London and Tokyo, 1996

Betterton, Sheila, *Quilts and Coverlets from the American Museum in Britain*, The American Museum in Britain, 1997

Bird, Adren J., Steven Goldsberry, J. Puninani Kanekoa Bird, *The Craft of Hawaiian Lauhala Weaving*, Honolulu, 1982

Black, John, *British Tin-glazed Earthenware*, Princes Risborough, 2001

Blackwood, Beatrice, *The Technology of a Modern Stone Age People in New Guinea*, Oxford, 1964

Blair, Mary Ellen and Laurence, *The Legacy of a Master Potter, Nampeyo and Her Descendants*, Tucson, Arizona, 1999

Bléhaut, Jean-François, *Iban Baskets*, Sarawak Literary Society, 1994

Bobart, H. H., *Basketwork through the Ages*, 1st ed. 1936, London, 1997

Book of Woodworking, London, 2001

Bossert, Helmuth Theodor, *Folk Art of Europe*, London and New York, 1954

Bramwell, Martyn, ed., *The International Book of Wood*, London and New York, 1976

Brandford, Joanne Segal, *From the Tree Where the Bark Grows: North American Basket Treasures from the Peabody Museum*, Cambridge, Mass., 1984

Braun, Barbara (ed.), text by Peter G. Roe, *Arts of the Amazon*, London and New York, 1995

Brody, J. J. et al., *Mimbres Pottery, Ancient Art of the American Southwest*, New York, 1983

Bromberg, Erik, *The Hopi Approach to the Art of Katchina Doll Carving,* West Chester, Pennsylvania, 1986

Bühler, Alfred, Eberhard Fischer and Marie-Louise Nabholz, *Indian Tie-dyed Fabrics*, Ahmedabad, 1980

Bunzel, Ruth L., *The Pueblo Potter, A Study of Creative Imagination in Primitive Art*, London and New York, 1972

Burkett, M. E., *The Art of the Felt Maker*, Kendal, 1979

Burnham, D. K., *A Textile Terminology: Warp and Weft*, Toronto, 1981

Butcher, Mary, *Contemporary International Basketmaking*, exh. cat., London, 1999

———, *Willow Work*, London, 1986

Butler, Louise (ed.), *Scotland's Crafts*, Edinburgh, 2000

Campbell, Margaret, Nakorn Pongnoi, Chusak Voraphitak, *From the Hands of the Hills (Thai Hilltribe Crafts)*, Hong Kong, 1981

Carey, Margaret, *Beads and Beadwork of East and South Africa*, Princes Risborough, 1986

Cave, O., and J. Hodges, *Smocking: Traditional and Modern Approaches*, London, 1984

Charleston, Robert J. (ed.), *World Ceramics, An Illustrated History*, London, New York, Sydney and Toronto, 1968

Chinn, Gary, and John Sainsbury, *The Carpenter's Companion*, London and Sydney, 1980

Clabburn, Pamela, *Beadwork*, Aylesbury, 1980

———, *Samplers*, Princes Risborough, 1977

Clarke, Duncan, *African Hats and Jewellery*, Rochester, 1998

———, *The Art of African Textiles*, San Diego, 1997

Clunie, Fergus, *Yalo i Viti, a Fiji Museum Catalogue*, Suva, 1986

Coe, Ralph T., *Sacred Circles: Two Thousand Years of North American Indian Art*, exh. cat., London, 1976 and Kansas City, Missouri, 1977

Coghlan, Herbert Henery, *Notes on the Prehistoric Metallurgy of Copper and Bronze in the Old World*, Oxford, 1951, 1975

Coles, Janet, and Robert Budwig, *The Complete Book of Beads*, London, 1990

Collingwood, P., *The Techniques of Ply-split Braiding*, London, 1998

———, *The Techniques of Sprang*, London and New York, 1974

———, *The Techniques of Tablet Weaving*, London and New York, 1982

———, *Textile and Weaving Structures: A Source Book for Makers and Designers*, London, 1987

Connors, Mary, *Lao Textiles and Tradition*, Oxford, New York and Kuala Lumpur, 1996

Conway, Susan, *Thai Textiles*, Bangkok, 1992

Cooper, Emmanuel, *The Potter's Book of Glaze Recipes*, London and New York, 1980

———, *Ten Thousand Years of Pottery*, 4th edn, London and Philadelphia, 2000

Cooper, Ilay, Barry Dawson and John Gillow, *Arts and Crafts of India*, London and New York, 1996

Coote, Jeremy, Chris Morton and Julia Nicholson, *Transformations: The Art of Recycling*, exh. cat., Oxford, 2000

Cort, Louise, and Nakamura Kenji, *A Basketmaker in Rural Japan*, Smithsonian Institution, Washington, D.C., in association with Weatherhill, New York and Tokyo, 1994

Coulter, Lane and Maurice Jr Dixon, *New Mexican Tinwork, 1840–1940*, Albuquerque, 1990

Crampton, Charles, *Cane Work*, Leicester, 1948

Crews, Patricia Cox, and Ronald C. Naugle, *Nebraska Quilts and Quiltmakers*, University of Nebraska Press, Lincoln, 1991

Crill, Rosemary, *Indian Ikat Textiles*, London, 1998

Davies, Lucy, and Mo Fini, *Arts and Crafts of South America*, London, 1994, and San Francisco, 1995

Davison, Julian, and Bruce Granquist, *Balinese Architecture*, Hong Kong, 1999

de la Bédoyère, Guy, *Pottery in Roman Britain*, Princes Risborough, 2000

Deuss, Krystyna, *Indian Costumes from Guatemala*, London, 1981

DeWald, Terry, *The Papago Indians and their Basketry*, Tucson, Arizona, 1979

D'Harcourt, Raoul, *Textiles of Ancient Peru, and their Techniques*, Mineola, NY, 1962

Dillingham, Rick, *Fourteen Families in Pueblo Pottery*, Albuquerque, New Mexico, 1994

——— with Melinda Elliot, *Acoma and Laguna Pottery*, Santa Fe, New Mexico, 1992

Dixon, M., *The Wool Book*, London, 1979

Dockstader, Frederick, *Weaving Arts of the North American Indian*, New York, 1993

Draper, Jo, *Post-Medieval Pottery, 1650–1800*, Princes Risborough, 2001

Dubin, Lois Sherr *The History of Beads: from 30,000 B.C. to the Present*, London and New York, 1987, 2004

Dyrenforth, Noel, *The Technique of Batik*, London, 1988

Earnshaw, Pat, *The Identification of Lace*, Princes Risborough, 2000

Edgeler, Audrey and John, *North Devon Art Pottery*, North Devon Museums Service, n.d.

Eicher, Joanne, *Nigerian Handcrafted Textiles*, Ife, 1976

Eisman, Jr, Fred B., *Ulat-Ulatan, Traditional Basketry in Bali*, Bangkok, 1999

Emery, I., *The Primary Structure of Fabrics, An Illustrated Classification*, Washington, D.C., and London, 1980, reprinted 1994

Esterly, David, *Grinling Gibbons and the Art of Carving*, London, 1999

Faegre, T., *Tents, Architecture of the Nomads*, New York, 1979

Fagg, William, *Yoruba Beadwork, Art of Nigeria*, New York, 1980

Fahr-Becker, Gabriele (ed.), *The Art of East Asia*, vols 1 and 2, Cologne, 1999

Farrelly, David, *The Book of Bamboo: A Comprehensive Guide to this Remarkable Plant, Its Uses, and its History*, London and San Francisco, 1996

Faulkner, R., *Japanese Stencils*, Exeter, 1988

Feder, Norman, *American Indian Art,* New York, 1995

Feest, Christian F., *Native Arts of North America*, London and New York, 1992

Fehérvári, Géza, *Ceramics of the Islamic World in the Tareq Rajab Museum*, London and New York, 2000

Feltham, Jane, *Peruvian Textiles*, Aylesbury, 1989

Feltwell, John, *The Story of Silk*, Stroud, 1990

Ferrier, R. W., *The Arts of Persia*, London and New Haven, 1989

Fisher, Nora (ed.), *Mud, Mirror and Thread: Folk Traditions of Rural India*, Ahmedabad and Middletown, New Jersey, 1993

Fitzgibbon, Kate, and Andy Hale, *Ikat, Silks of Central Asia, The Guido Goldman Collection*, London, 1997

———, *Ikats, Woven Silks from Central Asia, The Rau Collection*, Oxford and New York, 1988

Frame, Mary, *Andean Four-Cornered Hats*, exh. cat., Metropolitan Museum of Art, New York, 1990

Franses, Michael, *The Great Embroideries of Bokhara*, London, 2008

Fraser-Lu, Sylvia, *Handwoven Textiles of South-East Asia*, Oxford and Singapore, 1988

Freestone, Ian, and David Gaimster (eds), *Pottery in the Making, World Ceramic Traditions*, London and Washington, D.C., 1997

Fuhrmann, B., *Bobbin Lace: A Contemporary Approach*, New York, 1985

Gabriel, Sue, and Sally Goymer, *The Complete Book of Basketry*, London, 1991

Gao, Hanyu, *Chinese Textile Designs*, London, 1992

Garrett, Valery, *Chinese Clothing: An Illustrated Guide*, Oxford and Hong Kong, 1994

Gavin, Traude, *The Women's Warpath, Iban Ritual Fabrics from Borneo*, Los Angeles, 1996

Geijer, Agnes, *A History of Textile Art*, London and Totowa, N.J., 1979

Gibson, Thomas, *Feather Masterpieces of the Ancient Andean World*, exh. cat., Thomas Gibson Fine Art, London, 1990

Gillow, John, *African Textiles: Colour and Creativity Across a Continent*, London and San Francisco, 2003

———, and Nicholas Barnard, *Traditional Indian Textiles*, London and New York, 1991

———, and Barry Dawson, *Traditional Indonesian Textiles*, London and New York, 1992

———, and Bryan Sentance, *World Textiles: A Visual Guide to Traditional Techniques*, London and Boston, 1999

Gittinger, Mattiebelle, *Splendid Symbols, Textiles and Tradition in Indonesia*, 1984

———, and Leedom Lefferts, *Textiles and the Thai Experience in Southeast Asia*, Washington, D.C., 1992

Gittinger, Mattiebelle, *Master Dyers to the World: Technique and Trade in Early Indian Dyed Cotton Textiles*, Washington, D.C., 1982

Griswold, Lester, *Handicraft: Simplified Procedure and Projects*, 9th edn, New York, 1952

Grossert, J. W., *Zulu Crafts*, Pietermaritzburg, 1978

Guy, John, *Woven Cargoes, Indian Trade Textiles in the East*, London and New York, 1998

Haddon, A. C., and L. E. Start, *Iban or Sea Dayak Fabrics and their Patterns, a Descriptive Catalogue of the Iban Fabrics in the Museum of Archaeology and Ethnology, Cambridge*, 2nd ed., Cambridge, 1982

Hall, Rosalind, *Egyptian Textiles*, Aylesbury, 1986

Hamer, Frank and Janet, *The Potter's Dictionary of Materials and Techniques*, 4th edn, London and Philadelphia, 1997

Harris, Jennifer, *5000 Years of Textiles*, London and Washington, D.C., 1993

Harvey, Janet, *Traditional Textiles of Central Asia*, London and New York, 1996

Harvey, Virginia I., *The Techniques of Basketry*, London and Seattle, 1986

Hasselrot, Jonas, *Korgar, Tradition Och Teknik*, Stockholm, 1997

Hauser-Schäublin, B., Marie-Louise Nabholz-Kartaschoff and Urs Ramseyer, *Balinese Textiles*, London, 1991

Hayes, Allan, and John Blom, *Southwestern Pottery, Anasazi to Zuni*, Flagstaff, Arizona, 1996

Hayward, Helena, ed., *World Furniture: An Illustrated History*, London and New York, 1967

Hecht, A., *The Art of the Loom*, Seattle, 1989

Heinbuch, J., *A Quillwork Companion*, Liberty, Utah, 1990

Hemming, Steve, and Philip Jones, *Ngurunderi, An Aboriginal Dreaming*, exh. cat., South Australian Museum, Adelaide, 1989

Herald, Jacqueline, *World Crafts: A Celebration of Designs and Skills*, London, 1992 and Asheville, North Carolina, 1993

Heseltine, Alastair, *Baskets and Basketmaking*, Shire, Princes Risborough, 1982, 1996

Hessel, Ingo, *Inuit Art: an Introduction*, London and New York, 1998

Hilliard, Elizabeth, *The Tile Book, Decorating with Fired Earth*, London and San Francisco, 1999

Hiroa, Te Rangi (Peter H. Buck), *Arts and Crafts of Hawaii*, section iv, Twined baskets, Honolulu, 1964

Hitchcock, Michael, *Indonesian Textiles*, 1991

Hitkari, S. S., *Phulkari, The Folk Art of Punjab*, New Delhi, 1980

Hooper, Luther, *Hand-Loom Weaving: Plain and Ornamental*, London and New York, 1979

Hooper, Steven, ed., *Robert and Lisa Sainsbury Collection, Volume II: Pacific, African and Native North American Art*, New Haven and London, 1997

Hopper, Robin, *Functional Pottery, Form and Aesthetic in Pots of Purpose*, London and Iola, Wisconsin, 2000

Hope, Colin A., *Egyptian Pottery*, Princes Risborough, 2001

Horse Capture, George P., *Robes of Splendor*, Nashville, Tenn., 1993

Horsham, Michael, *Shaker Style*, London, 2000

Hucko, Bruce, *Southwestern Indian Pottery*, Las Vegas, Nevada, 1999

Hughes, Robert, *Amish, The Art of the Quilt*, London and New York, 1990, 1994

Hull, Alastair, Nicholas Barnard and José Luczyc-Wyhowska, *Kilim, The Complete Guide*, London and San Francisco, 1993

———, and Nicholas Barnard, *Living with Kilims*, London and New York, 1988

Humphrey, C., *Samplers*, Cambridge, 1997

Hunter Whiteford, Andrew, *Indian Arts*, New York, 1973

Impey, O. R., *Japanese Netsuke in Oxford: From the Ashmolean Museum, Pitt Rivers Museum and the Museum of the History of Science*, Oxford, 1987

Irwin, John, and Margaret Hall, *Indian Embroideries*, Ahmedabad, 1973

———, *Indian Painted and Printed Fabrics*, Ahmedabad, 1971

Isaacs, Jennifer, *Hermannsburg Potters, Aranda Artists of Central Australia*, Sydney, 2000

Jackson, Albert, and David Day, *Collins Complete Woodworker's Manual*, London, 1996

Jacobs, Julian, *The Nagas: Hill Peoples of Northeast India, Society, Culture and the Colonial Encounter*, London and New York, 1990

James, George Wharton, *Indian Basketry*, New York, 1901, 1909, 1972

Japanese Crafts, a Guide to Today's Traditional Handmade Objects, Tokyo, 2001

Jereb, James F., *Arts and Crafts of Morocco*, London, 1995 and San Francisco, 1996

Johnson, Kay, *Basketmaking*, London, 1991

Johnstone, Pauline, *A Guide to Greek Island Embroidery*, London, 1972

———, *Turkish Embroidery*, London, 1985

Jones, Suzi (ed.), *Pacific Basket Makers, A Living Tradition* (catalogue), Fairbanks, Alaska, 1990

Kalter, Johannes, *The Arts and Crafts of the Swat Valley. Living Traditions in the Hindu Kush*, London and New York, 1991

Kalter, Johannes, *The Arts and Crafts of Turkestan*, London and New York, 1984

———, and Margareta Pavaloi, *Uzbekistan, Heirs to the Silk Road*, London and New York, 1997

———, Margareta Pavaloi and Maria Zerrwicke, *The Arts and Crafts of Syria*, London and New York, 1992

Kapp, Kit, *Mola Art from the San Blas Islands*, 1972

Kasparian, Alice, *Armenian Needlelace and Embroidery*, McLean, Virginia, 1983

Kennedy, Alan, *Japanese Costume, History and Tradition*, Paris, 1990

King, J. C. H., *First Peoples, First Contacts: Native Peoples of North America*, London and Cambridge, Mass., 1999

Knowles, Sir Francis H. S., *Stone-Worker's Progress: A Study of Stone Implements in the Pitt Rivers Museum*, Oxford, 1976

Konieczny, M. G., *Textiles of Baluchistan*, London, 1979

Kooijman, Simon, *Polynesian Barkcloth*, Princes Risborough, 1988

———, *Tapa on Moce Island, Fiji, a Traditional Handicraft in a Changing Society*, Leiden, 1977

Krishna, Rai, Anand and Vijay, *Banaras Brocades: Structure and Functioning*, Varanasi, 1966

Küchler, Susanne, and Graeme Were, *Pacific Pattern*, London, 2005

Lamb, Venice, *West African Weaving*, London, 1975

Lamb, Venice, and Alastair, *Au Cameroun, Weaving, Tissage*, Douala, 1981

———, *Sierra Leone Weaving*, Hertingfordbury, 1984

Lamb, Venice, and Judy Holmes, *Nigerian Weaving*, Lagos, 1980

Lane, Robert E., *Philippine Basketry, An Appreciation*, Manila, Philippines, 1986

Larsen, Jack, Alfred Bühler and Garret Solyom, *The Dyer's Art*, London and New York, 1976

Leach, Bernard, *A Potter's Book*, 3rd edn, London, 1976

Lee, Molly, *Baleen Basketry of the North Alaskan Eskimo*, Barrow, Alaska, 1983

Lewis, David, and Werner Forman, *The Maori: Heirs of Tane*, London, 1982

Lewis, Paul and Elaine, *Peoples of the Golden Triangle, Six Tribes in Thailand*, London and New York, 1984

Ling Roth, H., *The Maori Mantle*, Bedford, 1979

Lobb, Allan, *Indian Baskets of the Northwest Coast*, Portland, Oregon, 1978, 1990

Love, George, *The Theory and Practice of Woodwork*, London, 1969 and 1981

Lynton, Linda, *The Sari: Styles, Patterns, History, Techniques*, London and New York, 1995

Mack, Dan, *Simple Rustic Furniture: a Weekend Workshop with Dan Mack*, Asheville, 1999

Mack, Daniel, *The Art of Rustic Furniture: Traditions Techniques and Inspirations*, New York, 1996, 2001

Mack, John, *Malagasy Textiles*, Princes Risborough, 1989

Majlis, Brigitte Khan et al., *Batik: From the Courts of Java and Sumatra*, London, 2000

Mallinson, J., N. Donelly and Hang Ly, *H'mong Batik*, Chiang Mai, 1988

Mansfield, Janet, *A Collector's Guide to Modern Australian Ceramics*, Seaforth, N.S.W., 1988

Mason, Otis T., *Aboriginal Indian Basketry*, Glorieta, New Mexico, 1902, 1972

Maxwell, Robyn, *Textiles of South-East Asia, Tradition, Trade and Transformation*, Oxford and Melbourne, 1990

McEwan, Colin, Cristiana Barreto and Eduardo Neves, *Unknown Amazon: Culture in Nature in Ancient Brazil*, exh. cat., London, 2001

McNeese, Tim, *The Illustrated Myths of Native America: The Southwest, Western Range, Pacific Northwest and California*, London and New York, 1999

Mead Moko, Hirini, *Te Toi Whakairo: The Art of Maori Carving*, Auckland, 1999

Meisch, L. A. (ed.), *Traditional Textiles of the Andes: Life and Cloth in the Highlands*, The Jeffrey Appleby Collection of Andean Textiles, exh. cat., Fine Arts Museums of San Francisco, 1997

Meyer, Anthony J. P., *Oceanic Art*, Cologne, 1995

Middleton, Sheila Hoey, *Traditional Korean Wrapping Cloths*, Seoul, 1990

Miller, Bruce W., *Chumash: A Picture of their World*, Los Osos, California, 1988

Mingei: Two Centuries of Japanese Folk Art, Tokyo, 1995

Minick, Scott, and Jiao Ping, *Arts and Crafts of China*, London and New York, 1996

Misago, Célestine Kanimba and Mesas, Thierry, *Artisanat au Rwanda. la vannerie*, Rwanda, 2000

Bibliography

Mohanty, B. C., *Brocaded Fabrics of India*, Ahmedabad, 1984

Morphy, Howard, and Elizabeth Edwards, eds, *Australia in Oxford,* Oxford, 1988

Morrell, Anne, *The Techniques of Indian Embroidery*, London and Loveland, Colorado, 1994

Morris, B., *Victorian Embroidery*, 1962

Mowat, Linda, Howard Morphy and Penny Dransart (eds), *Basketmakers: Meaning and Form in Native American Baskets*, Oxford, 1992

Mullins, Barbara, and Douglas Baglin, *Aboriginal Art of Australia*, Marleston, 1999

Munan, Heidi, *Sarawak Crafts: Methods, Materials and Motifs,* Oxford, Singapore and New York, 1989

Murfitt, Stephen, *The Glaze Book, a Visual Catalogue of Decorative Ceramic Glazes*, London and Iola, Wisconsin, 2002

Murphy, Veronica, and Rosemary Crill, *Tie-Dyed Textiles of India: Tradition and Trade*, London and New York, 1991

Nabholz-Kartaschoff, Marie-Louise, *Golden Sprays and Scarlet Flowers, Traditional Indian Textiles from the Museum of Ethnography* [Basel, Switzerland], Kyoto, 1986

Naylor, Rod, *Woodcarving Techniques*, London, 1979

Neich, R., and M. Pendergrast, *Traditional Tapa Textiles of the Pacific*, London and New York, 1997

Nicholson, Paul T., *Egyptian Faience and Glass*, Princes Risborough, 1993

Oakes, Jill, and Rick Riewe, *Our Boots, An Inuit Women's Art*, London and New York, 1996

O'Connor, D., *Miao Costumes from Guizhou Province, South West China*, exh. cat., James Hockney Gallery, W.S.C.A.D., Farnham, 1994

Oelsner, G. H., *A Handbook of Weaves*, New York, 1975

Onions, C. T. (ed.), *The Oxford Dictionary of English Etymology*, Oxford, 1976, 1982

Paine, Sheila, *Embroidered Textiles, Traditional Patterns from Five Continents with a Worldwide Guide to Identification*, London and New York, 1990, paperback 1995

Parker, A., and A. Neal, *Molas: Folk Art of the Cuna Indians*, Barre, Mass. and New York, 1977

Pastor-Roces, Marian, *Sinaunang Habi, Philippine Ancestral Weave*, 1991

Paul, Frances, *Spruce Root Basketry of the Alaska Tlingit*, Sitka, Alaska, 1944

Pegrum, Brenda, *Painted Ceramics, Colour and Imagery on Clay*, Marlborough, 1999

Pendergrast, M., *Kakahu, Maori Cloaks*, Auckland, 1997

———, *Te Aho Tapu, The Sacred Thread*, Auckland, 1987

Perryman, Jane, *Traditional Pottery of India*, London, 2000

Peterson, Susan, *The Living Tradition of María Martínez*, Tokyo and New York, 1989

Pettersen, Carmen L., *Maya of Guatemala, their Life and Dress*, Seattle, 1976

Phillips, E. D., *The Royal Hordes, Nomad Peoples of the Steppes*, London and New York, 1965

Phillips, Tom (ed.), *Africa, The Art of a Continent*, exh. cat., Munich and New York, 1995

Pickering, Brooke, W. Russell Pickering and Ralph S. Yohe, *Moroccan Carpets*, Chevy Chase, MD, 1994

Picton, John, *The Art of African Textiles, Technology, Tradition and Lurex*, London, 1995

———, and John Mack, *African Textiles*, London, 1979, 2nd ed. 1989

Posey, Sarah, *Yemeni Pottery*, London, 1994

Pownall, Glen, *Know your Maori Carving,* Paraparaumu, 1994

Proctor, M., *Victorian Canvas Work, Berlin Wool Work*, London and New York, 1972

Puketapu-Hetet, Erenora, *Maori Weaving*, Auckland, 1999

Puls, H., *The Art of Cutwork and Appliqué: Historic, Modern and Kuna Indian*, London, 1978

———, *Textiles of the Kuna Indians of Panama*, Princes Risborough, 1988

Rajab, Jehan, *Palestinian Costume*, London and New York, 1989

Ranjan, M. P., Nilam Iyer, Ghanshyam Pandya, *Bamboo and Cane Crafts of Northeast India*, New Delhi, 1986

Rathbun, W. J., *Beyond the Tanabata Bridge: Traditional Japanese Textiles*, exh. cat., The Art Institute of Seattle, Washington, 1993

Reigate, E., *An Illustrated Guide to Lace*, Woodbridge, 1986

Reswick, Imtraud, *Traditional Textiles of Tunisia and Related North African Weavings*, Los Angeles, 1985

Roffey, Mabel, *Simple Basketry*, Pitman, London and New York, 1930

Rossbach, Ed, *Baskets as Textile Art*, London and New York, 1973

———, *The New Basketry*, London and New York, 1976

Ryan, Judith, and Anna McLeod, *Tikwani, Contemporary Tiwi Ceramics*, exh. cat., Melbourne, 2002

Ryan, M. G., *The Complete Encyclopaedia of Stitchcraft*, London, 1981

Saint-Gilles, Amaury, *Mingei, Japan's Enduring Folk Arts*, Rutland, Vermont and Tokyo, 1998

Saitoti, Tepilit Ole, *Maasai*, New York, 1980 and 1993

Sandberg, Gösta, *Indigo Textiles: Technique and History*, London and Asheville, N.C., 1989

———, *The Red Dyes, Cochineal, Madder and Murex Purple: A World Tour of Textile Techniques*, Asheville, North Carolina, 1997

Sarabhai, Mrinalini, and Jasleen Dhamija, *Patolas and Resist-Dyed Fabrics of India*, Ahmedabad, 1988

Saul, M., *Shells*, New York, 1974

Sayer, Chloë, *Arts and Crafts of Mexico*, London and San Francisco, 1990

———, *Mexican Textile Techniques*, Aylesbury, 1988

———, *Mexican Textiles*, London, 1990

Schevill, Margot Blum, *Evolution in Textile Design from the Highlands of Guatemala*, Berkeley and Seattle, Washington, 1985

Schiffer, Nancy, *Baskets*, Pennsylvania, 1984

Scott, Philippa, *The Book of Silk*, London, 1993

Seike, Kiyoshi, *Japanese Joinery,* New York and Tokyo, 1999

Sekijama, Hisako, *Basketry: Projects from Baskets to Grass Slippers*, New York and Tokyo, 1986

Sellschop, Susan, Wendy Goldblatt and Doreen Hemp, *Craft South Africa, Traditional, Transitional, Contemporary,* South Africa, 2002

Selvanayagam, Grace Inpam, *Songket, Malaysia's Woven Treasure*, Oxford and Singapore, 1990

Sentance, B., *Basketry: A World Guide to Traditional Techniques*, London and New York, 2001

———, *Ceramics: A World Guide to Traditional Techniques*, London and New York, 2004

———, *Wood: The World of Woodwork and Carving*, London and New York, 2003

Seward, L., *The Country Quilter's Companion*, London, 1994

Seymour, J., *The Forgotten Arts, A Practical Guide to Traditional Skills*, London, 1984

Shadbolt, Doris, *Bill Reid*, Vancouver, Toronto and Seattle, 1986

Shaw, Ian, and Paul Nicholson, *British Museum Dictionary of Ancient Egypt*, London, 1995

Shaw-Smith, David, *Traditional Crafts of Ireland*, London and New York, 2003

Sichel, Marion, *Japan*, London and New York, 1987

Sieber, Roy, *African Furniture and Household Objects*, London, New York and Bloomington, Indiana, 1980

Simmons, D. R., *Te Whare Runanga: The Maori Meeting House,* Auckland, 1997

Smith, Monte, *The Technique of North American Beadwork*, Ogden, Utah, 1983

Sparkes, Ivan G., *Woodland Craftsmen*, Princes Risborough, 1997; exh. cat., 1972

Spring, Christopher, *African Textiles*, Wakefield, RI, 1989

———, and Julie Hudson, *North African Textiles*, London and Washington, D.C., 1995

Start, Laura E., *The McDougall Collection of Indian Textiles from Guatemala and Mexico*, Oxford, 1948

Starzecka, D. C., ed., *Maori Art and Culture*, London, 1996, 1998

Stillman, Yedida Kalfon, *Palestinian Costume and Jewelry*, Albuquerque, 1979

Stillwell, Alexandra, *Cassell Illustrated Dictionary of Lacemaking*, London, 1996

Stockley, Beth (ed.), *Woven Air*, exh. cat. (of Bangladeshi textiles), Whitechapel Art Gallery, London, 1988

Stone, Caroline, *The Embroideries of North Africa*, Harlow, 1985

Stone-Miller, Rebecca, *To Weave for the Sun, Ancient Andean Textiles in the Museum of Fine Arts, Boston*, London and New York, 1994

Dato'Haji Sulaiman Othman, et al., *The Crafts of Malaysia*, Singapore, 1994, 1997

Swain, Margaret, *Ayrshire and Other Whitework*, Princes Risborough, 1982

Talwar, Kay, and Kalyan Krishna, *Indian Pigment Paintings on Cloth*, Ahmedabad, 1979

Taylor, Colin F., ed., *The Native Americans: The Indigenous People of North America*, London, 1991, 1995

Taylor, Roderick, *Embroidery of the Greek Islands and Epirus*, Yeovil, New York, 1998

———, *Ottoman Embroidery*, London and New York, 1995

Teiwes, Helga, *Hopi Basket Weaving, Artistry in Natural Fibres*, Tucson, Arizona, 1996

Thom, Ian M., ed., *Robert Davidson: Eagle of the Dawn*, London and Seattle, 1993

Thompson, Jon, *Carpets from the Tents, Cottages and Workshops of Asia*, New York, rev. ed. 1988

Thurman, C. C. M., *Textiles in the Art Institute of Chicago*, Chicago, 1992

Tomalin, Stefany, *The Bead Jewelry Book*, Newton Abbot and Chicago, 1997

Traditional Crafts in Britain, London, 1982

Traditional Crafts in Britain, Woodcarving Magazine, London, 1982

Trowell, Margaret, *African Design*, New York, 3rd edn, 1971

Tsultem, N., *Mongolian Arts and Crafts*, Mongolia, 1987

Turnbaugh, Sarah Peabody, and William A. Turnbaugh, *Indian Baskets*, West Chester, Pennsylvania, 1986

Van Lemmen, Hans, *Delftware Tiles*, Princes Risborough and Woodstock, New York, 1998

Veldhuisen, Harmen, *Batik Belanda, Dutch Influence in Batik from Java*, Jakarta, 1993

Verdet-Fierz, Bernard and Regula, *Willow Basketry*, Loveland, Co., 1993

Villegas, Liliana and Benjamin, *Artefactos: Colombian Crafts from the Andes to the Amazon*, New York, 1992

Visonà, Monica Blackmun, Robin Poynor, Herbert M. Cole, Michael D. Harris, Rowland Abiodun and Suzanne Preston Blier, *A History of Art in Africa*, London, 2000 and New York, 2001

Volbach, Fritz, *Early Decorative Textiles*, London and New York, 1969

Wada, Yoshiko, Mary Kellogg Rice and Jane Barton, *Shibori, The Inventive Art of Japanese Shaped Resist Dyeing, Tradition, Techniques, Innovation*, Tokyo, 1983
Walker, Philip, *Woodworking Tools*, Princes Risborough, 2000
Walpole, Lois, *Creative Basket Making*, London and Cincinnati, Ohio, 1989
———, *Weave Coil and Plait Crafty Containers from Recycled Materials*, Wellwood, UK, 1997
Ward, Gerald W. B. et al., *American Folk*, exh. cat., Museum of Fine Arts, Boston, 2001
Wardle, P., *A Guide to English Embroidery*, London, 1970
Warming, Wanda, and Michael Gaworski, *The World of Indonesian Textiles*, Tokyo, 1991
Warren, William, and Luca Invernizzi Tettoni, *Arts and Crafts of Thailand*, London, 1994, and San Francisco, 1996
Warshaw, Josie, *The Potter's Guide to Handbuilding*, London, 2000
Wasserspring, Lois, *Oaxacan Ceramics, Traditional Folk Art by Oaxacan Women*, San Francisco, 2000
Weir, Shelagh, *Palestinian Costume*, London and Austin, 1989
———, and Serene Shahid, *Palestinian Embroidery, Cross stitch Patterns from the Traditional Costumes of the Village Women of Palestine*, London, 1988
Wendrich, Willeke, *Basketry in Egypt: Ancient Traditions, Modern Applications* (Slide set), Manchester, 1994
———, *The World According to Basketry: An Ethno-Archeological Interpretation of Basketry Production in Egypt*, Leiden, 1999
Whiteford, Andrew Hunter, *North American Indian Arts*, New York, 1973
———, *Southwestern Indian Baskets: Their History and Their Makers*, Seattle, 1988
Wien, C. A., *Log Cabin Quilt Book, Complete Patterns and Instructions for Making All Types of Log Cabin Quilts*, London and New York, 1984
Wilcox, R. Turner, *Folk and Festival Costume of the World*, New York, 1965, London, 1989
Wildschut, William, and John Ewers, *Crow Indian Beadwork*, New York, 1959
Wilson, Verity, *Chinese Dress*, London, 1990
Wright, Dorothy, *The Complete Book of Baskets and Basketry*, Newton Abbot, 1977
Wulff, Hans, *The Traditional Crafts of Persia, their Development, Technology, and Influence on Eastern and Western Civilizations*, London and Cambridge, Mass., 1966
Yefimova, L., and R. Belogorskaya, *Russian Embroidery and Lace*, London and New York, 1987
Zaman, Niaz, *The Art of Kantha Embroidery*, Dhaka, 1993

Museums and Collections

Australia
ADELAIDE
National Textile Museum of Australia
Urrbrae House
Fullarton Road
Urrbrae
Adelaide
South Australia (5064)

South Australian Museum
North Terrace
Adelaide
South Australia (5000)
T 08 82077500
www.samuseum.sa.gov.au

AUSTRIA
VIENNA
Museum für Völkerkunde (Museum of Ethnology)
Neue Burg
A-1010 Vienna
T 43 1 534 30
www.ethno-museum.ac.at

BALI
UBUD
Neka Art Museum
Ubud, Gianyar 80571
www.museumneka.com/

BELGIUM
ANTWERP
Etnografisch Museum (Ethnographic Museum)
Suikerrui 19
B 2000 Antwerp
T 03 220 86 00
museum.antwerpen.be/etnografisch_museum/

BRUSSELS
Musée du Costume et de la Dentelle
6 rue de la Violette
1000 Brussels

Musées Royaux d'Art et d'Histoire
10 Parc du Cinquantenaire
1040 Brussels
www.kmkg-mrah.be/

TERVUREN
Musée de l'Afrique Centrale Royal
13 Steenweg op Leuven
3080 Tervuren
Brabant
T 02 7695211
www.africamuseum.be/

BOLIVIA
LA PAZ
Museo Nacional
Calle Tihuanacu 93, La Paz

Museo Nacional de Etnografía y Folklore (Museum of Ethnography and Folklore)
Calle Ingani 942
La Paz
www.musef.org.bo/

BRAZIL
RIO DE JANEIRO
Museu do Indio
Rua das Palmeiras 55
Botafogo
Rio de Janeiro 22270-070
T 021 2862097
www.museudoindio.org.br/

SÃO PAOLO
Museu do Folclore (Folklore Museum)
Pavilhao Garcez
Parque Ibirapuera
01000 São Paolo

BRUNEI
BEGAWAN
Brunei Museum
Kota Batu
Banda Seri
2018 Begawan

BULGARIA
SOFIA
Etnografski institut s muzej kam Balgarska akademija na naukite (National Ethnographic Museum of the Bulgarian Academy of Sciences)
ul Moskovska 6a,
1000 Sofia

CAMEROON
YAOUNDE
National Museum of Yaounde
Direction des Affaires Culturelles
Yaounde

CANADA
OTTAWA
National Museum of Natural Sciences
MacLeod and Metcalfe Sts
Ottawa, Ontario KIA OM8

Royal Ontario Museum
100 Queen's Park
Toronto
Ontario M5S 2C6
T 416 586 5549
www.rom.on.ca

VANCOUVER
Museum of Anthropology
c/o University of British Columbia

6393 Marine Drive NW
Vancouver
British Columbia V6T 1Z2
T 604 822 5087
www.moa.ubc.ca

VICTORIA
Royal BC Museum
675 Belleville Street
Victoria
British Columbia V8W 9W2
T 250 356-BBCM /226
www.royalbcmuseum.bc.ca

CHINA
BEIJING
Museum of the Cultural Palace of National Minorities
Changan Street
100 000 Beijing

GUIYANG
Guizhou Provincial Museum
Beijing Road
Guiyang
550 000 Guizhou

KUNMING
Yunnan Provincial Museum
2 May Day Road
Dongteng St
Yuantong Shan Hill
Kunming, 650 000 Yunnan
www.chinamuseums.com/yunnan.htm

COLOMBIA
BOGOTÁ
Museo Etnográfico de Colombia
Calle 34
No. 6–61 piso 30
Apdo. Aéreo 10511, Bogotá

CZECH REPUBLIC
PRAGUE
Náprstkoro Muzeum asijskych, africkych a americkych kultur (Náprstkoro Museum of Asian, African and American Culture)
Betlemské nám 1
11000 Prague
T 02 22221416

DENMARK
COPENHAGEN
Nationalmuseet (National Museum)
Prinsens Palais
Frederiksholms Kanal 12
1220 Copenhagen
T 33134411
www.natmus.dk

Museums and Collections

ECUADOR
CUENCA
Centro Interamericano de
Artesanías y Artes Populares
(CIDAP)
Hermano Miguel 3–23 La Escalinata
Cuenca
T 593 7 2840919/2829451
www.cidap.org.ec

Museo y el Parque Arqueológico
Pumapungo
Calle Larga near Huayna Capac
Cuenca
T 283 1255
www.www.museos-
ecuador.com/bce/html/home/
evento_9_0.htm

QUITO
Museo Etnográfico de Artesania
de Ecuador
Reina Victoria N26–166 & La Niña
Quito
T 223 0609
www.sinchisacha.org

FIJI
SUVA
Fiji Museum
Suva
Viti Levu
T 679 331 5944
www.fijimuseum.org.fj

FRANCE
CADENET
Musée de la Vannerie
La Glaneuse
Avenue Philippe de Girard
84160 Cadenet
T 04 90 68 24 44

PARIS
Musée de l'Homme
Palais de Chaillot
17 place du Trocadéro
75116 Paris
T 01 44 05 72 72
www.mnhn.fr

Musée National des Arts d'Afrique
et d'Océanie
293 avenue Daumesnil
75012 Paris
T 01 44 74 84 80
www.museums-of-paris.com

VALLABRÈGUES
Musée de la Vannerie
5 rue Carnot
30300 Vallabrègues
T 04 66 59 23 41

GERMANY
BERLIN
Museum für Völkerkunde,
Staatliche Museen zu Berlin –
Preußischer Kulturbesitz
Lansstrasse 8
14195 Berlin
T 030 2660
Staatliche Museen zu Berlin
www.smb.spk-berlin.de

COLOGNE
Rautenstrauch-Joest-Museum für
Völkerkunde der Stadt Köln
Ubierring 45
50678 Cologne
www.museenkoeln.de/rautenstrauch
-joest-museum/

FRANKFURT AM MAIN
Museum der Weltkulturen
(Ethnography Museum)
Schaumankai 29
60594 Frankfurt am Main
T 69 21235913
www.mdw-frankfurt.de

MUNICH
Staatliches Museum für
Völkerkunde München
Maximilianstr 42
80538 Munich
T 089 21 01360
www.koenige-in-afrika.de

STUTTGART
Linden-Museum Stuttgart-
Staatliches Museum für
Völkerkunde
Hegelplatz 1
70174 Stuttgart
T 0711 2022408
www.lindenmuseum.deCentral

GHANA
ACCRA
Ghana National Museum
Barnes Rd
Accra

GREECE
ATHENS
Museum of the Greek Folklore
Society
12 Didotou St
Athens

GUATEMALA
GUATEMALA CITY
Museo Nacional de Artes e
Industrias Populares
(National Museum of Popular Arts)
Avenida 10, No. 10–70, Zona 1
Ciudad de Guatemala
T 2380334

HUNGARY
BUDAPEST
Néprajzi Múzeum (Ethnographic
Museum)
Kossuth Lajos tér 12
1055, Budapest
T 01 3326340
www.neprajz.hu

INDIA
NEW DELHI
Crafts Museum
Pragati Maidan
Bhairon Road
110001 New Delhi

INDONESIA
JAKARTA
Museum Textil
Jl. K. Satsuit Tuban 4
Jakarta

ITALY
FAENZA
Museo Internazionale delle
Ceramiche
(Museum of International Ceramics)
Via Campidori 2
48018 Faenza
T 0546 21240
www.micfaenza.org/index.htm

MILAN
Museo di Arte Estremo Orientale e
di Etnografia
(Museum of Far Eastern Art and
Ethnography)
Via Mosé Bianchi 94
20149 Milan
T 024 38201

ROME
Museo Nazionale Preistorico
Etnografico Luigi Pigorini (Luigi
Pigorini Museum of Prehistory and
Ethnography)
Viale Lincoln 3
00144 Rome
www.pigorini.arti.beniculturali.it/

JAPAN
OSAKA
Kokuritsu Minzokugaku
Hakubutsukan (National Museum
of Ethnology)
10–1 Senri Banpaku Koen,
Suita-Shi
Osaka 565–8511
T 06 876 2151

Museum of Textiles
5–102 Tomobuchi-Cho, 1–Chome
Miyakojima-Ku, Osaka

Nihon Kogei-kan (Japanese Folk
Art Museum)
3–7–6 Namba-naka, Naniwa-ku,
Osaka
T 06 6641 6309

TOKYO
Nihon Mingeikan (Japanese Folk
Art Museum)
4–3–33 Komaba, Meguro-ku,
Tokyo
T 03 3467 4527
www.mingeikan.or.jp/Pages/
entrance-e.html

LAOS
VIENTIANE
National Museum
Saysettha District, Vientiane

MALAYSIA
KINABALU
Sabah State Museum
1239 Gaya St
Kota Kinabalu
www.mzm.sabah.gov.my/

KUCHING
Sarawak Museum
Jalan Tun Haji Openg
93566, Kuching
T 082 44232
www.museum.sarawak.gov.my/
indexeng.htm

MEXICO
MEXICO CITY
Museo Nacional de Artes e
Industrias Populares del INI
Avenida Juárez 44
06050 Mexico City
T 05 5103404

Museo Nacional de Culturas
Populares
Avenida Hidalgo 289, Coyoacán
Mexico City

OAXACA
Museo Regional de Oaxaca
Alcalá Street, Oaxaca
T 951 5162991

TONALÁ
Museo Nacional de la Cerámica
(National Museum of Ceramics)
Constitución 104
Tonalá, Guadalajara

MOROCCO
MARRAKESH
Bert Flint Museum
Maison Tiskiwin Marrakech
8 Rue de la Bahia
Marrakesh

THE NETHERLANDS
DELFT
Nusantara Ethnographical
Museum
Agatha Plein 4
2611 HR Delft

LEEUWARDEN
Keramiekmuseum Princessehof
(National Museum of Ceramics)
Grote Kerkstraat 11
8911 DZ, Leeuwarden, Friesland
T 058 2948958
www.princessehof.nl

LEIDEN
Rijksmuseum voor Volkenkunde
(National Museum of Ethnology)
Steenstraat 1
2312 BS Leiden
T 071 5168800
www.rmv.nl

ROTTERDAM
Wereldmuseum Rotterdam
(Museum of Ethnology)
Willemskade 25
3016 DM, Rotterdam
T 010 2707172
www.wereldmuseum.rotterdam.nl

NEW ZEALAND
AUCKLAND
Auckland Institute and Museum
Auckland Domain
Auckland 1000
T 09 3090443
www.aucklandmuseum.com

ROTORUA
The New Zealand Maori Arts and
Crafts Institute
Hemo Road
Rotorua
T 64 7 348 9047
www.nzmaori.co.nz

WAITANGI
Waitangi National Reserve
Waitangi National Trust, Paihia
Tau Henare Drive
Waitangi, Bay of Islands
T 649 402 7437
www.waitangi.net.nz

WELLINGTON
Te Papa, Museum of New Zealand
Te Papa Tongarewa
Cable St
Wellington 6020
T 04 3817000
www.tepapa.govt.nz

NIGERIA
LAGOS
Nigerian Museum
Lagos

PAPUA NEW GUINEA
PORT MORESBY
National Museum and Art Gallery
Waigini
Port Moresby

PERU
CUSCO
Museo Inka
Cuesta del Almirante 103
Cusco
T 084 22 2271
Pre-Columbian Andean culture

LIMA
Museo Nacional de Antropología y
Arqueología
Plaza Bolivia s/n
Pueblo Libre
Lima
T 01 635070

PHILIPPINES
MANILA
National Museum of the
Philippines
P. Burgos St, Rizal Park
1000, Manila
T 02 5271215

POLAND
WARSAW
Muzeum Azji i Pacyfiku (Asia and
Pacific Museum)
ul. Solec 24
00-467 Warsaw
T 022 6296724
www.muzeumazji.pl

PORTUGAL
LISBON
Museu Etnográfico da Sociedade
de Geografia de Lisboa
(Ethnographical Museum)
Rua Portas de Santo Antão 100
1150-269 Lisbon
T 213425401

ROMANIA
BUCHAREST
Muzeul National de Istorie a
României
(Romanian National History
Museum)
Calea Victoriei nr. 12
79740 Bucharest
T 40 21 315 82 07
www.mnir.ro/index_uk.html

RUSSIA
ST PETERSBURG
Muzej Antropologii i Etnografii im.
Petra Velikogo (Peter the Great

Museum of Anthropology and
Ethnography)
Universitetskaja Nab 3
199034 St Petersburg
T 812 3280712

State Museum of Ethnography
ul. Inzenernaya, 4–1
St Petersburg

SAMOA
APIA
Falemataaga-Museum of Samoa
Beach Road, Apia
Upolu
T 63415

SOUTH AFRICA
CAPE TOWN
South African Cultural History
Museum
49 Adderley St
Cape Town
T 021 4618280

SPAIN
BARCELONA
Museu Etnològic (Ethnography
Museum)
Passeig Santa Madrona
08001 Barcelona
www.museuetnologic.bcn.es

MADRID
Museo Nacional de Etnología
(Ethnography Museum)
Alfonso XII, 68
28014 Madrid
T 915306418

SWEDEN
GOTHENBURG
Etnografiska Museet
(Ethnography Museum)
Norra Hamngatan 12
41114 Gothenburg
http://www.etnografiska.se/

STOCKHOLM
Folkens Museum Etnografiska
(National Museum of Ethnography)
Djurgårdsbrunnsvägen 34
102 52 Stockholm
T 08 51955000
www.etnografiska.se

Nordiska Museet (The National
Museum of Cultural History)
Djurgårdsv. 6–16
115 93 Stockholm
T 08 51956000
www.nordiskamuseet.se

SWITZERLAND
BASEL
Museum für Völkerkunde und
Schweizerisches Museum für
Volkskunde Basel
Augustinergasse 2
4001 Basel

ST GALLEN
Völkerkundliche Sammlung
Museumstrasse 50
9000 St Gallen

THAILAND
CHIANG MAI
Hill-tribe Museum and Research
Rama 9 Park, Chotana Road
Chiang Mai
T 210872, 221933

UNITED KINGDOM
BATH
The American Museum in Britain
Claverton Manor
Bath BA2 7BD
T 01225 460503
www.americanmuseum.org

BELLANALECK
The Sheelin Antique Irish Lace
Museum
Bellanaleck
Enniskillen, Co. Fermanagh
Northern Ireland, BT92 2BA
T 028 6634 8052
www.irishlacemuseum.com

BIDEFORD
Burton Art Gallery and Museum
Kingsley Road
Bideford
Devon EX39 2QQ
T 01237 471455
www.burtonartgallery.co.uk

BRISTOL
City Museum and Art Gallery
Queens Road
Bristol BS8 1RL

CAMBRIDGE
Fitzwilliam Museum
Trumpington Street
Cambridge CB2 1RB
T 01223 332900
www.fitzmuseum.cam.ac.uk

University Museum of
Archaeology and Anthropology
Downing St, Cambridge CB2 3DZ
maa.cam.ac.uk/

EAST MOLESEY
Embroiderers' Guild Museum
Collection
Apartment 41, Hampton Court
Palace

East Molesey, Surrey KT8 9AU
www.embroiderersguild.com/
collection/

EDINBURGH
Royal Museum of Scotland
Chambers Street
Edinburgh EH1 1JF

EXETER
The Royal Albert Memorial
Museum & Art Gallery
Queen Street
Exeter EX4 3RX
T 01392 665858

HONITON
Allhallows Museum
High Street
Honiton, Devon EX14 8PE
www.honitonmuseum.co.uk/

LONDON
The British Museum
Great Russell Street
London WC1B 3DG
T 020 7636 1555
www.britishmuseum.org/

Horniman Museum
100 London Road, Forest Hill
London SE23 3PQ
T 020 8699 1872
www.horniman.ac.uk/

Victoria and Albert Museum
Cromwell Road
London SW7 2RL
T 020 7942 2000
www.vam.ac.uk/

NOTTINGHAM
Lace Centre
Severns Buildings, Castle Road
Nottingham NG1 6AA

OXFORD
Pitt Rivers Museum
South Parks Road
Oxford OX1 3PP
T 01865 270927
www.prm.ox.ac.uk

UNITED STATES OF AMERICA
ALBUQUERQUE,
NEW MEXICO
Indian Pueblo Cultural Center
2401 12th Street NW
Albuquerque, NM 87104
T 800 766 4405
www.indianpueblo.org

CAMBRIDGE, MASS.
Peabody Museum of Archaeology
and Ethnology
11 Divinity Av
Cambridge, MA 02138
www.peabody.harvard.edu

DENVER, COLORADO
Denver Art Museum
100 W 14th Av Pkwy
Denver, CO 80204
T 303 640 4433
www.denverartmuseum.org

DRAGOON, ARIZONA
The Amerind Foundation
2100 N Amerind Road
Dragoon, AZ 85609
T 520 586 3666
www.amerind.org

HAINES, ALASKA
Sheldon Museum
11 Main St
Haines, AK 99827
T 907 766 2366
www.sheldonmuseum.org

HONOLULU, HAWAII
Bishop Museum
1525 Bernice Street
Honolulu, HI 96817-0916
T 808 847 3511
www.bishopmuseum.org

JUNEAU, ALASKA
Sealaska Heritage Institute
1 Sealaska Plaza, Suite 301
Juneau, Alaska
T 907 433 4844
www.sealaskaheritage.org

KLAMATH FALLS, OREGON
Favell Museum of Western Art and
Indian Artifacts
125 West Main St
Klamath Falls, OR 97601
T 541 882 9996
www.favellmuseum.org

LA JOLLA, CALIFORNIA
Mingei International Museum
of Folk Art
4405 La Jolla, CA 92037
www.mingei.org/

LOS ANGELES, CALIFORNIA
Southwest Museum of the
American Indian
234 Museum Drive
Los Angeles, CA 90065
www.southwestmuseum.org

NEW YORK
The Metropolitan Museum of Art
1000 Fifth Avenue
New York, NY 10028
www.metmuseum.org/

National Museum of the American
Indian
Smithsonian Institution
George Gustav Heye Center
1 Bowling Green
New York, NY 10004
www.nmai.si.edu

Museums and Collections/Acknowledgments/Sources of Illustrations

NORRIS, TENNESSEE
Museum of Appalachia
Hwy 61, Norris, TN 37828
T 423 494 7680
www.museumofappalachia.org

PHOENIX, ARIZONA
The Heard Museum
2301 North Central Avenue
Phoenix, AZ 85004
T 602 252 8840
www.heard.org

SALEM, MASS.
Peabody Essex Museum
East India Square
Salem, MA 01970
www.pem.org/

SAN DIEGO, CALIFORNIA
Museum of Man
San Diego
Balboa Park
1350 El Prado
San Diego CA 92101
T 619 239 2001
www.museumofman.org

SANTA FE, NEW MEXICO
Museum of International
Folk Art
706 Camino Lejo
Santa Fe, NM 87505
T 505 476 1200
www.moifa.org

Wheelwright Museum of the
American Indian
704 Camino Lejo
Santa Fe, NM 87505
T 505 982 4636
www.wheelwright.org

SEATTLE, WASHINGTON
National Museum of Natural
History
Seattle Art Museum
Volunteer Park, Seattle, WA 98122

SECOND MESA, ARIZONA
Hopi Cultural Centre
Second Mesa
Hopi Reservation, AZ 86043
T 520 734 6650

5 Miles W of 87 Route 264
Second Mesa, AZ 86043
www.hopiculturalcenter.com

TUCSON, ARIZONA
Arizona State Museum
University of Arizona
Tucson, AZ 85721-0026
www.statemuseum.arizona.edu

UKIAH, CALIFORNIA
Grace Hudson Museum and the
Sun House
431 S Main Street
Ukiah, CA 95482
www.gracehudsonmuseum.org

YOSEMITE, CALIFORNIA
Indian Cultural Museum
Museum Bldg
Yosemite National Park
Yosemite, CA 95389
T 209 372 0281

ZUNI, NEW MEXICO
A:shiwi A:wan Museum and
Heritage Center
1222 Highway 53
Zuni, NM 87327
T 505 782 4403
www.ashiwi-museum.org

Acknowledgments

A great deal of this book is based on research carried out on our own travels, but it would not have been possible without consulting the researches of others in both books and collections and just talking to people who have been there, seen it or done it.

Particular thanks are owed to Clive Loveless for generously allowing us access to his archives, and his introductions and support. Our projects would not have been so successful without the help of Alastair and Hazel Hull at Haddenham Gallery in Cambridgeshire.

Many people lent images, allowed us to photograph their objects or provided information and technical support, including the following: Kay Anderson; James and Pauline Austin; Jenny Balfour-Paul; Ellen Bjørnsen; Bradworthy Primary School, Devon; Mary Butcher; Todd Calhoun; Gabriel Casey; Rosemary Cathcart; John Christian of Boquio Iron and Glass, Cornwall; CIDAP; Francisco López Cisnero; Duncan Clarke, Adire African Textiles; Peter Collingwood; David Cook Galleries, Denver; Becki Daniel; Angela Davies; Dave Dawson; Joyce Doel; Emma and CJ; Rosie Ford; Michael Franses; John Gardener; Rachel Geller; John Gillow; Grant at Long Ago and Far Away; Richard and Patricia Hann; Andrew Hewson; Janet Harvey; Jonas Hasselrot; Ronald Henderson; Rick Huteson; Alan and Julia Jarret; Kay Johnson; Zachary Jones at Sealaska Heritage Institute, Juneau, Alaska; Roy Lamur; Leonard Lovejoy at Crafted Nature; Clive Loveless; Daniel Mack; Pippa Moss; Dr Paul Nielsen; Sheila Paine; Ruben Proaño; Gordon Reece; Edward Rozylowicz; Andrew Sanigar; Michael and Sandra Schwab at Many Horses; Paul and Christine Sentance; Barry Trice; Mircea Ungurean; J. P. Uranker; Peter Vincent; Satsuki Wakane; Ian West and Stephanie Woolf

Thank you also to all those anonymous craftspeople who made so many of the uncredited objects that appear in this book. If I have omitted credit I apologise, but please let me know so that I may correct this in future editions.

Sources of Illustrations

The following abbreviations have been used: *a* above; *b* below; *c* centre; *l* left; *r* right; *t* top

All line drawings are by Bryan Sentance

James Austin 1, 6*b*, 20*bc*, 28*al*, 28*bl*, 40*br*, 50*l*, 53*l*, 68, 69*r*, 74*ar*, 74*b*, 75*b*, 81*r*, 82 *background*, 84*ar*, 84*r*, 85*r*, 87, 90*a*, 90*b*, 92*bl*, 93*a*, 93*b*, 100*bl*, 101*b*, 101*ar*, 102*r*, 103 *all*, 107*l*, 107*br*, 120*l*, 127*l*, 127*br*, 128*l*, 134*r*, 136, 142*l*, 142*r*, 143, 144*a*, 145*l*, 145*r*, 146, 147*l*, 147*r*, 148*l*, 148*r*, 149, 150*r*, 153, 159*a*, 159*b*, 164*c*, 166*br*, 167, 168*ar*, 168*br*, 171*a*, 174*b*, 194*ar*, 196, 197*r*, 198*r*, 200*a*, 200*b*, 201*a*, 203*b*, 208*r*, 209*r*, 209*r*, 211, 225*b*; Jenny Balfour-Paul 214*r*, 216*b*; Ellen Bjørnsen 88*al*; Courtesy of Mary Butcher 29*l*, 53*r*, 92*br*, 220*br*; Courtesy of Duncan Clarke, Adire African Textiles 141 all; Courtesy of Peter Collingwood 220*ar*, 221, 222*l*; Courtesy of David Cook Galleries 42*b*; Richard Hann 5*l*, 17, 30*a*, 30*b*, 31, 134*c*, 135, 151, 152*a*, 152*b*; Courtesy of Janet Harvey 182*a*, 182*b*, 183*r*, 185*l*, 185*r*, 199*r*; Jonas Hasselrot 89*r*, 91*l*,

92*al*; Courtesy of Alastair Hull 8, 168*bl*, 178, 179*l*, 179*r*, 173*l*, 173*r*; Kay Johnson 225*ar*; Courtesy of Long Ago And Faraway 22*b*; Private Collections Courtesy of Clive Loveless' archives 124 *background*, 131, 153*b*, 155, 172, 176*l*, 177, 183*l*, 190*b*, 191*l*, 213, 217, 219 *all*, 222*r*; Courtesy of Clive Loveless and Andrew Hewson 218; Courtesy of Clive Loveless and the Textile Gallery, London 164 *background*, 184; Courtesy of Daniel Mack 32*l*, 32*r*, 33*r*; Courtesy of Many Horses Jewelry Supply and Artwork 38*r*; Courtesy of M'Art 88*c*, 88*r*, 89*l*; Edward Rokita 57*b*; Courtesy of Royal British Columbia Museum 25*al*, 25*bl*; Edward Rozylowicz 56, 57*al*, 57*ar*; Courtesy of Sealaska Heritage Institute 27*l*; Bryan Sentance 2, 4, 5*r*, 6*a*, 6*b*, 7*t*, 7*r*, 10*ar*, 11*ar*, 13*al*, 13*br*, 15, 16*l*, 16*r*, 18, 19*a*, 20*al*, 21, 22*ar*, 23*t*, 23*c*, 26*b*, 27, 28*ar*, 33*l*, 36, 37*l*, 37*r*, 38*l*, 39*l*, 39*r*, 40*al*, 40*ac*, 41*l*, 41*r*, 42*al*, 42*ar*, 42*c*, 43*a*, 44*l*, 44*r*, 45*l*, 45*r*, 46*t*, 46*br*, 47*br*, 48*l*, 49*al*, 49*ar*, 49*br*, 51, 52*al*, 52*bl*, 54 *all*, 55, 58*l*, 58*r*, 59*a*, 59*b*, 60*al*, 60*c*, 60*ar*, 61, 62, 63, 64 *all*, 65*a*, 65*b*, 66*a*, 66*b*, 67, 69*al*, 69*c*, 70 *all*, 71, 72 *all*, 73 *all*, 75*a*, 76 *all*, 77*a*, 77*b*, 78 *all*, 79, 80*a*, 80*b*,

81*al*, 82*c*, 83 *all*, 84*l*, 86*al*, 86*br*, 91*br*, 94 *all*, 95, 96*l*, 96*r*, 97, 98*l*, 98*r*, 99*l*, 99*r*, 100*a*, 102*al*, 102*c*, 104*l*, 104*r*, 105 *all*, 106*l*, 106*r*, 107*ar*, 108*l*, 108*r*, 109*l*, 109*r*, 110*l*, 110*r*, 111 *all*, 112 *all*, 113, 114, 115 *all*, 116 *all*, 117 *all*, 118, 119 *all*, 123*al*, 124*al*, 124*br*, 125, 126*a*, 126*bl*, 127*tr*, 127*c*, 128*ar*, 129, 130 *all*, 132 *all*, 133*l*, 133*r*, 134*al*, 137, 138 *all*, 139*a*, 139*b*, 140, 144*b*, 150*al*, 152*al*, 156*a*, 156*b*, 157, 160, 162*a*, 162*b*, 163*a*, 163*b*, 165*r*, 166*al*, 167*l*, 169, 170*a*, 170*c*, 171*b*, 175*al*, 175*b*, 176*c*, 176*r*, 180 *all*, 181*al*, 181*r*, 186*l*, 186*r*, 187, 188 *all*, 189*l*, 189*r*, 191*r*, 192*a*, 192*b*, 193*l*, 193*r*, 194*al*, 194*b*, 195*l*, 195*r*, 196, 199*l*, 201*b*, 202*a*, 202*b*, 203*al*, 206*r*, 207*l*, 208*l*, 210*l*, 210*r*, 212*a*, 215*l*, 220*l*, 223, 224, 225*al*, 226, 227*ar*, 227*br*, 228 *all*, 229 *all*, 230, 231*l*; Paul Sentance 29*a*; Polly Sentance 11*b*, 12*r*, 14, 34*bc*, 34*br*, 35, 46*bl*, 47*al*, 48*r*, 50*r*, 52*r*, 120*r*, 121, 122, 123*r*, 161*l*, 161*r*, 166*ar*, 174*a*, 175*ar*, 198*l*, 205*l*, 205*r*, 206*l*, 207*r*, 212*b*, 214*l*, 216*a*, 227*l*, 231*r*, 240; Smugmug 60*br*; J. P. Uranker 34*ar*; Peter Vincent 24, 204

Index

Index

Painted tinwork figure
of the skeletal Caterina,
Oaxaca, Mexico